The Mysteries of the Caucasus

The Mysteries of the Caucasus

Dorota Gierycz

To order additional copies of this book, contact:
Xlibris Corporation
1-888-795-4274
www.Xlibris.com
Orders@Xlibris.com
81801

Contents

Preface 7

Acknowledgments 9

Introduction 11

Chapter 1   Welcome to the Aitar Hotel 13

Chapter 2   Abkhazia: The Illusion of Freedom 19

Chapter 3   Country Roads...31

Chapter 4   The Aitar Women 37

Chapter 5   Displaced and Abandoned 56

Chapter 6   Dachas of the Communist Bosses 62

Chapter 7   Of Peacocks and Swans 75

Chapter 8   Sochi..78

Chapter 9   Gori and Stalin's Birthplace 87

Chapter 10   Kodori Gorge...95

Chapter 11   Smiling Faces 103

Chapter 12   Maria 107

Chapter 13   Sergio: Death in Baghdad 112

Chapter 14   The Caucasian Roulette 131

Chapter 15   Tbilisi, Mon Amour...136

Chapter 16   Kitty 142

Chapter 17   Shevardnadze: Hero of Perestroika or "Silver Fox"
              of the Caucasus?..147

Chapter 18   Rose Revolution or Masquerade?........................162

Chapter 19   Shevardnadze: An Afterword.............................176

Chapter 20   Russia, Georgia, and Their Leaders 181

Chapter 21   UNOMIG: Mission Impossible.........................191

Chapter 22   Abashidze and the Council of Europe:
              An Odd Alliance..200

Chapter 23   Democracy of the Fist:
              The Georgian Crisis of 2007............................207

Chapter 24   The Summer of Olympics, 2008........................218

Chapter 25   The Rose Revolution: Six Years On...................228

Chapter 26   Feeling Abandoned: The International Community......238

Chapter 27   In the Opposition Club 243

Epilogue..253

Selected Bibliography...255

Abbreviations 285

About the Author..287

Preface

I am again walking through the streets of Tbilisi. It is the summer of 2009, about six years since my first visit to Georgia in the year of the Rose Revolution. As in that fateful year, Rustaveli Avenue is again blocked by crowds of demonstrators. Traffic is diverted away from the front of parliament. The demonstrators are peaceful, well-organized, and determined. Like six years ago, they carry signs calling for fair elections and democracy and stand in groups talking and gesticulating excitedly.

I have an uneasy feeling that time stopped, that I am again in the midst of the Rose Revolution. Am I really? Have the crowds ever left the streets of Tbilisi, or have they been demonstrating all along, all this time? I must find out.

I want to write about Georgia. I want to tell the story of a tiny country in the Caucasus, a country largely unknown to the world.

"Georgia? You're going to Georgia?" some colleagues asked in 2003, hearing of my new posting. "It is good that you will be closer after all these distant assignments."

"Closer?"

"Yes, in Georgia. Atlanta?"

"No, Tbilisi. The Caucasus."

"Oh, that Georgia. But isn't it dangerous? It is a communist country. And there is the war in Chechnya."

And now, today, it is itself at war with Russia.

I am again asked the same: "Why do you go there? That's the country at war. Russian tanks are all over the place."

*   *   *

"Why do you write about Georgia?" friends ask.

"You have been all over the world and lived in many countries," say others. "Why Georgia, a small insignificant country?"

7

I have no logical answer.

"I simply fell in love with Georgia and its people," I tell them. "And love is irrational."

That I know is not convincing.

"I want to talk about my fascination with the country whose very existence is often not only unknown, but also whose essence remains a mystery to even those to whom it is familiar."

Acknowledgments

I thank all of the friends, colleagues, and the family who encouraged this project, in particular Olga Alexakos and Michael Gierycz whose enthusiasm for it was infectious.

I am grateful for helpful conversations and storytelling during my visits to Sukhumi and Tbilisi.

Special thanks to my Georgian friends, who wish to remain anonymous for their assistance, unique inside knowledge, and trust.

Shavonna Maxwell provided me with most valuable advice and assistance in bringing this book to its current shape.

Last but not least, I want to express my appreciation for the assistance provided by the Xlibris team—Jethro Aragon, Victor Balon, Kay Benavides and Janeth Pareno.

Introduction

Georgia is a small country, roughly seventy thousand square kilometers (about the size of Ireland) with just over 4.6 million people, located in the North Caucasus, bordering Russia, Turkey, Azerbaijan, and Armenia. It is a country at the crossroads of Europe and Asia, Christianity and Islam, European culture and that of never-conquered Caucasian tribes. It is a multiethnic, Christian nation with a long tradition of freedom, diversity, and close ties to Europe and an equally strong sense of independence, honor, and mystery resulting from its nesting in the Caucasus.

Georgia was, economically, the most prosperous of the former Soviet republics and politically the most open. The combination of a well-developed agricultural sector, attractive seacoast, and enduring sense of national identity enabled her to maintain relative prosperity and, in the case of the Georgian intelligentsia, close cultural links with the West, both rare in the Soviet system.

Georgia's perennial lean toward the West and the repression of Russia, her imperious and powerful neighbor to the north, has led to bloodshed at critical points in Georgian history. The Stalin years were particularly brutal. Anti-Russian demonstrations in Tbilisi were brutally put down on Khrushchev's orders in 1956: Georgia had been the first to test Khrushchev's new policy course before the workers' protests in Poznan, Poland, and before the uprising in Hungary later that same year. In 1989, in the same manner, month, and city, Georgians challenged Gorbachev and tested his policies of *glasnost* and *perestroika*. Again, there were dead and wounded.

Georgian independence, though finally achieved in 1991, has not, in the years since, lead to her independence from Russian influence. The long frozen conflict over Abkhazia and South Ossetia and the clash over Georgia's demand and aggressive attempts to join Europe and Russia's attempt to keep Georgia in its sphere of influence culminated in the 2008 late-summer war between the two countries, defining not only the current chapter of Georgian-Russian relations, but also reflecting the changing power structures in the Caucasus and beyond.

It is against this background that the author, a former senior United Nations official stationed in Sukhumi and Tbilisi, tells the stories of people in Abkhazia and Georgia proper, intertwined with astute and timely analysis of the political events that have shaped the small Caucasus nation in the years since she gained her independence—from the rise and fall of Shevardnadze, the hero of *perestroika* and the West's favorite "democrat," to the era of Saakashvili, the proclaimed "beacon of democracy," increasingly authoritarian and challenged by a discontented public. The analysis is also anchored in Georgia's history and collective memory, indelibly marked by the lasting impact of the brutal rule of Stalin and Beria and the ever-present shadow and interference of Russia.

The series of essays collected here provide firsthand accounts of the effect of these events and history on the daily lives of the ordinary people who suffer their consequences. It tells the story of the struggle for economic survival of women in Abkhazia and the ongoing struggle for democracy and a life free of political repression in Georgia. It also provides sharp and candid political analysis—and criticism—of the United Nations and the international community's role in the protracted Abkhazian-Georgian conflict, the state of the current political crisis in Georgia and the Caucasus more broadly, and the relations between Putin and Saakashvili and their respective countries.

Through this well-researched collection of essays, the author provides the close-up, personal insight and expert analysis of an experienced professional and scholar into this largely unknown yet majestic and strategically important region along the Black Sea coast.

Chapter 1

Welcome to the Aitar Hotel

As the plane approached the landing in Sukhumi, capital of the de facto state of Abkhazia, the various small figures were becoming increasingly visible, taking on the shapes of cars, men in uniforms, buildings, and animals. These miniature forms seemed to be lost in the endless blue of the sea and sky, the green of the subtropical forest, the brightness of the sun, and the glare of the snow-tipped mountains in the horizon. Although I knew that I was about to land in one of the most devastated parts of the world, I had the sudden sense of entering a dreamland. In that instant, I wished to believe that the reality would be closer to the magic of the moment rather than that of the collection of colorless reports I had studied prior to my arrival.

As soon as the plane hit the ground, I faced reality close-up. The cars turned out to be the well-known white UN four-wheel drives accompanied by a separate set of armored vehicles, and the buildings were a collection of dilapidated walls looking precariously close to losing their balance at any moment. The UN receiving staff, although formally polite, seemed worried and tired. The employees of the local Abkhaz administration, on the other hand, were openly suspicious and determined to complicate rather than facilitate our entry.

The formalities were endless. Only nature held its early promise: the lavish tropical green remained intertwined with the blue of the sea, and the ever-present white peaks of the mountains looked as they had from afar. And they would always be there, the one constant in the good and bad days to follow.

I was quite pleased to see the familiar face of Edin, a Bosniak, who had been one of the drivers at the UN Mission in Bosnia and Herzegovina (UNMIBH) in Sarajevo. In Sukhumi, he worked as a security officer at the UN Observer Mission in Georgia (UNOMIG), an obvious promotion and change in status. In the car, we immediately started talking.

"Yes," he confirmed, "it is a very bad day. This morning, thirty-seven convicts broke out of the prison. Some were committed for murder so there is a real security concern."

In the short distance between the airport and our destination, the Aitar Hotel, which hosted both UN headquarters and living quarters in Sukhumi, Edin made contact with UN headquarters on the car radio. "Charlie, Charlie, this is Alfa 157." He explained that even in more normal circumstances there were strict security regulations. Mission staff outside of the compound were obliged to report to UNOMIG security every half hour. Whether you were in town, out shopping, taking a walk, or having coffee, you were not to miss a call. It sounded strange to me, but I was about to learn many more things that were to make this posting truly unusual.

Edin dropped me in the middle of the courtyard of the Aitar where I was supposed to be met by someone "in charge" to guide me further through the endless arrival formalities. I was tired. I wanted to rest, take a shower, and drink a coffee. I had gotten up at 5:00 a.m. and had yet to recover from the sudden transfer from my previous posting in Sarajevo.

As the person "in charge" was apparently busy elsewhere, I was pointed to the Staff Club where I could get some coffee and wait. So far, so good; nobody seemed to be in a hurry. After a while, a local employee came and retrieved my luggage. He was neither particularly courteous nor talkative. I followed hoping to be led to my new accommodation where I could take a shower and rest.

My luggage was placed in a filthy room equipped with a limp chair and spotted mattress. I was told that it was a "transit room," and I assumed that it was a kind of storage for the belongings of newcomers. Still, I was concerned that the army of ants I saw roaming about the room would enter my suitcases and that the dust and pervasive smell of mold might permeate my clothes.

I started asking around and inquiring about when I could move to my actual accommodation and what it was like, and I kept getting evasive replies: "You were not on the list of today's arrivals. They did not expect you," or "There is a shortage of accommodations. That is the way things are here," or "What did you expect? We live like this. This is not New York."

It took me a while to comprehend that the ant-ridden "transit room" was intended to be my accommodation for an unspecified period of time. I found that hard to believe and ran immediately to the Office of Personnel for further clarification.

"Yes," the chief of personnel answered, "that is what it means. It happened to me as well upon my arrival two weeks ago. I agree that it is not acceptable, but nobody seems to be bothered by it. There is an official explanation that there is nothing else."

After a moment, she added, "I wonder if it is happening to women only. I have not heard of men in senior positions ending up in such rooms. You are right to complain. I will do my best to help."

And she did. I spent only one night in the "transit room." That night, however, stays among my most dreadful and unforgettable of memories. Tired and resigned, I resolved to put up with the circumstances and survive quietly until the morning, passing away the hours reading. However, when I re-entered the room, I could not bear the reality: cold wind was blowing through a broken window; cockroaches were running about in all directions; the ants were attempting to feast on my luggage, which, as a result, looked like termite hills; the mattress on the bed was torn and the bedsheets spotted. In the dim light of a single bulb, the dark spots on the walls and ceiling appeared more like markings one would find in a prison cell than in a hotel room.

Acting on impulse, I turned and ran to call for assistance, for room cleaners, for the hotel manager, anyone. I ran up the stairs, looking for any sign—an open door, a reception—any place with light, food, warmth, and above all, human beings to whom I could tell my ordeal.

By chance, I came upon the Military Club as it was the only open place in the building. It was a midsize room with a few tables, a television, a bar, and a food corner where meals were prepared on two electric plates; a bit bare but nonetheless bright and warm. A few men in uniforms were sitting around. In a state of total frustration, I began demanding access to the hotel administration. It took some time and a lot of persuasion by my newly met colleagues before I was to understand or accept that hotel services were only available during strictly defined hours; that the Aitar management should not be disturbed by clients such as myself and approached only through "proper channels," that is, through a designated UN mission official; and finally, that nothing could be done at that hour in any case.

With hindsight, I can well imagine the impression my sudden appearance in the Military Club must have created. Two of the military invited me to their table. They tried to calm me down and convince me to have some warm food and a glass of wine. I joined them, grateful for their camaraderie. "Welcome to the Aitar," they raised the toast. We laughed. It was the first time I had laughed since landing in Sukhumi. They tried to explain the rules of the game at the Aitar. I admit difficulty (again) understanding, or rather accepting, what I heard. I remember repeating that hotels were for patrons, that the management had certain obligations toward its clients, and that I had to speak to the manager who obviously must have a phone number and somehow be accessible.

After the dinner, my new colleagues accompanied me back to my room and provided me with some emergency assistance: clean bedsheets "borrowed" from somewhere, extra blankets, and a towel. Anatoly fixed the broken window with a piece of newspaper, scotch tape, and paper boxes. Jean-Luc brought in an antibug spray retrieved from the German medical team to use against the cockroaches. This is how, reconciled with my fate, I survived my first night in Abkhazia.

The next day, I discovered that news of my complaint had quickly spread about the mission compound. There only for a few hours, I had already become, unwillingly, the center of a controversy.

"Welcome to the Aitar. So you are the one complaining around. Good for you!" I was greeted by some.

"You should know that this is not New York, and we come here to serve in hardship conditions," admonished others.

The story was watched closely by many, by those who sympathized with my position but dared not speak up in their own cases, and by those who identified hardship with negligence and filth and were either not disturbed by it or did not want to antagonize the local authorities running the establishment about it. But I would not comprehend this dichotomy until much later.

During those first days, I also tried to understand why I should live in the Aitar at all, especially if there was a shortage of proper living quarters at the hotel. After exploring Stalin's *dacha* (summer home) next door, I wanted to know why it was not possible for me to move there, at least temporarily. The distance from both the Aitar and Stalin's dacha to Beria's dacha, where my office was located, could be covered by car in five minutes.

"It is not possible because of security constraints," I was told.

"So why do high-level representatives of governments and international organizations stay there during their visits to Sukhumi? I am much less attractive as a political target," I would respond.

"They come with their own close protection" was the reply.

I was not convinced. If the place was really that dangerous, a two-person close protection would not be of much use. Moreover, countries like the United States and the United Kingdom were particularly concerned about the safety of their citizens. They would not leave the safety of their political representatives to chance.

Other colleagues voiced different concerns. The mission was classified by the United Nations as a hardship posting and that classification brought with it a few additional entitlements. Some feared that if some staff members were to live outside of the UN compound in more acceptable conditions, the additional entitlements would be withdrawn. They would not believe that a mission's "hardship" status was based on a clearly defined set of criteria and that the housing situation of individual mission staff was not one of them. Staff accommodation was the subject of different regulations, varying mission by mission based on assessment of the local security conditions. Thus, at many UN hardship missions, staff were housed in a variety of privately arranged quarters once security requirements were met. I tried to explain this point, but some colleagues remained unconvinced and were instead annoyed that my "rocking the boat" could potentially put their entitlements in jeopardy.

I faced a similar reaction with regard to my office. It was a nice large room on the ground floor of Beria's dacha with trees and plants growing into the windows. It was terribly neglected, however. I did what I thought was obvious: I requested a thorough cleaning and airing and removal of the obsolete and worn-out furniture. With a few plants, carpet, a shelf of books, lamps for the desks, and some vases for fresh flowers, it began to look and feel nice and cozy. I could work there.

Colleagues who had been working at the Dacha, as the office was called, claimed that the room had been changed beyond recognition. Suddenly it was spacious, comfortable, and filled with sea air, and the scent of flowers entered through the windows.

"Is it the same room?" some wondered. "How so? It is so pleasant and people-friendly."

The number of visitors began to grow, all curious about the new shape of the office. I was surprised by its popularity.

"Is it so unusual to create a pleasant working environment?" I asked. "That's the minimum we can do in such difficult conditions. We owe it to ourselves and our local counterparts. And it does not require a lot of time or resources."

I also emphasized the support that I had received from the mission's administration. Although my requests were modest and amounted only to some minor reparations and furniture replacements, they were done fast and with a rare enthusiasm.

After a while, I began to understand that it was rather unusual for staff to make any requests at all and that some colleagues liked my "daring" attitude, one they dared not display themselves.

"You are right," agreed some. "But we feel that it is not good to put forward any demands. Some people may not like it."

I could not understand such self-imposed constraints. Then one of the local staff looked at me with concern and said, "*Eto nielzia.*"

That was the first time that I heard the term *nielzia*. *Nielzia* refers to an unwritten prohibition, an invisible, impersonal barrier preventing people from asking, querying, or contesting. It does not have to be substantiated or justified—it just is.

This mentality, that of *nielzia*, would remain present during my days in Abkhazia.

Chapter 2

Abkhazia: The Illusion of Freedom

Abkhazia occupies a small but attractive piece of land on the south shore of the Black Sea. It is home to the Black Sea Riviera, the site of the most popular vacation resorts of the former Soviet Union: Sukhumi, Pitsunda, Novi Afon, and Gagra. Historically, it has been part of Georgia, with varying degrees of autonomy, striving for independence. Unlike Georgians, most Abkhaz are Muslims, others are Christians, some nonreligious. The Abkhaz attitude toward religion, however, has been a secular one; and religion has not served as a social dividing factor. At least not yet.

Much attention has been attached to the Abkhaz language, national identity, and cultural traditions. The struggle for independence has been fought in the name of each of these values. Their linguistic identity, however, remains problematic. In 1989, over 90 percent of the Abkhaz claimed to know their mother tongue, and close to 80 percent identified Russian as their second language; in reality, most of them do not know Abkhazian well. Even today, most newspapers are published in Russian, though by law, they must include a certain quota of articles in Abkhaz. One of the two TV channels is in Russian. And it is impossible to find a sufficient number of Abkhaz-speaking journalists, teachers, and other professionals. Since Russia's recognition of Abkhaz independence in 2008, which has been accompanied with a constant influx of Russians, the use of the Abkhaz language has been in further decline.

It too remains unclear how many Abkhaz actually live in Abkhazia. At the beginning of the twenty-first century the optimistic estimation was around 150,000. The Abkhaz often explained the low figure as stemming from the history of deportation and repression of their people. In the 1800s, for example, many Abkhaz fled to Turkey in the wake of Russian ethnic cleansing; their number there today most likely exceeds those living in Abkhazia.

The Abkhaz struggle for independence has, indeed, been long. With the collapse of czarist Russia in 1918, Georgia reached an agreement with Abkhazia granting her broad autonomy. That agreement was later codified in the 1921 Georgian Constitution. However, with the end of Georgian statehood later that same year, the arrangement was rendered obsolete. The period of troublesome Georgian-Abkhazian relations followed.

* * *

The Abkhaz claim that their oppression began with two Georgians, Joseph Stalin and Lavrenti Beria, and continued with a third, Eduard Shevardnadze. In 1931, Stalin made Abkhazia an autonomous republic within Georgia, and soon after, Beria took charge of the region. In 1936, he allegedly murdered Nestor Lakoba, the old Abkhaz communist leader (he died during a visit to Beria). Lakoba had used his friendship with Stalin to protect Abkhazia from political repression and terror. Soon after his death, Beria ordered a large-scale "georgianification" of the region: Abkhaz schools were closed, the language banned, and Georgians took over most public positions. In the years that followed, thousands of Georgians were forcibly resettled to Abkhazia where they had already constituted the largest ethnic group.

The tide of history changed for Abkhazia after Stalin's death in 1953 and Beria's execution some months later. Moscow adopted a largely pro-Abkhaz policy. Although the Abkhaz constituted only a quarter of the population, they soon occupied all important party and government posts in the republic. They were also disproportionately represented in the local parliament. The Abkhaz's enhanced status provoked discontent among Georgians, who believed themselves to be victims of discrimination.

For the Abkhaz, the Georgian attitude only served to encourage them to push for full republic status within the USSR and later demand complete independence in the years of *perestroika* and upon disintegration of the Soviet Union. On July 23, 1992, Abkhazia was finally declared independent by her leader, Vladislav Ardzinba. The move enjoyed full Russian support, which saw Abkhazian independence as a means of weakening the newly independent Georgia. (Georgia had achieved her independence in 1991.) And Ardzinba was Moscow's man of confidence. He had the required background: He graduated from the History Department, Sukhumi Pedagogical Institute and studied for many years the oriental history and culture in Moscow. In Tbilisi he held the post of the Director of the Abkhaz Institute of Language, Literature and History and focused in his work on dissention between Georgian and Abkhaz languages and cultures. Allegedly, however, he did not know the Abkhaz language; and his Georgian was not much better.

The Georgian Parliament quickly rejected the Abkhaz declaration of independence and proclaimed it invalid. Nonetheless, some believe that at this point full autonomy for Abkhazia could have been negotiated and may have saved the day. But the Georgians were not ready for it.

The fighting broke out in Abkhazia in August of 1992. It began with social unrest in the streets and quickly escalated into a series of violent confrontations. Georgia had already deployed its military in response to the Abkhaz's independence declaration. Georgia's national guard forces, under orders from the defense minister, Tengiz Kitovani, marched into Sukhumi where they were met with massive resistance by Abkhaz forces, who were assisted by volunteers from the North Caucasus. The North Caucasus militia was comprised of a mixture of Russian, Chechen, and Kazak nationalists as well as some members of the Russian military. Faced with this massive resistance, Georgian forces fled in disarray as there was neither a strong unified command nor sufficient equipment to sustain an attack. Thereafter, Abkhaz forces and their allies gained control over most of the Abkhazian territory.

An exact historical record of these events is difficult to reconstruct. There are varying accounts, highly charged emotional stories from the battlefield and tales of diplomatic efforts riddled with broken promises and half-hearted agreements. What is undeniable is the enormous destruction to the infrastructure, livelihoods, and social fabric left in the wake of the fighting. The Soviet Riviera was in ruins. Thousands were left dead, wounded, and displaced. Atrocities had been committed against civilians by both sides. The war forged a deep divide between ethnic Georgians and the Abkhaz, a division that has been continually exploited politically since.

Indeed, the war came at a politically sensitive time for Georgia. The newly independent republic was only in its second year as a sovereign and suffering from internal political turmoil. The three-person state council—with Shevardnadze at the helm and Kitovani and Jaba Ioseliani—was in the midst of a power struggle with the political supporters of the country's ex-president, Zviad Gamsakhurdia. Abkhazia just became one more war front.

Fearing that the conflict and separatist tendencies could spill over into neighboring Russian republics, Russian President Boris Yeltsin brokered a cease-fire agreement between Shevardnadze and Ardzinba in Moscow on September 3, 1992. The agreement provided that "the territorial integrity of the Republic of Georgia will be ensured" and that Russia would be the guarantor of the agreement's enforcement. Georgian forces withdrew from the war zone.

Soon afterward, however, the fighting resumed. Abkhaz forces took advantage of the lull in hostilities and took over northern Abkhazia. The September 3 agreement became the first of many cease-fires and treaties to be violated with no consequences for their violators.

Further talks involving Georgian, Abkhaz, and Russian leaders—interrupted by occasional skirmishes and provocations—followed but were, in the end, ineffective. A lasting solution did not get any closer; high tensions and mistrust prevailed. Moscow finally brokered a further cease-fire agreement between Abkhazia and Georgia, signed in Sochi on July 27, 1993. As soon as Georgia met its main obligation under the agreement and withdrew heavy equipment from the conflict zone, the Abkhaz launched a full-scale offensive and took control of the entire Abkhaz prewar territory. It was a repeat of the 1992 postagreement events. President Shevardnadze accused Russia of complicity and providing arm supplies and assistance to Abkhazia.

In the meantime, supporters of the ousted Georgian ex-president, Zviad Gamsakhurdia, launched a parallel offensive. Gamsakhurdia returned from Grozny and called on Georgians to demote the "junta of Shevardnadze." His forces quickly took control of western Georgia and its capital Zugdidi and forced Shevardnadze to run to Moscow for help despite his grievances against Russia. Yeltsin assented and Russian troops moved in quickly, defeating Gamsakhurdia and reinstating Shevardnadze.

The cost to Georgia was high. Russia dictated the terms of its subsequent military protection: Georgia would join the Commonwealth of Independent States (CIS); ensure Russian access to its Black Sea ports and four Russia military bases (Soviet-era legacies) remaining on Georgian territory in Gudauta, Akhalkalaki, Vaziani (outside Tbilisis), and Batumi; and agree to the deployment of a CIS peacekeeping force to maintain separation of the warring parties along the cease-fire line.

The events of 1993 demonstrated that Georgia was, indeed, a failed state and practically at the mercy of Russia, her much-despised archenemy. And Abkhazia, like South Ossetia, had became a useful instrument for Russia as it maneuvered to retain its dominance in the Caucasus and exact revenge on Georgia for her own (successful) independence efforts. The events that year also confirmed that Georgia could not count on any reliable support from the West, a reality that remains unchanged today. The only political compromise Russia was willing to assent to was the establishment of the United Nations Observer Mission in Georgia (UNOMIG), which was formed on August 24, 1993. But the mission's mandate was very limited and strictly observatory—to monitor the agreed cease-fire. However, it remains the only case where the UN engaged in a conflict involving Russia.

Over the next fifteen years, a multitude of peace initiatives, diplomatic maneuverings, and multilateral and bilateral meetings would be undertaken; none would bring about a breakthrough. How could they? The positions of the two adversaries were basically nonreconcilable. The Abkhaz's uncompromising demand for independence could not be satisfied by Georgian belated offers of autonomy. Georgia's agreements with Russia could not be revoked without serious consequences for Georgia and implications for East-West relations. There was also no mood among international partners to challenge Russia regarding the inherent conflict posed by its declared role as a neutral peace guarantor and mediator and its de facto role in maintaining and controlling the "frozen conflict," whether directly or by proxy, effectively preventing any lasting solution.

So diplomatic initiatives and negotiations, some even innovative, came and went. No serious attempt was made to take stock and reflect upon the causes for the continued diplomatic failures. Meanwhile, tensions between Abkhazia and Georgia continued to fluctuate between small skirmishes and provocations and wars of words and more serious violent attacks on territories and installations and against the inhabitants of the conflict area.

*   *   *

In the years since the 1992-93 war, Abkhazia has skilfully used the time to move toward consolidating her independence. In November 1994, Abkhazia adopted a new constitution and elected a parliament and president. Each of these acts was in violation of all previous agreements recognizing the territorial integrity of Georgia. In 1996, Georgia managed to successfully lobby the CIS to impose an economic blockade on Abkhazia at its Moscow summit. Undeterred, that same year Abkhazia held parliamentary elections and, in 1999, re-elected the incumbent president, Ardzinba, to another term. In sum, Abkhazia established itself as a de facto independent state, holding regular elections for its de facto president and parliament, despite the lack of formal recognition by any country.

Abkhazia also had the de facto support of Russia, which strongly condoned her independence efforts. Although Russia officially expressed support for the unquestionable principle of Georgian territorial integrity, numerous Russian politicians and institutions treated Abkhaz leaders in a manner usually reserved for state officials and made public statements and took other actions in clear support of the Abkhaz "separatists." The Russian government—in the name of democracy and separation of powers—did not intervene or condemn such activities, such as state visits by Vladimir Zhirinovsky and other Russian parliamentarians to Abkhazia and formal relations between the city of Moscow and Sukhumi, proclaimed "sister cities" by Yuri Luzhkov, the Muscovite mayor. Russia also remained silent when Abkhaz wines, labeled under the Abkhaz flag, appeared in Russian shops in the middle of Georgian-Russian wine war. While extension of Russian citizenship to the inhabitants of Abkhazia was in accordance with the Russian law entitling citizens of the former USSR to citizenship of Russia, the opening of Russia's borders to Abkhaz products was, formally, in violation of CIS economic sanctions.

Russia also enjoyed (and exploited) multiple roles in the international and bilateral efforts aimed at resolving the Abkhazian-Georgian conflict. The northern power played the role of peace guarantor, peacekeeper, impartial member of various international negotiating bodies, and acted as Georgia's military and economic ally within the CIS and on the UN Security Council where it had veto power, to mention a few. Russia also exerted de facto influence over all key Abkhaz policy decisions. Abkhazian leaders were handpicked and totally dependent on Moscow—they had Russian nationality and consulted with Moscow on the "Abkhaz" position to be taken at all international forums. Abkhazia's long-serving de facto president, Ardzinba, spent most of his time while in office in Moscow, allegedly due to poor health.

Therefore it came as a surprise when, in 2004, the Abkhaz tried to take the presidential elections into their own hands. Russia had taken it for granted that Raul Khadjimba, the Moscow-backed candidate with a KGB background, would win. Numerous Russian politicians had publicly expressed their support for his candidacy—in their personal capacities, of course. The winner turned out to be Sergei Bagapsh, an independent candidate and local businessman married to a Georgian woman. Months of tensions, threats, confusion, and political maneuvering followed the elections, ending with Russia being forced to finally take the election result seriously. Power-sharing arrangements were worked out, and Bagapsh was proclaimed the (de facto) president of Abkhazia. In 2008, he became Abkhazia's first *de jure* president, at least for Russia and Nicaragua, which had recognized Abkhazian sovereignty.

The 2004 elections gave clear indication that Abkhaz feelings toward Russia were more complex than they appeared on the surface. Despite her historical grievances against Russia, Abkhazia perceived Russia as her only effective protector against Georgia and political supporter as she moved toward independence. Russia was the only country to open its borders and markets to the Abkhaz. Moreover, the memories of the Georgian invasion in 1992 and the destruction that followed pushed the Abkhaz toward accepting a close association with Russia, and all the attendant consequences of such a relationship, to include Russian control and interference in Abkhaz internal affairs and grant of Russian citizenship to her inhabitants.

The Abkhaz nonetheless increasingly came to resent the humiliation, persistent misery, poverty, and lack of prospects, which they attributed to local authorities and their Russian masters. The Abkhazian people wanted to be treated in a respectful manner, not as a pawn in a great power's world game.

It was during my visit to Abkhazia during the 2004 electoral crisis that I heard the first voices of criticism. Some local men supporting Bagapsh, leaning against a lorry parked close to his office in Sukhumi, loudly proclaimed: "They should not be too sure of themselves. We will stand by Sergei. He is our man. He lives here, we know him," said one of them. "We do not need another president who lives in Moscow and sends us instructions from there—"

"And who will be on permanent sick leave in Russia," a young boy interjected.

"If they like Khadjimba, they can give him a nice post in Russia. Keep him there if he is so good. We do not need him. We have enough of *siloviki* here," another chimed in.

"Some people may be afraid that it is *our* Rose Revolution," a tall, thin man added. "They kicked out a Moscow man in Tbilisi, and we are doing the same here. At least, it may look that way."

"Psst, do not talk stupidly. It has nothing to do with Georgia," the first man hissed, nervously looking around. "Such stupid talk is not helpful. Somebody may hear it. And Bagapsh is not Saakashvili. He is not America's guy. He is from here, and he has friends and connections in Moscow as well."

The usually reserved receptionist at the Aitar Hotel, Galina, welcomed me with the comment: "Let us hope that something will change. All we want is a normal life, and up to now, we have not moved in that direction. There have always been obstacles. We all know that the Georgians ruined our country and our lives, but the war ended many years ago. There is no explanation for why we should live in these conditions now."

Vala, a cleaning lady, stopped watering flowers at the entrance and joined us.

"I do not even want anything for myself, but I want a different life for my grandchildren. My children's lives have already been ruined by the war. But my granddaughter is very intelligent, an excellent student, and I wonder what she can do in the future. She cannot even get a proper education here—she cannot learn foreign languages, travel, or see anything beyond the mess of Sukhumi.

"We do not even feel ourselves anymore in what degradation we live," she went on. "We have gotten used to it. Yesterday evening, when I was about to finish my duty, I was told by one of the girls that there was a vacant apartment in the building. I took the opportunity to quietly use the bathroom—taking a bath and washing my hair in hot water.

"Later on, when I arrived at home, I said to my family, 'I had a lucky day today [*U mienia sievodnia prazdnik*]. I bathed in hot water!' So that is our life."

But while there was no love lost between the Abkhaz and Russians, Georgia was perceived as the principal enemy of Abkhazia, the source of her misfortune, fear, and economic degradation and the cause for her dependency on Russia.

*   *   *

With the Rose Revolution and change in political leadership in Georgia, there was some hope of a possible Georgian-Abkhazian settlement or, at least, the opening of a meaningful dialogue. The Abkhaz never had high expectations for Saakashvili, but given their hatred for Shevardnadze, Saakashvili was at least a change. Soon, however, old feelings of bitterness and suspicion returned.

I was told in Sukhumi that the Georgian border at the cease-fire line remained closed to the Abkhaz as before. Sofiko, one of the Aitar women, told me that her cousin, fed up with the misery and lawlessness in Abkhazia, decided to go to Zugdidi to get Georgian documents rather than take a Russian passport. He had intended to find relatives in Tbilisi and somehow settle there. He did not get far. On the Georgian side of the cease-fire line, he was treated like a criminal by the Georgian authorities. He had expected support but was detained and interrogated instead. After a while, he managed to escape and return to Sukhumi. I heard similar stories from others who had tried to discretely inquire about obtaining Georgian papers and temporary support should they decided to resettle in Georgia proper. They were met with bureaucratic rigidity, political hostility, and suspicion.

I could not believe my ears. I rather expected that Saakashvili would have learned from recent European experiences and would apply the tactics so successfully used by West Germany. I could envisage special "hospitality" centers in areas bordering Abkhazia welcoming visitors, encouraging contacts, and offering assistance to those who wanted to see their families in Georgia proper. With donor money flowing in from the West after the Rose Revolution, some basic arrangements of this kind could have been easily made.

As for the Georgian people, most of my Georgian interlocutors remained skeptical about prospects for improvement in Georgian-Abkhazian relations. But they had not been particularly preoccupied with the matter either or motivated to use the change in the political climate on the heels of the Rose Revolution to attempt at least informal dialogue with the people of Abkhazia. They also believed that, in any case, such efforts would not be allowed by Russia.

Georgian opinions essentially fell into one of two categories, the first being: "The Abkhaz are bad and hate Georgians, ally with our enemies, and do not properly appreciate the possibility of being part of Georgia. All complaints about Georgian atrocities and destruction of Sukhumi in the early 1990s are exaggerated. Georgians were fighting for the right cause as Abkhazia had always been a part of their territory. The fault for the violence lay with the Abkhaz, encouraged by the Russians. The Abkhaz betrayed Georgia, their historical homeland, and chased Georgians out of Abkhazia, destroying and appropriating Georgian homes and properties and depriving them of the land of their ancestors. There is no way of talking to the Abkhaz except from the position of force. Their leaders and others guilty of treason and responsible for the massive killing of Georgians should be brought to justice and punished. Until then, there is no room for any dialogue."

And the second view being: "The Russians are to blame. The Abkhaz and Georgians lived for centuries in peace. It was only during Soviet times that, due to political manipulation, relations started to deteriorate. If left to themselves, if left free of Russian interference, they would have found ways to communicate and live together as before. After all, there are common economic interests and demands of daily life—transportation, local trade, housing—that would be much easier solved with even minimum cooperation between the two adversaries. However, as long as Russia retains influence over developments in Abkhazia and has a say in the so-called peace process between the parties, nothing can change. Russian control of the 'frozen conflict' provides the optimal conditions for Russia to exercise its authority over the region."

I found too that—notwithstanding the Georgians' usual openness, worldly sophistication, and eagerness to talk politics—the subject of Abkhazia was taboo. There was simply no way to have a rational conversation on the topic. Anti-Abkhaz and anti-Russian feelings predominated. The image of the enemy blinded even the most astute. The hatred of pro-Russian leaders in the separatist provinces had extended itself to the general population. There was no reflection on the condition of the people, the Abkhaz and South Ossetians, who had little control over the situation. Nor was there a discussion about ways to initiate dialogue and open up the lines of communication with each other, except possibly immediate family members.

Abkhazian views mirrored those of Georgians. What the Georgians thought of the Abkhaz was reflective of how the Abkhaz perceived Georgians. They differed only in their respective views of Russia.

*   *   *

In the summer of 2009, I met with former Georgian President, Eduard Shevardnadze. Commenting on the situation in Abkhazia, he expressed the view that the Abkhaz leaders had made a serious mistake. Expounding further, he remarked, "They will be quickly outnumbered by Russians, and they will have no voice in their country. They may soon vanish all together." He also expressed disappointment in Bagapsh who, years ago, he had supported for the position of the second secretary of the Komsomol of Georgia.

The situation in Abkhazia has changed drastically. The events since the 2008 Georgian-Russian war over South Ossetia and Russia's subsequent recognition of Abkhazia and South Ossetia as sovereign states, suggest truth in Shevardnadze's words.

First and foremost, the economic takeover of the fledgling de facto state by the Russians—of Abkhaz commercial markets and property in Abkhazia—is undeniable. In the past, there were no official investments, and Russians acquired property informally as Abkhazia was still officially recognized by her northern neighbor as part of Georgia. With independence (as recognized by Russia), all bilateral relations, to include trade and economic relations, could be (and have been) formally established. As a consequence, Russian investors and banks have moved in, construction of Russian-financed hotels and tourist establishments have began in force, and numerous properties have officially changed hands into Russian hands.

While the influx of money is very much needed in Abkhazia, Russian investment and Russian money has meant Russian decision making, shared only with a narrow segment of the population—the local economic and political elite loyal to Russia. The same applies to the socio-political system. Considering the authoritarianism of the Russian regime, the precarious security situation in Abkhazia and in the Caucasus more generally, and deep Abkhaz dependence on Russia, Abkhazia is not going to be a liberal democracy. It is yet to be seen which decisions will be taken by Abkhaz authorities and which will be dictated by the Russians. The incident involving Russian replacement of Abkhaz border police in August 2009, despite protests and resistance from the Abkhaz, may be foretelling of future such conflicts.

Further, the steady increase in the number of Russians coming to Abkhazia, over time, can only serve to further weaken the Abkhaz in their own land. The recent construction of a Russian military base on Abkhaz territory, ostensibly "to protect it from possible attacks by Georgia," implies not only another massive influx of Russians during the period of construction, but also their constant military and political presence—these are strictly Russian-led activities.

And it is a numbers as well as power struggle. As all Abkhaz are Russian citizens the distinction can, with time, become blurred, the Abkhaz may find themselves indistinguishable, melded into a Russian-dominated society. The irony is poignant: the Abkhaz struggle for independence has been fought in the name of national identity and sovereignty, precisely to preserve her cultural traditions and language. Not only may the Abkhaz soon find themselves a minority in their own land (which they may already be), they may soon find that it is they who are unwelcome.

Chapter 3

Country Roads

I was looking forward to my first trip from Sukhumi to Gali, in the southern region of Abkhazia. It was only about one hundred kilometers away, so I was surprised by the estimated two hours the trip was projected to take. I was even more astonished by the amount of formalities and preparations: prior to departure, we had to check the security situation; upon leaving, we had to travel by convoy with at least two people in one car or, if required by UN security, with two cars; and at various points along the road, we had to contact the mission by radio using a specially assigned code. After leaving Sukhumi, however, certain of these requirements became more understandable.

The journey to Gali City, the regional capital, amounted to navigating around the multitude of potholes and animals, which had overtaken the road. Cows and pigs ran freely about, far outnumbering the humans and vehicles, and they did not have to report "Charlie, Charlie" to headquarters every thirty minutes. On sunny days, the cows would lay down in the center of the road, as that, it was said, provided them protection from the flies that would otherwise disturb their sleep.

The terrain along the road to Gali City, although green and rich in vegetation, was largely marked by the skeletons of abandoned houses, fruit gardens overtaken by weeds and herds of unsupervised animals. The region—which had been a main supplier of nuts, oranges, mandarins, and tea to Soviet republics—now looked like a ghost area. There were hardly any people around. The few inhabited houses we saw along the way often did not differ much from the abandoned ones. It looked as if nature in all her forms—from the free-roaming animals to the wild overgrowth of green foliage and dense subtropical rainforest—had reclaimed what was once human space. Only remnants of formerly cultivated gardens and fields, paved roads, and properly kept houses and villas remained.

The Gali region had been abandoned and neglected for many years, since the Georgian-Abkhazian war in 1992-93. Sparsely populated, only occasionally would a human shadow emerge in the distance, from the corner of a garden, in the bush or just behind a window's shade. For us, the civilians stationed in Sukhumi, it was impossible to establish any contact with them. Only when we were accompanied by our military observers, particularly those who had been in the region for a while, was there a chance for direct, though quite formal, contact. I was struck by how uncomfortable, fearful and poor the people looked: a devastated people in a devastated environment. They looked around nervously and tried to keep conversations short, seemly always relieved when we were about to depart.

We could only speculate as to the reasons behind such behavior: the recent experience of war atrocities; the uncontrolled criminality and harassment in the region; abuse by local authorities; their own possible illegal occupation of another's property; an unwillingness to breach the local code of silence?

*   *   *

Who were these people? Mainly ethnic Georgians and Mingrelians who had lived in the Gali region both before and during the war, and had remained there after the war. They were the people who had never left. Thus, only a small number of Gali inhabitants were returnees, internally displaced persons (IDPs), those who had left for Georgia proper during the war and subsequently returned. Living conditions for IDPs in Georgia proper were dreadful and the people lacked future prospects, but it was not easy to return to Abkhazia.

The right of return of former Abkhazian inhabitants, mainly ethnic Georgians, had been at the center of international negotiations since the war. Their voluntary and safe return should have been organized in accordance with the rules of the United Nations High Commissioner for Refugees (UNHCR) and facilitated by the international community (IC) as part of the peace process. But such conditions did not exist in Abkhazia, particularly in the lawless Gali. And although the Abkhaz side, supported by Russia, insisted that it was prepared to receive potential returnees, Georgia, the UNHCR and the IC all had serious reservations.

Abkhazia was not recognized as a state, but the Abkhaz controlled the territory. As with any such control it came with a set of legal obligations that the controlling authority, here the Abkhaz, had toward the inhabitants, without prejudice to their status. These obligations included respect of the inhabitants' basic human rights and freedoms and protection of their security. In the case of returnees, the controlling authority was obligated to facilitate the returnees' resettlement to their abandoned properties and homes, at least to the extent possible. Abkhaz authorities, however, were reluctant to admit the existence of such obligations. They were mainly concerned with "security" in the sense of the territorial security of Abkhazia, particularly in the Gali region, which was vulnerable to Georgian armed attacks, not the security of the inhabitants.

Georgian concerns were the exact opposite and focused on the protection of her citizens from harassment by Abkhaz security forces. For years, Georgian authorities had insisted upon opening a UNOMIG human rights office in Gali and placing a UN police component in the region. That could have strengthened regional security and addressed the concerns of all parties. But the Abkhaz were not prepared to allow any kind of international supervision of the return process, or the human rights situation more generally, in the Gali region. Rather, Abkhaz authorities, backed by Russia, undertook steps to sabotage such efforts.

Thus, security remained one of the principle obstacles to return. Cases of arbitrary house searches and arrests and abuses by local security forces against ethnic Georgians were widespread in Gali. The insecurity was further exacerbated by the general lawlessness and frequent acts of criminality, mainly armed robbery and theft, committed by unknown perpetrators. It was assumed that some of these acts were done in cooperation with the local security, or even the Russian-led CIS peacekeepers, or at least with their full knowledge and consent. It was also understood that the perpetrators would never be found and goods never returned. That had much to do with political intimidation. Ethnic Georgian returnees were even more at risk than the Georgians who had never left Gali. Local authorities were especially suspicious of those who had spent considerable time in "enemy" territory, alleging them to be spies against Abkhazia or involved in some other subversive activities.

There was also a question of status. The returnees did not want to be registered as Abkhaz citizens. From their perspective, it was both wrong politically and against their sense of identity. While they wanted to return to their homes and property, they did not accept the idea of Abkhazian statehood. It would have been viewed as an act of treason against Georgia, and they were, first and foremost, Georgians.

The problem was further compounded by the absence of transparency in the return process. In the years following the 1992-93 war, the formal demands imposed on returnees by Abkhaz authorities were never made clear and kept changing. Even the contents of the papers the returnees were required to sign largely remained a mystery, and the practical consequences of signing them never coherently explained. It appears as well that the nature of the formalities too were arbitrary and depended on the point in time, location, policy of the local authorities, and random decisions of individual officials. Indeed, for several years, from 2001 to 2004, Abkhaz authorities insisted that the papers served only an administrative purpose, a form of registration. We, along with our colleagues at the UNHCR, had a number of conversations with Abkhaz officials on this issue:

"Does the form include a 'loyalty clause,' a confirmation of loyalty to the Abkhaz 'state'?"

"No, it only requires a statement on the respect for law and order. You always have to respect the laws of the country of residence, no?"

We never managed to get beyond such superficial exchanges. It was also close to impossible to get a copy of the "registration" form and, if we did, to be sure that it was both valid and complete.

The Abkhaz claimed that they had the right to know who lived in their territory, where they lived, and to whom each plot of land belonged. They justified the registration requirement on security grounds as well. Georgia had never stopped in its attempts to undermine Abkhaz rule and often supported criminal elements in the area. Until the Rose Revolution, to the extent Georgia was a state, it was a failing one. It was thus often hard to say which criminal element committed what attack—Georgians, the Abkhaz, Russians, or some multiethnic group—and on whose orders. The security situation proved so fragile that the UNHCR and UNDP were forced to leave the region following attacks on Abkhaz positions and installations in Gali, in 2000, fighting which saw widespread destruction of property and house burning and political repression.

Another alleged consequence of the "paper signing" by returnees was possible conscription into the Abkhaz army. Returnees claimed that this had been the case in the past, and that as non-Abkhaz, they should not be subjected to serving in the Abkhaz military, a military meant to be used against Georgia. The Abkhaz denied the practice, which is illegal under international law, but most IDPs with sons at risk of being drafted nonetheless stayed out of Gali, where the conscription was allegedly taking place. As a result, the vast majority of returnees to Gali were elderly, people who over time increasingly lost the capacity to work their plots or maintain their war-scarred, dilapidated homes. To aid them, younger family members and friends from Georgia proper, excepting men who were potential military conscripts, began visiting in the summer to work the land and maintain the property. To earn income, their relatives also tried to transport as many agricultural goods as possible back across the cease-fire line into Georgia proper.

These undertakings were not without risks. Invariably, there was the possibility of arrest or harassment by Abkhaz security forces either on the family farm itself or at the "border" crossing, the latter always being a tedious and an uncertain affair. There was no transportation connecting the main cities on either side, and the long bridge over the Inguri River at the cease-fire line had to be crossed by foot. Thus, the amount of goods that could be taken on any one-time journey had to be restricted to what could be placed in a pushcart or carried.

The contents of such belongings were subject to inspection and "customs" and, in the worst case, confiscation. On the Abkhaz side, there were obviously no established tariffs and decisions were arbitrary, amounting to a sharing of the spoils. On the Georgian side, the police also had to get a cut. Thus the poorest of the poor — the IDPs — were forced to carry the burden of corruption and pay with their meager goods at both ends. Sometimes they were even forced to pay third parties, namely the Russian peacekeepers who, tasked with supervising the cease-fire line, had the right to monitor all "security-related" activities.

In addition to official corruption, the IDPs were also vulnerable to armed robbery. Although the harvest season always resulted in a corresponding rise in attacks on farmers, no security measures where taken by authorities to protect them. The Russian peacekeeping force also turned a blind eye to the theft, or rather, according to some, took part in it. Despite these risks, the summer migration steadily increased, driven primarily by the desperation of the IDPs.

With the 2008 Georgian-Russian war and the recognition of Abkhazian independence by Russia, all such contacts abruptly stopped. Abkhazia became totally inaccessible to Georgians, and the situation of the inhabitants in the Gali region further deteriorated. Completely isolated, they have allegedly been subjected to increased repression and forced dispossession of their property, but there is no way to verify these reports.

Chapter 4

The Aitar Women

The Aitar employed a lot of locals as cleaners, manual workers, guards, receptionists, and clerks. As they were paid symbolically, they worked symbolically. There was an assumption that they would find extra income—in dollars, no less—by providing a sundry of personal, individually proffered services to foreigners. For the local people, employment at the Aitar was therefore perceived as a privilege, a once-in-a-life opportunity—a chance to escape poverty and daily misery, a means to access a better world.

The Aitar had two canteens, the Civilian and Military clubs, and a café. Each required the services of caters and bartenders to attend to the patrons, and the services of handymen to deal with endlessly malfunctioning electrical wiring, coffee machines and cookers, and that of the unhinged doors and broken windows. There were also two masseurs and a hairdresser operating on the premises. Most of the employees, with the exception of the handymen, were women. They were of all ages, smart, most attentive to their appearance and hardworking. They were also quite determined and often unscrupulous, looking to get as much as they possibly could out of the circumstances: they would charm, oblige, cheat, take on any additional work or transaction on the side, anything to get ahead. Life had taught them to trust no one. They were quite suspicious of us, the foreigners, the Aitar administration, and local authorities, and above all, each other.

The Aitar women were also intensely competitive. Despite the existence of unwritten rules demarcating their respective territories (rules I never fully grasped) and a hierarchy of jobs, they would occasionally get into disputes and open disagreements. Backbiting and gossip was the way of life and survival. They aggressively fought for patrons, employing all available means, to include their connections in the Aitar administration and among UN employees, to secure them.

Most Aitar women were the only bread winners in their families, families which often had numerous dependents, including men. Some tried to explain why the men had to stay home instead of taking up available work. They spoke proudly of the important positions their husbands had held before the war "in the good old times."

"My husband had been a factory director with a lot of subordinates under him," Vera, one of the room cleaners, explained. "What could he do in these ruins around us nowadays? There is no work for him matching his qualifications. He cannot do work like this," she said, pointing to the filthy floors, streams of spider webs, and broken installations.

The Construction Workers

I was particularly moved by the situation of the women working in construction, renovating hotel apartments. As day contractors, they were somewhere near the bottom of the Aitar's social structure. They were considered outsiders by those who were regularly employed and often lived on the premises. They interacted neither with the Aitar women nor hotel inhabitants. I came across them when I started following the renovation of my newly assigned apartment. The scene reminded me of something out of a Dickens novel or one of those old movies portraying nineteenth century capitalism and the desolate conditions under which laborers were forced to work.

I saw two human skeletons covered in dust and dirt moving about the mess of bricks, shattered glass, and broken furniture. In the dimness of the light, it took me a while to recognize that they were women—skinny, severely malnourished and prematurely aged. How old could they be? In their late thirties, early forties? Clearly, they would be considered young or just entering middle age by standards in the West. How different must their lives and mind-sets have been.

They were surprised by my appearance and embarrassed by their poor condition. They nervously started brushing off their dark cloth and cleaning their palms to respond to my outstretched hand. They murmured their names and bowed and then they started explaining that they did their best.

"We really work very hard, we want you to know," said one.

"We have just one pair of scissors to cut the wallpaper and a big hammer. We do not even have a pair of protective gloves. We have to do it all with bare hands."

"Pssst, do not talk too much," interrupted the other.

"I just came here to thank you for your hard work and introduce myself," I mumbled, now saddened by my perceived role. "I am impressed by how hard you work—only women can do such a job in these conditions. And I will benefit from your work as I will move in here."

I looked around again, disbelieving the place could ever be habitable. "How can you work in such conditions? Don't you have protective cloth? Proper tools?"

They glanced at each other and started to relax, even smile. They were reassured that I did not come from the Aitar administration and did not intend to report them. After a while, they probably concluded that I was one of those foreign women around the compound who was not fearful of the administration or local authorities and—although curious, assertive, and sometimes irritating—was sympathetic to them. Thus, I felt that they began to enjoy my presence. We started chatting.

I asked if we could have a cup of coffee. As there were no coffee facilities around, I wanted to invite them to the compound canteen or my VIP room, but they declined. They did not want go anywhere in such shape, and in any case, they were not supposed to mingle with the residents of the compound. Why not, I wanted to know. *Eto nielzia*—simply, one should not, they told me.

Again, *nielzia*—a prohibition, the reasons for which are neither stated nor questioned, but must be in all circumstances obeyed. It is a way of thinking, of existing. It is impersonal, a general norm governing people's lives.

The word—and the mentality it represented—was unfailingly present throughout my time in Abkhazia. I will always associate it with life in Sukhumi, a lasting legacy of its Soviet past.

The *"nielzia"* mentality permeated all aspects of life in Abkhazia. It supported the political and social hierarchy in various institutions, enabling dismissal, out-of-hand, unwelcome queries and suppression of any form of dissent. To conform, one simply refrained from asking inconvenient questions, in public and in private. So pervasive was *"nielzia"* that it had even entered the vocabulary and culture of the UN office in Sukhumi and influenced the behavior of some UN staff.

The coffee problem was solved by bringing a pot of coffee and sweets to the construction site. The women were truly moved. We kept talking. They told me about their families and their lives before the war and about their difficult work at the Aitar which, despite the meager wages and unhealthy conditions, was very precious to them. It was the means by which their families could be provided for and their families were the central focus of their universe; they had no personal expectations. We also touched on a lighter, more noncontroversial subject: the beauty of Abkhazia.

From time to time, they looked nervously around to make sure that our coffee break was not being watched. I tried to assure them that there was nothing wrong with having a coffee break in the midst of their endless work day and that I would take responsibility if anyone questioned my presence on the premises. After all, the unit they were working on was going to be my future apartment.

Afterward, I tried to discreetly inquire if the UN, the hotel's main client, could somehow influence the treatment of hotel employees.

"It is not our business. We have enough problems with the Aitar administration. They can refuse to extend the lease and cause us a lot of trouble" was the answer. "Do not get involved in that."

"And what about international human rights standards?"

"They do not apply to UN staff." I had heard that before. "But they are not UN employees," I said, trying another line of argument.

"This is not an independent state. If you ask them to apply international standards in Abkhazia, they would use it as proof of her independence."

I gave up. I did not want to get into a discussion about the responsibilities of a power controlling a territory toward the inhabitants of that territory, a discussion which would have been useless in any case. It was not up to me to organize training for UN staff on international legal standards, but I was disappointed by the lack of compassion.

Tonya

I moved to the VIP room while awaiting renovation of my permanent accommodation. It was a luxury suite by Aitar standards: It was small but clean and even had a bedside lamp with a bare bulb.

As soon as I arrived, I heard a knock at the door. I saw a strong, sturdy, carefully dressed midaged woman with bleached blond hair and gold teeth. She introduced herself as Tonya and wanted to know if I already had somebody "to work for me." No, I did not, but my mind was not on such practicalities.

"Please can I do the work for you?" she continued. "I have nobody to work for at the moment, and if we do not agree now, the girls will convince you later to accept somebody else." Half absentmindedly, I promised not to get into any arrangement until the two of us met again and discussed the matter.

After Tonya's departure, I received numerous calls from other women employed at the Aitar wanting to work for me. I resisted the pressure of their hard sales although it took me a while to understand the system.

Tonya started "working for me" to our mutual satisfaction. One day, looking at my French books spread out all over the apartment, Tonya asked me, *"Parlez-vous francais"*? Yes, I know what it means, I still remember. There was a time when I studied French as well, at school in Leningrad, now St. Petersburg."

She tried to recall a French song. *Un, deux, "trois"* . . . I do not remember anymore. It's been so many years." She sighed, her expression changing. Her down-to-earth, heavy presence and determined face suddenly became dreamy and distant with thoughts of school, the friends of her youth, the bridges over Neva, the dreams.

"I still have a good friend there, Natalia. We are from the same school, the same neighborhood, and still very close although fate separated us for years and made our respective lives very different.

"I made mistakes for which I can only blame myself," Tonya continued. "I was young and attractive. I liked to go out, dance, and dress well. My mother understood it. She knew that my youth would not last forever and encouraged me to enjoy life."

After graduation from high school, Tonya did not go to university. She thought she would one day, but in the meantime, she got a job as a clerk in an office. Soon after, she went on holiday to Sukhumi, one of the most popular vacation destinations in the Soviet Union those days.

"You can't imagine how beautiful and elegant it was," she told me. "People were well dressed. There were posh cafés, beaches lined with umbrellas and children's playgrounds, parks and seaside promenades, and supermarkets better supplied than those in Moscow.

"The world was wonderful, and I met a very good-looking young man. He was a 'local.' We fell in love and a few months later got married." She quickly left Leningrad, her job, her friends, and her mother. She was rushing to embrace her new life, life in this paradise on earth with the man she loved.

"I can't believe it myself today," Tonya mused. "But that was it."

They settled down. She took care of the household and worked a lot during the summer in local restaurants. Soon their son, Alosha, was born. The happiness, however, did not last long. She noticed that her husband secretly drank. With time, his drinking habits became obvious and led to all kinds of trouble typical for families of alcoholics.

"He was not violent," Tonya said, "but he spent all the money and all his time drinking. He had a lot of company to do it. Most local men were like this, and most women quietly accepted their drinking ways. I went through hell with a small child without means and steady employment. I tried to save him, sent him to doctors and for counseling. No other women did that. They believed that it was the male role to drink and that I was lucky that he did not harass me.

"The treatment and my efforts led nowhere. With time, my husband lost every bit of self-respect and ruined his health. He died prematurely, leaving us with nothing. I had to start from scratch and struggle to provide for my son. And then, this dreadful war came, this madness. There is nothing worse than a war. But at this point in my life, I could not return to Leningrad. I had to stay here.

"My deepest regret is that I did not see my mother for years. I always thought that one day I would be able to support her. I was wrong. Now she is gone, and I miss her terribly.

"Natalia did much better," Tonya said. She stayed and studied in Leningrad. She married well, meaning to someone who was educated, worked as a *naucznyj sotrudnik* (academic teacher) at the Technical University, did not get into any political trouble, and most surprisingly, did not drink. Natalia did not have children, which was rather rare among Russian women of their generation but seemed not to mind it. Instead, she enjoyed concerts and the theater, read a lot, dressed well, and filled her apartment with luxury goods, at least luxurious compared to her contemporaries, including Tonya. By now, she too was a widow—the predominant status of midaged women in the former Soviet Union—but it had not changed her lifestyle. She remained elegant, well-preserved, and had developed a habit of taking in homeless cats.

Visiting Natalia was one of the bright points in Tonya's life. But those were rare visits. St. Petersburg was far away and even the cheapest transportation meant a lot of money by Sukhumi standards. The women of Tonya's generation were not in the habit of spending on themselves. But Tonya had another reason to go. Her only grandson lived close to St. Petersburg with his mother, her ex-daughter-in-law. Their story was as common as Tonya's own. Tonya's son had been born of a Russian-Abkhaz union. His wife was Georgian. And like Tonya and her husband, her son and his wife met in Sukhumi, on the beautiful Black Sea Riviera, where they both had been born and brought up. They fell in love, married, and had a son.

But times changed with the Abkhazian-Georgian war. Georgian troops marched through Abkhazia, leaving behind burnt cities, destroyed houses, fleeing crowds, and dead bodies. Abkhaz shock turned into outrage, sparking even stronger nationalism and anti-Georgian sentiment. "You can either be with us and against them or a declared enemy of every Abkhaz" was a predominant attitude. There was no other choice.

Eka, Tonya's daughter-in-law, suffered the same fate—the loss of home, destruction of Sukhumi—as others. But she was Georgian and devastated by the death of young Georgian soldiers and civilians as well. She considered the war a tragic misunderstanding rather than a devilish Georgian plot. She tried to reason and understand the situation in her own way, a way different from that of her neighbors and in-laws. So she became suspect.

Tonya shook her head. "I never believed it, but she was perceived as a traitor. She talked to the Georgian invaders so people thought that she was against us. She had to flee. She took her son along."

Tonya stopped and seemed to look off at some distant point, lost in her memories.

"With the war, my son lost his job and his family. He started drinking like his father and prematurely aged. Once the war ended, he moved in with me so I could take care of him. He is improving, he is a good boy, but he keeps bad company. That makes things difficult. They always tease him and call on him to have a beer. Once they start drinking, they cannot stop. Finally, he and Eka divorced, but it was done through the lawyers. She never came back to Abkhazia."

Tonya put her strong, worn-out hands on top of the broom but did not move.

"My daughter-in-law told me that she had nothing against me. She said I could visit her any time I want and take the boy for vacation, but not to Abkhazia. She would never permit that. She does not have a grudge against her husband, so he can see his son as well, but not to take him away."

So Tonya tried to clean as many apartments as possible to save money for her son and herself to travel to the North to see her grandson. Afterward, she planned to reward herself with a rare treat. She would extend her trip to St. Petersburg and stay with Natalia.

Tonya's postwar life had had some bright points. She met a man with whom she had settled, a man who was widowed like herself, a retired colonel, one of the defenders of Sukhumi who was highly regarded for his achievements during the war. Like Tonya, he had one child and one grandchild that he supported. They also lived abroad, in Armenia. He did not drink, looked good, and respected her. It goes without saying that she was the main income and care provider, but he tried to help. He bred hens and worked as a handyman in the neighborhood. He did not mind it despite his prestigious military career. He also received a small pension. It was not surprising then that other women envied her stroke of personal luck. Her son was also gradually recovering from his depression and alcoholism and had even began to do part-time work around the neighborhood.

"There is justice in the world," Tonya concluded, "sometimes at least."

*   *   *

When I returned to Sukhumi in the summer of 2004, I contacted Tonya and asked if she could care for my living quarters. I also warned her that there were now two of us, as my cat, Kitty, would be coming with me.

This time I got a regular apartment—a far better place than the "transit room" of my first night ever in Abkhazia—one I could even put up with for a few weeks. Still, I felt some unease moving into such a neglected place, which, despite all Tonya's efforts, could not be properly cleaned.

Tonya and Kitty got along extremely well. Kitty seemed to enjoy the place although it was much smaller than our Tbilisi apartment. She adjusted immediately and developed an enormous appetite. It must have been the effect of the magical Abkhazian coastal climate. But Tonya was concerned.

"She should not eat so much. It is not healthy, especially in the evening."

"Do not worry, Tonya. She does not sleep much at night. It is her playtime. Plus, she is used to having a buffet and eating whenever she wants. She regulates it herself."

Tonya remained unconvinced. It took her a while to accept Kitty's unorthodox ways. One day, she turned to Kitty and said, "My friend in St. Petersburg has a nice cat, but her cat is not as nice as you. I already wrote her about you, and she is upset. She believes that her cat is the most beautiful in the world, but it is fat."

She started to laugh. "You should not eat too much so you can keep your figure." Kitty looked at her, narrowed her green eyes, and meowed.

Actually, all the Aitar women liked Kitty in spite of her Georgian origin. And she, in turn, free of any ethnic prejudice, liked everything in Sukhumi. The small size of the apartment caused her to occasionally do some damage: knock over the reading lamp, bite a cable, clear off my dressing table of all its cosmetics. On one such occasion, Tonya reported, laughing, "*Vasha koshka huliganka*" (your cat is a hooligan). Indeed, compared to the scared and neglected cats around the Aitar premises, Kitty seemed to be the personification (or catification?) of energy and independence, a truly free Caucasian spirit. She also began contributing to the housekeeping, catching insects, especially cockroaches. Occasionally, during the night, she would proudly bring her trophies to my bed. Unfortunately, some of them were still alive.

"You are lucky you do not have mice," one of the colleagues told me. "They just reappeared in my apartment despite the many cats around the compound. I do not know what to do about it," he complained.

Adopt one of them was my advice, but I don't think he followed it.

I was getting a lot of questions about Kitty. It was not surprising considering the monotony of life in Sukhumi. Moreover, unlike in Tbilisi, there were not many foreigners traveling through Sukhumi with pets. With time, however, her increasing popularity started to worry me. Kitty's good-natured disposition was apparently not her only winning quality. For instance, one of the women at the Aitar wanted to know if at birth she had been the only cat. When I confirmed she was, she exclaimed, "I knew it, she is a real Siberian cat! With this huge tail, long and strong coat, and big collar, she had to be. But I wanted to be sure. Real Siberians have only one baby.

"In Krasnodar, they pay eight hundred dollars for such cats."

My heart sank. I worried suddenly that this rumor might encourage a theft. Not that I believed my cat would go for such a high price on the market. For me, she was priceless, but that was different. And my concern was justified. Although the compound was protected, there had been some cases of robbery. Outside its gates reigned lawlessness and criminality. Nobody would have been bothered by the theft of a cat, even mine, certainly not the hotel administration. For them, Kitty was an illegal occupant.

I shared my concerns with Tonya who got serious about it. "When you are in the office, I will try to be around as much as I can. I will also talk to some of the women—those whom I trust—and we will keep an eye on her."

They did. We both survived the remaining weeks at the Aitar and returned to our comfortable apartment in Tbilisi, at Chavchavadze Avenue 20.

Mothers, Sons, and Daughters

Anna and Jan

Anna had two sons. One, already a family man, was close by in Abkhazia. The second, Jan, was a student in Poland. Although she was still supporting the older son, most of her savings went to the younger one. He was already in the second year of the law faculty at Poznan University, and she was hoping for a brighter future for him. With that in mind, she had abandoned her prestigious job as a schoolmaster and began cleaning rooms at the Aitar. She worked hard, tried to get as many clients as possible, and save as much as possible. Despite the drastic change in profession, Anna maintained some of her lifelong habits: she stayed slim, dressed smart, read, smoked, and drank coffee. In rare free moments, she socialized with the Abkhaz intelligentsia, Polish minority, and small Catholic community.

When I met her in April 2003, she was counting the days to the summer holiday, which her youngest son would be spending in

Sukhumi. I had readily accepted the invitation to her home to meet him and hear about his life and achievements in a better world in Poland. Anna believed that Jan would settle down there after graduation, that she would visit him, and finally see the country of her ancestors. That would be the crowning joy of her efforts, the endless hours of grueling work—the cleaning, washing, and scrubbing of the floors at the Aitar—and validate her choice that many questioned, especially her former teaching colleagues who ridiculed her new "profession."

Not seeing her for a while around the compound, I asked about Anna. I was told that she had the flu. It had to be a chronic case, I thought, as she had been away on sick leave for several weeks. I started to worry. It was out of the ordinary. Abkhaz women were used to working under all circumstances. Nobody, including they themselves, cared if they were sick or healthy. None of the Aitar women would put their jobs and earnings at risk, particularly not Anna.

I asked Tonya about it, who admitted that she had been concerned as well. She had wanted to visit Anna, but her suggestion was not welcomed. She told me that Anna had also been ill a few months earlier. She had a "button" on her breast and had gone to Sochi to have it removed. She wanted it done quickly, cheaply, and discretely. She could afford neither a break in earnings nor a rumor about her suitability for the job. As there were no health services in Sukhumi, she made arrangements in Sochi. She had returned to work just three days later, looking terrible, but worked nonetheless, smoking, and pretending that all was resolved. She never went back to see the doctor.

Soon after, news hit the Aitar that Anna was in critical condition. Her eldest son had informed the administration and wrote his brother in Poland, telling him to return home. It was against Anna's wishes who, until her last breath, insisted that she would recover and make it back to work in a few days.

Jan was shocked. He had no clue that his mother had been ill. She died twenty-four hours after his arrival.

"She should have taken care of herself," Tonya told me. "Her younger son is devastated. He ran away. His older brother blames him for his mother's death. Jan was her favorite and the oldest boy always envied him."

"Where has he gone?" I asked. "I hope he will continue his studies in Poland. He has a scholarship and that is what she would want him to do."

"I do not know," Tonya said doubtfully. "I heard that he is not as good of a student as his mother claimed. That was more a story for her, but who knows."

"Is there any way to contact him?" I wanted to know.

"I do not think so. He is not around, and nobody knows of his whereabouts. And what good was it for?" Tonya repeated, shaking her head. "To kill herself for nothing."

Elena and Gala

Elena worked as a school teacher in Sukhumi teaching Russian. She occasionally came to the Aitar to give Russian lessons to some UN employees. She was proud of her job and social position. She believed that, unlike the other women, she had maintained her professional and social status. She also had a respectable family: a handsome, educated husband and two children, a son who studied in Russia and a daughter. It was rather unclear what the husband did except that he was well-read and played piano.

Elena did not interact with other Aitar women. She used to go straight to the accommodation of her foreign students without looking at anybody on the compound. She would not interact with any local employee, except the hotel director, who she claimed was a family friend. She was convinced that she personified dignity, patriotism, and success, that she was a model Abkhaz woman envied by the others. She wanted her daughter, Gala, to follow in her footsteps. But Elena was aware that Gala had much yet to learn to assimilate those values, and she would have to undertake the noble task of helping her.

Elena understood that times had changed and that, unlike her son, the daughter wanted to enjoy the company of other Sukhumi youth rather than work hard and collect degrees. It took her a while to complete a degree at the local university although the level of teaching and requirements were not too high. The problem with her unsatisfactory attendance was overcome through family connections to the dean of the faculty. She graduated, not with honors but with an equivalent of a master's, the standard degree awarded at all Soviet and post-Soviet universities. The dean's assistance had to be properly gratified by the family by some tangible means. It was not clear what form this gratification took, but it obviously involved a substantial amount of the family's savings, obliging Elena to take on some extra foreign students.

After a while, another problem emerged. One summer day, despite her careful makeup and hair style, Elena looked tired, pale, and distressed. She had dark circles under her eyes, could not concentrate on the text, and was visibly nervous. No longer able to contain her problem, she burst out, "It is difficult to understand our times, the young people in particular, but one should try."

She laughed nervously and shook her head. Finally, she shared with me the story:

The night before, she had been awakened by a call from the police. It was her daughter who had called. She had been arrested for misbehavior, drunkenness, and insulting the police. The girl was beside herself, outraged, and locked up at the police station. It had taken a mix of threats, promises, and name-dropping for her to convince the policemen to allow her to call her family, otherwise no one would have bothered. They were a respected, well-connected family, not a poor one. That was very important.

Elena rushed to the police station. Alone. She did not want to disturb her husband who was asleep and tired after the late night dinner she had prepared after returning from school. She was glad to see that her daughter was OK, just nervous and agitated. The two young men with whom she had been arrested were also there with their parents on the way. Elena was relieved when she realized that nothing serious had happened. The youth had been on the streets after midnight in violation of the curfew. That was all. She argued with the police but in the end agreed to "reach an understanding" with them to avoid destroying her daughter's record and exposing the family's good name to local gossip. Now, as she reflected on the night's events, she was trying to convince not only me, but also herself that all was fine and nothing had happened.

"The young people and girls nowadays are different. They want to enjoy life, go out, and dance in discos. They do not want to take on so quickly family duties as we did," she mused.

As a teacher, she said, she was confronted with it on a daily basis. It was normal. But the youth in Sukhumi, unfortunately, did not have the same possibilities as those in other countries. But then, her daughter was different: "Our police should know better who is who in Abkhazia. So maybe I should complain about the incident after all." On the other hand, she said she would talk to her daughter once they had both calmed down. She should not endanger her reputation and expose herself to such risks. And there were security considerations. There were still some criminal elements around and enemies of Abkhazia who wanted to destabilize the situation. So maybe the police had a point, she thought.

"I do not know what to do," she said, resigned. "But we cannot allow our daughter to be treated like this as if she were just a common girl from Sukhumi."

"What about professional interests of your daughter? What does she want to do in the future?" I asked.

"She does not know yet," Elena replied. "In the present circumstances, there are no prospects. The young people need time to find inspiration, so in the meantime, they enjoy life."

"And what about her living expenses, the need to contribute to the household, or at least earn pocket money?" I added.

"No," she said matter-of-factly. "She is too young, just twenty-three, and we are very proud that she has everything at home so she does not have to work. You should see her. She is very beautiful and very well-dressed. She has really good taste for clothes and art. You would not confuse her with any other girl on the street, certainly not these cheaply dressed women in the Aitar."

Her face brightened; she smiled.

"I hope that one day she will find a proper husband and that I will have some grandchildren. It is time that we have more pure Abkhaz around."

Soon after our talk, Elena decided that it was time for her daughter to vacation away from Sukhumi, to see the world. They decided that Gala would go to Moscow to stay with some family friends. But that meant extra expenses as life in Moscow was costly, even if the lodging was free. She would also need presents for her hosts, money to buy some new clothes, and tickets to theater and cinema. To make sure Gala felt fine in Moscow, she might have to go with her to neighboring Sochi to purchase a few outfits prior to her departure. It would force her to suspend our lessons for a while. It would also speed up her lodging project.

"Didn't I tell you about it?" she asked. "About the project?"

I was quite intrigued. "No."

Elena had played with the idea for a while and finally it was about to materialize. She would rent the ground floor of her house to Russian tourists. Although it would restrict their living space and limit them to the upper floor for three months, they were prepared to sacrifice their comfort for a while. She would have to adapt the rooms for her Russian summer tenants. She wanted to install as many beds or mattresses as possible, four or five per room. Fortunately, Russians were not demanding and were more interested in low prices than privacy. All they needed was the magic of the seashore, sunny skies, emerald waters, and a peaceful environment. It was the latter that slightly troubled Elena. If there were any extraordinary tensions between Abkhazia and Georgia, any incidents along the cease-fire line, or even hostile rhetoric from Georgian politicians, all her efforts could be in vain. For her, as many other Abkhaz families, the summer season presented a unique opportunity to earn.

Thus, our lessons were interrupted, and Elena got busy with her new project. It seemed that the room letting worked. She immediately began outlining plans for expansion. The next summer, she planned to put even more space in her house to use and get permission to use some public buildings that were vacant during the school-holiday season. She was determined to use her connections with Abkhaz authorities and Russians stationed in Sukhumi. She was quite optimistic and grew increasingly self-confident as she discovered her new entrepreneurial skills. She was eager to earn more money to support her family, to maintain the living standard to which they were accustomed.

I heard less, however, about her second project, her daughter's vacation in Moscow. The subject of the daughter would return three months later. Gala was back and was involved in a "minor" drinking-and-driving accident. She had not been behind the wheel. It was her friend, a nice boy from a good Abkhaz family. The boy, however, went with fists against the policemen; and Gala verbally harassed the victims of the crash and threatened them with her connections. This time, the story got out as the policemen and the victims' families went on the public offensive. Somebody made photos; somebody complained to the authorities.

Elena interrupted her teaching for some weeks and never explained the reason. She also stopped talking about her family.

Sofiko

It was a sunny day in Sukhumi, like many before it, when Sofiko heard the sound of guns and the engine-rumbling of planes and suddenly saw houses blowing up, vehicles burning, and people fleeing in panic in all directions. It was her city, the city where she had spent vacations since childhood, where she had made countless of friends, where her parents had a nice dacha, where she had fell in love. She went first with her neighbors, following the crowds fleeing the Georgian attack, seeking protection behind the changing fronts. Later, she had to go into hiding because she was Georgian herself, and the Abkhaz were on the counteroffensive. Finally, when the Georgian troops lost the battle and she realized that her beautiful land would belong to the Abkhaz, she decided to stay and adapt.

Why did she stay? She got caught up in the war. Her mother had been killed by a falling roof. Her father had left hastily with the Georgian troops. She had not heard from him for many years. So she stayed in Abkhazia with distant relatives, a mixed Abkhazian-Georgian couple with strong pro-Russian sentiments. She married a man who did not stop loving her, even with her being Georgian. She quickly learned how to conceal her Georgian identity, of which she had never been aware until that fateful summer in Abkhazia. She went on with life trying to be like everybody around her. It was not difficult in a society where destruction, poverty, and the absence of even the most basic necessities forced all to struggle for daily survival.

With years, she adjusted and lived with her Abkhaz husband in a shack that had once been the home of her in-laws. Her work—preparing the daily supply of homemade lunches at the Military Club in the Aitar—provided her with a small but steady income and, more importantly, access to the international community, the outside world. That made her life different, more interesting, and worthy. She interacted with people from all over the world. She heard their stories and envied their self-confidence and wealth. Most were polite and respectful, easier to attend to than the local dignitaries. She even picked up some English phrases. Occasionally, she would get some tips and small gifts. Sofiko would have loved to prepare other meals for her clients—breakfast, dinner, snacks, even open a stand selling homemade cakes—but she knew she could not. *Nielzia.*

Access to jobs at the Aitar was strictly, though informally, regulated. I never quite understood who had the final say on such matters. The hotel administration, feared and disliked, obviously played a role in controlling access to the earning possibilities that the Aitar generated. Without the administration's consent, employment was impossible. Any announcement posted on the walls or passed around by word of mouth used to bring in hundreds of candidates. None of the jobs required formal qualifications or degrees, making selection even more dependent on personal and family connections, political loyalties, favoritism, and sympathies of those running the enterprise. Obviously, there was no tradition of transparency or open competition. One can only imagine what the stakes were to get a job, what consideration had to be paid. The UN, although the Aitar's principal client (it rented out most of the premises), was still merely a tenant and had no involvement in running the hotel or selecting its employees.

There was another informal constraint on individual earnings. The Aitar employees, independent of their respective occupations—whether room cleaners, street sweepers, peacock attendants, gardeners, cooks, clerks, garbage collectors, handymen, electricians, bartenders, cashiers, construction workers, carpenters, receptionists, concierges, or masseurs—each closely monitored the others' activities in order to prevent uneven earning and preferential access. The rules seemed to be strictly defined: the number of clients, either for laundry, cooking, or room cleaning, was determined by some unspoken agreement, for instance. The peer pressure was strong and disregard for the existing modalities might have led to social ostracism and the loss of one's job.

Years after the war, Sofiko learned that her father was alive and living somewhere in a large IDP center outside of Tbilisi. She never managed to see him as Tbilisi was separated from Abkhazia by invisible walls—bureaucratic, political, ideological, and psychological.

Like most inhabitants of Abkhazia, Sofiko did not have proper travel documents to go beyond its territory. As Abkhazian statehood was not recognized, their local "passports" had no legal value. Formally, all inhabitants of Abkhazia were still Georgian citizens and entitled to Georgian passports, but it did not work that way. Passports had never been issued to those in Abkhazia as the war and the separation of Abkhazia from Georgia took place soon after Georgia proclaimed her independence. With the dysfunction of the Georgian state and the territorial separation of Abkhazia, it was practically impossible to apply for a passport. It was also politically risky: the Abkhaz authorities and people of Abkhazia would consider it treason if discovered. As the only acceptable solution to the political crisis from the perspective of the Abkhaz was an independent Abkhazia, personal compromises were not allowed.

Sofiko also knew of some discouraging examples, cases of Abkhazian inhabitants who had tried discreetly to obtain Georgian passports or leave for Georgia proper counting on the support of Georgian guards at the cease-fire line. They failed and were met with suspicion and hatred. Contrary to Tbilisi's official "one Georgia" policy, the inhabitants of Abkhazia were not welcome. Sofiko hoped that might change with the new Saakashvili government, a logical expectation that has not materialized.

Sofiko had one more increasingly popular option: to apply for a Russian passport. As her previous passport (a travel document serving as a passport) was issued in the USSR, whose successor was Russia, she could obtain a Russian passport. This course of action was strongly supported politically though it inevitably led to the strengthening of Russia's grip on Abkhazia. The Georgians, of course, were opposed as it created a situation where most of the inhabitants of her separatist territory were Russian citizens. As for Sofiko, although torn between her Georgian and Abkhaz identities, with strong preference for the latter, she did not feel like being a Russian.

The fate of Sofiko's father was even more distressing. Soon after the war, he started counting the days in the IDP center, looking forward to his return to Abkhazia. He expected the Georgian army to reorganize and re-enter Abkhazia—this time successfully. He made sure that the authorities would draft him, that he would have a second chance to regain the motherland and his property. He went around Tbilisi speaking to his former comrades, military officials, and even some members of the government to make sure that he would not be forgotten. Some encouraged him to be ready at any time and even told him about advance preparations; others were evasive and unwilling to talk. He waited for an announcement by the president, which was never made. He expected a call from the military command, but it never came. Finally, he waited for an international crisis to put an end to the injustice.

The world will not tolerate it, he thought.

The world, however, did not move. Days, weeks, months, and years were passing; and nothing was happening. He could only expect the highest intervention—where people failed, God should act. Something must happen: a plague, an earthquake, a tsunami. But the world stood still in the Caucasus.

Without the possibility of travel to Tbilisi, Sofiko had to rely on occasional contacts to receive bits of news about her father. Although far from being well-off herself, she always tried to send him a small sum of money or a gift. The news about his living conditions was truly disturbing. Like other IDPs, he lived in a desolate building with a leaking roof and without basic utilities like electricity, heating, and running water. Contrary to official IDP regulations, he only irregularly received his monthly entitlement of 14 lari (US$7), and often only half that amount.

After about a decade of living in such conditions, it seemed that Sofiko's father was affected both physically and mentally. He had become a bitter man, sick and tired of life. He seemed even to have a grudge against his daughter, whom he believed to be living comfortably in Abkhazia, among the enemies of Georgia, failing to support her ailing father.

Chapter 5

Displaced and Abandoned

The war, which resulted in the defeat of Georgian forces and the loss of two Georgian provinces, Abkhazia and South Ossetia, produced over three hundred thousand internally displaced persons or IDPs, people who fled the breakaway provinces to Georgia proper. When they initially left in the midst and aftermath of the 1992-93 war, everybody thought it would be temporary. Although there was no certainty as to exactly when they would be allowed to return, nobody believed that the loss of these territories—and thus the IDPs estrangement from their homes and land—would be permanent.

With the passage of time, the story of the tragedy of Georgian IDPs began to unfold: they lost their homes and possessions; their families were often scattered about the Caucasus and politically divided; they were displaced not knowing for how long, crippling their ability to plan for their futures; they felt that their sacrifices were not properly appreciated, and even felt themselves a burden on society.

With time, they developed a grudge against the Georgian authorities who had used them in the past to defend the motherland, only to later abandon them like outcasts. They, the Georgians who had tried to defend Abkhazia and the civilians who had fled with them when the war was lost, were never fully embraced by the Georgian state or society. At the beginning, they were the intense focus of local and international politics. Soon, however, their hero status and standing as symbols of the victimization of the entire country—that of all Georgians—gradually gave way to social fatigue and frustration with the thousands of IDPs occupying scarce living space and draining public resources. Thus, sympathy and generosity were replaced by indifference, resentment, and even hostility. Some tried to stay with relatives but in time found themselves downgraded from welcomed guests to nuisances, notwithstanding the famed Georgian hospitality traditionally meted out to visitors. Most were housed in public facilities, hotels, schools, and newly constructed government complexes converted into IDP centers.

These centers too, with time, acquired a bad name. They deteriorated into slum conditions and chronically lacked basic services, services which were cut off or severely restricted due to the lack of funds and maintenance. The authorities often claimed not to have sufficient resources to remedy the problems and laid blame on the IDPs for the dilapidated condition of the facilities, theft of building fixtures and other components for sale on the market, and the general lack of safety, claiming that the IDPs robbed each other, endangering the community. Gradually, the areas around the centers, even in the best parts of the city, became known as "no-go" neighborhoods. Soon, people began reacting to IDPs with suspicion as well, causing them to become increasingly more isolated and bitter.

In the decade following the war, a new generation grew up with nothing other than an IDP identity, facing poverty, prejudice, and exclusion. Kids from such backgrounds had almost no opportunity to benefit from education or cultural life. Even those in Tbilisi were beset by this fate and suffered from a related sense of inferiority, which prevented them from developing normal friendships with children from non-IDP families and from being treated as equals in the schools.

The IDPs also complained of being financially abused by the authorities. A multimillion dollar budget was established to aid the IDPs, from which they received approximately US$7 per person, per month in assistance. This amount did not include allotments for investments in the infrastructure of IDP facilities, which should have come from other budgetary or donor allocations. During my time in Georgia, nonpayment, partial payment, and irregular payment of IDP allowances was common. The funds appeared to melt at several stages. At the central level, there lacked certainty as to the actual number of IDPs; the three-hundred-thousand figure was the product of an estimation conducted in the early 1990s and had never been updated. On average, IDPs received their monthly entitlements, which were meager to begin with, only six to nine times a year. Somewhere between the central level and the middle men at the regional level and in the IDP centers, the balance of the funds disappeared. Some of the middle men imposed a "tax" on IDP recipients, dispersing only a portion of their monthly allowance and deducting the rest for "services."

There was also no transparency in the management of the IDP centers, and it appeared as if nothing had ever been done, or at least done properly. Even if the money came from foreign donors, thorough supervision was lacking. Theoretically, the IDPs were represented at all levels of government—in parliament, in government institutions, at the regional level, and in the IDP centers themselves—and should have been able to defend their interests. The reality, however, was quite different. The representatives were part of the problem, and when IDPs from time to time complained and accused their representatives of misuse of funds and unfair distribution of goods, nothing ultimately happened to anyone and nothing changed. The allegations were either not substantiated or the principal complainers paid-off with a token monetary payment or some goods, with promises for more in the future. But most—after a decade of depravation, dejection, and abuse—had lost the will to fight.

It is difficult to determine who to blame most for the situation. Georgia was essentially a failed state with no functioning central authority for the better part of the early 1990s. But after some passage of time, I was amazed that the international community had not put more pressure on Georgian authorities to redress the issue. It was a public secret: everybody knew it, only the wilfully ignorant did not. And it was easy to reach the IDP centers in Tbilisi or Zugdidi to verify the facts. Every visit to an IDP center and every meeting with IDPs led to the same repeated accusations of theft and mistreatment, to no avail. Even the occasional high-level discussion of the issue resulted in no action.

"We will look into the matter, but the facts you give us are not necessarily correct" was among the milder responses to my queries. Others simply dismissed the issue outright or changed the subject, discussing the occupation of Abkhazia and the gross human rights violations committed there against Georgians, or some other matter. I attempted various formal and informal interventions, but all in vain.

I had hoped that soon after the Rose Revolution this abuse would stop, but it took much longer to work out a comprehensive solution to the problem. Some were of the opinion that the matter would have not been addressed at all but for the influx of new IDPs from South Ossetia forcing the government's hand following the August 2008 war; at that point, something had to be done to address the crisis; otherwise, officials risked the spectacle of thousands of desperate people filing into the city center of Tbilisi, camping out next to the political demonstrators if they failed to act. This forced them to deal with the matter of "old" IDPs as well, many of whom by that time had been evicted from most collective housing centers (most of which had been closed and converted into commercial buildings). Only some of these IDPs had by then received some form of financial compensation or alternative accommodation.

With the loss of 150 villages along the former demarcation line between South Ossetia and Georgia proper in 2008, the government, with international assistance, including from the UNHCR, built a few refugee settlements along the road between Tbilisi and Gori for the new IDPs. They were monstrous, barrackslike, low-quality constructions. They did not have proper foundations and insulation, and the walls were cracked and often molded. But they were constructed fast, in accordance with UNHCR standards, and sheltered thousands of families.

I visited some of these shelters. They consisted, on average, of two to four rooms, some with and some without indoor bathrooms, electricity, running water, and a small garden in front. They also varied in the amount of living space, land, and furnishings allocated to each home. Their inhabitants often attributed the differences in the allocations to individual connections with Georgian authorities or their own representatives, political loyalty, or bribes. But in a change from the past, all the IDPs confirmed that they were regularly receiving their monthly entitlements, now 28 lari per month, per person. And unlike six years prior, there were no "taxes" imposed or bribes extracted.

Most people living in the IDP centers came from much better conditions. They were Georgians who had lived on the outskirts of South Ossetia in traditional homes, close to Georgia proper. Their main income had been from farming, and they were having difficulty adjusting to their new "homes" after being uprooted from their prior lives without means. Marina and her two adult sons were such a family.

"We left with very limited belongings," Marina told me. "We left our house, our farm, and all the goods we had accumulated over our entire lives. We simply fled. Now you see how we live. We have nothing, and we will likely not be able to go back, that is now apparent. And it is impossible to live in this ghetto."

"It is not only about the living conditions. It is about the sick atmosphere and the political oppression. They try to exploit our misfortune and manipulate us," Vladen, Marina's son added. "They were using the accommodation and settlement formalities to review the electoral lists, checking who would vote and for whom. That allowed them to remind people how they should vote. It is not surprising that the great majority voted for Saakashvili."

"We did not," his brother informs us. "So soon after I lost my job as a teacher. Perhaps by chance. We know that our activities are monitored and that, for example, your visit will be reported."

"To whom? By whom?"

"People here live in such misery that they are ready to sell each other out for some lari, better accommodation, a more fertile garden, or a job. Plus, we live on top of each other and have nothing to do. It is natural in such circumstances to find many willing informers. We also have our *sonder-commandos* to bring people in line if necessary. You can be beaten up or robbed, your car can be destroyed. They are paid 500 lari per month. That is a lot compared to our 28 lari."

I began to feel uncomfortable. *We shouldn't have come*, I thought. If, indeed, their house was under surveillance, their conversations were also likely being recorded.

"I do not care," Marina told me as if reading my thoughts. "I am not going to be intimidated. We have nothing to lose. We will fight. The world should know what we are going through, what is happening in this country."

On the way out, we met a BBC correspondent. She had come to speak with Marina, who, true to her promise, was fighting and telling the world her story.

It was much more difficult getting firsthand information about the old IDPs. They had been dispersed across the country, out of the sight and out of the mind of the public. From official sources at the UNHCR and in the Ministry of Refugee and Resettlement Affairs (MRA), I got confirmation that about 80 percent of the old IDP cases had been settled. The average IDP from the original wave of internal refugees was paid US$5,000 to US$10,000 in cash or in-kind through provisions of housing and an amount to recompense for their losses. Considering Georgian living standards, it was a fair deal, but the settlements bore no relation to the value of the property lost in Abkhazia and South Ossetia. However, compensating that loss was beyond the Georgian government's capacity and general international practice in such situations.

The only visible reminder of the tragic situation of the old IDPs that I came across was Beso, a veteran of the 1992-93 war in Abkhazia. He was begging close to the Courtyard Marriott Hotel at Freedom Square in the capital. He wore a torn military uniform fully decorated and exposing his badly healed wounds.

"I was in Sukhumi years ago," he told me. "I got multiple injuries, none of which were ever properly treated. My health was ruined. I was never able to work afterward. Yes, I got disability assistance, but the amount was very low, impossible to live on and support a family.

"My wife worked in the kitchen of one of the Tbilisi hotels so we could manage," he continued. "Unfortunately, she has been ill for the past two years and had to stop working. We have no money for medication. You can get very little nowadays through social health services and to pay privately is very expensive."

"Did you get compensation money?" I asked.

"Yes, I got it, but we used it for living and medical expenses. We did not need an apartment. We lived together with our cousin on the outskirts of town. It was cheaper."

After making a donation, I prepared to leave.

"I hate it," he shouted after me. "I hate it. I would never have expected years ago, when I fought for Abkhazia, that I would end up begging on the streets to pay for my wife's medication. I hate them all!"

Chapter 6

Dachas of the Communist Bosses

Abkhazia, the most attractive area along the Black Sea coast, was long known as the "Soviet Riviera." All top Soviet leaders—from Stalin to Gorbachev—had their dachas (summer homes) there. Foreign dignitaries from the fraternal order of communist countries and communist parties used to spend their holidays in Sukhumi, New Athos (Novi Afon), Pitsunda, and Gagra at local sanatoriums or party guesthouses. Most of these buildings have survived and, although neglected, can be visited today. Accessing them, however, can be a complicated affair as it is not clear who owns them, who manages them, or who profits from their use. While the sanatoriums are generally occupied by the Russian military today, the dachas of former dignitaries belong to the Abkhaz "government."

Given the fragility of the security and political conditions in the region, and the general suspicion that prevailed, visits to the dachas had to be cleared in advance by local authorities. Knowing (or finding out) who they were, however, was sometimes difficult without knowing the right informal channels to navigate. And even if the local authorities gave the green light for a visit—orally, of course, no paper trail—the current managers and/or occupants of the premises may not allow it. As they had no names or official identities, it was difficult to ensure their prior consent.

During my time in Abkhazia, I managed to visit a number of the dachas: each of the three Stalin kept in Sukhumi, Miusera, and Coldstream near Gagra; Shevardnadze's dacha in Pitsunda; and Gorbachev's in Agudzera. I also came to know well Beria's dacha in Sukhumi as it housed my office.

Beria's Dacha

"It's Beria's villa," I was informed upon my arrival. Edin, a UNOMIG security officer, pointed to the house on the hill, hidden behind the trees. "Your office will be there." I looked at him in disbelief not knowing if it was true or a joke.

"Beria's villa? You mean Lavrenti Pavlovich Beria, the chief of Stalin's security services, those with the multiple names and singular purpose? The man responsible for massive terror and extermination of millions? You mean *that* Beria, the face of the Stalinist system?"

"Your office is there," repeated Edin, visibly unsure of the historical details.

I looked up again and saw the contour of the building emerging from the overgrowth of trees and bushes. The car was moving slowly up the narrow, curving road. Soon the building became fully visible. It was old and gracious, built atop the hill, surrounded by a green park, which fell into the sea.

I tried to place my destination—my office—and its former owner in proper historical context. Beria, who lived from 1899 to 1953, is known mainly for the many atrocities he committed in Stalin's name: the torture, the show trials, the murder of millions. He was born close to Sukhumi, into a Mingrelian family. He studied architecture in Baku but soon joined Cheka, the former Soviet security service, and quickly moved up in its ranks. From 1931 to 1938, he lived in Tbilisi and ran Georgia as the party's top representative. In 1938, he assumed the helm of the NKVD, the infamous successor of Cheka, and went onto holding various other government and party posts overseeing Soviet security activities.

Unlike most in Stalin's entourage, Beria was intelligent, well-educated, and witty. He was also a skilled manager, excellent organizer, and workaholic; he could function for days without sleep. He was complex: a sadist who took pride in personally torturing his victims, a notorious womanizer and rapist, a loving husband, and a caring father.

"Let me have one night with him, and I will have him confessing he is the King of England," he used to boast of his victims' fate.

Beria was generally feared and mistrusted most by those in Stalin's inner circle, but he managed nonetheless to gain and maintain Stalin's confidence throughout his (Stalin's) life. He reorganized the NKVD into an effective terror organization, serving as the power base of Stalin's rule over the Soviet Union and beyond. He always treated Stalin with deference, never questioning his judgment or missing an opportunity to demonstrate his loyalty. His family befriended the Stalins, ensuring a Georgian touch in their private relations. There was always Georgian food and Georgian music, songs and stories awaiting Stalin, a fellow Georgian, at the Berias.

Soon after Stalin's death in 1953, Beria was arrested and executed. He was charged with inciting counterrevolution and hatred among the nations of the USSR, espionage and conspiracy. The mass atrocities and crimes against the country's people, however, were not part of the indictment.

So that, in short, was the man in whose house I would be working—the house he had designed and which had been stylishly maintained by his attractive, aristocratic Georgian wife, Nina; the house where they had lived in privilege and comfort, unlike the vast majority of their compatriots. Nina, who Stalin liked and respected, was a scientist, active professionally, sporty, and well-read. She played tennis and enjoyed literature, foreign films, and magazines generally not accessible in the USSR and considered foreign to the communist ideology of the time.

During their vacations in Georgia, the Berias and Stalins regularly visited each other at their respective dachas. The Berias also cared for Stalin's mother, Keke, and paid frequent visits to her apartment in Tbilisi. She enjoyed their company and allegedly kept Beria's portrait among the many pictures, photos, and letters of her own son. Beria also arranged and attended her funeral on Stalin's behalf in 1937.

The building had preserved its original shape. Its dark, wooden interior, spacious hall, broad and creeping stairs, and large paneled rooms showed no signs of modernization or renovation, emoting a sense of abandonment and solitude. From the moment I would enter the dacha in the months that followed, I would feel as if in the midst of history. My spacious yet neglected office—home to wild roses growing through the windows offering beautiful views of the sea below—made the whole scene even more mysterious and surreal. I wished the walls could talk.

How could this beautifully serene and luxurious space, the site of joyous family holidays, coexist with the brutality of Beria's profession—the torture, execution, deportation, rape, and murder he both ordered and committed?

I wished I could have shared these feelings with my parents from whom I had heard the name of Beria for the first time decades ago. For them, his contemporaries who lived through the Stalinist period in Poland, he symbolized the worst of the terror, oppression, and atrocities of that era. Who would have expected that, due to some unpredictable turns of history, their daughter would end up in his dacha as a UN senior political adviser, trying to heal the wounds of the Abkhazian-Georgian conflict, the seeds of which had been sowed in the czarist Russia and then successfully cultivated by Beria and Stalin. I am sure that my parents would have appreciated the irony.

*   *   *

I particularly loved the old, unattended park surrounding the dacha with its subtropical trees and overgrown lawns full of strawberries. They were always there, red and fresh. I loved picking them but soon noticed, with surprise, that I was the only one. In vain, I tried to encourage some of the local employees to join me. I was equally unsuccessful in my search to find out why not. Asking questions was simply not a part of the culture of the place. So it was a while before I had an opportunity to raise the issue with one of the local workers. He was repairing the doors of the dacha and could not easily escape me. I shared my surprise at being the only one fond of wild strawberries.

"But it is Beria's dacha," he stated.

"So what? Beria is not around. He has been dead for decades. The property is used by the UNOMIG, nobody else has the access, and the strawberries are delicious."

I did not get a response. He simply shook his head and the conversation ended.

None of my UN colleagues or local acquaintances shared my fascination with the dacha and its secrets. So I was happy to discover that the new arrival, Christopher, a consultant from Switzerland, had similar interests. He seemed to be familiar with the history of the region and was outspoken and curious. He worked hard on his project but, like me, tried to take advantage of the unique opportunity of being in Abkhazia, exploring and learning as much as possible. Outgoing, he was also adept at engaging people in conversation, never discouraged by the *nielzia* mind-set.

One day he visited the dacha. After a chain of staff meetings, he ended up in my office. We drank tea. I noticed that he was unusually quiet and serious. I was puzzled. What could be the matter? Finally, he admitted to feeling uneasy in the building and that it must have had something to do with its aura. It took him a while to clarify the point. In short, his unease had to do with the building's history and his assumption as to what must have occurred there during Beria's time.

"Have you noticed that some local staff do not like to stay alone in the building after office hours?" he asked me.

I had not. I probably had not been sufficiently observant.

I suddenly recalled, however, that recent literature on the subject increasingly suggested that Beria's atrocities were not limited to Lublianka and other infamous NKVD prisons and that his sadistic inclinations and personal involvement in torture were not restricted to his office hours or premises. His victims had often been friends, lovers, and close associates turned over to him as alleged enemies of the system, or unfortunates who had somehow crossed his path and been accused of treason as a consequence. A notorious womanizer, it is also likely that Beria used his authority to sometimes get rid of troublesome lovers, some of whom were the wives, daughters, sisters, and girlfriends of the victims begging for their lives.

So maybe Christopher had a point, maybe I had been not sufficiently sensitive to this "aura." He was probably not alone in his belief. Those who did not like the red strawberries might have had similar feelings. But how would I know? They would not talk about it. *Eto nielzia.*

But my discussions with Christopher did make me more attentive to the dacha's aura. On one occasion, in the midst of a rainy and windy evening, when we were bound to complete a report for the UN Headquarters in New York, we heard a noise coming from the kitchen. Nobody rushed to find out its source. After a while, however, we desperately needed coffee. According to dacha protocol, the cleaning ladies were solely responsible for attending to all kitchen matters. There were practical reasons for the rule. Firstly, the antiquated electrical equipment in the kitchen posed a serious danger to those not familiar with it. Secondly, the mission sought to employ as many local people as possible, reserving kitchen duty to the local staff facilitated this goal.

We asked who wanted a coffee but were met with a deadly silence. Even the cleaning ladies, normally very attentive, looked away. So in the chilled atmosphere, Christopher and I broke protocol and headed to the kitchen. Switching on the light, we noticed a shadow disappearing into a hole under the oven. We informed our colleagues that it must have been a rat, a rather obvious conclusion as the place was infested with rodents. Again, deadly silence; no one said a word. We continued looking around the kitchen, but the rat was gone. Christopher quipped that it must be the ghost of Beria. We laughed. I noticed, however, that we were the only ones amused by the joke. The others—who were standing outside the entrance to the kitchen—acted as if they were not even there. They appeared to notice and hear nothing. They neither wanted to enter the kitchen, nor drink the coffee. They ignored Christopher's joke.

The ghost of Beria was apparently still very much alive.

Stalin's Dachas

My acquaintance with Stalin's dacha in Sukhumi came next, in connection with my initial frustrations with the (dismal) living conditions at the Aitar. In response to my inquiry about possible alternative accommodation, out of the Aitar somebody pointed to the green hill behind it. "There is one of Stalin's dachas, and they have some rooms for rent, but it is expensive."

Undeterred, I took a car and drove in the pointed direction. I was stopped at the gate and, after a thorough interview and a couple of phone calls, allowed to drive farther on. Again, I found myself in a magical, neglected park draped in a lush mix of subtropical plants and trees. Once upon the time, it must have been carefully attended to and manicured.

The car climbed around a curvy road up the hill. At its top there were two houses: the first one, white and stylish, was obviously Stalin's dacha and the second an attachment. I was met by the manager who showed me available apartments in the white building. The view from all of them was breathtaking. The balsamic air, the breeze of the sea, and the aroma of the flowers filled the rooms. The apartments were by far better than anything else I had seen around, but there was something unnatural, artificial about them. They were sparsely furnished with small closets and a few chairs but adorned with some built-in luxury fixtures: a marble bathroom here, a large crystal mirror there. And the house was silent and seemed to be empty. There were no guests visible, no cars in the car park, no sounds of music from either a radio or TV.

I was quoted a price for an available apartment much higher than that charged at the Aitar but found it acceptable and offered to rent it for a month or two.

"Can I get it for a longer period of time if necessary? I will be here at least six months."

"It is possible, but it will depend on other requests," the manager replied. "Let us start with what I can offer right now, and we will worry about the rest later."

I thanked him and asked how I should contact him. He gave me a piece of paper with a phone number written thereon. No name, no letterhead.

"What is your name?" I asked. "I would like to refer to our conversation and know how to find you."

"I am Igor. But don't worry. The best is if you come in person. There is always somebody here to attend to our guests."

"Yes, but your security guards down the road?"

"Do not worry, now we know you."

My curiosity was piqued. "I have two more questions," I said. "First, is it possible to book a room for the summer? My family may be coming, and they cannot stay at the Aitar. UNOMIG is a nonfamily mission, and I have to make all necessary arrangements on my own. And if I make a reservation with you, could you ensure their entry into Abkhazia?"

"Do not worry. We can do anything you want."

"My second query is more immediate. Can I have a cup of coffee somewhere in the hotel? Do you have a café or a restaurant where I can go?"

"No problem. Please follow me."

I followed. He took me to the reception and vanished. The receptionist, an exceptionally talkative and curious woman, wanted to know everything about me. She made me a cup of coffee (Nescafé) and was quite enthused about the idea of my moving in. I thanked her, but I wanted to know if they had a regular café or restaurant in the hotel where I could go in the future.

"You are most welcome. Now you know me, so I can always make you a cup of coffee, and we can chat" was her eager response. "Please come whenever you want."

I thanked her, left the reception, and entered the deserted square in front of the hotel. I went toward the annex in search of some kind of restaurant or café. Considering the almost total lack of such basic services in Abkhazia and being impressed with the beauty and tranquillity of Stalin's dacha, I was hoping to find a place where I could spend a quiet moment over a glass of wine from time to time or have a nice dinner with some colleagues.

Unfortunately, the reality did not match my expectations. There was a kind of restaurant in the annex, but it more resembled a canteen common to Soviet-era hostels than a café. It was large, shabby and, like the rest of the house, practically deserted. One table was occupied by two men drinking beer. They wore black leather jackets and appeared typical of men in the region. They could have been security guards, businessmen, politicians, anything. I sat at one of the many vacant tables and waited for what would be next. After a while, I was approached by a tired and neglected-looking woman who asked me what I wanted. I requested a coffee.

"Are you a hotel guest?" she inquired.

"No, but I visited the hotel."

"In this case, you cannot get anything. We only serve hotel guests." I was positive that the two local men were not hotel guests but did not feel like arguing.

"Do you have many hotel guests?" I asked.

"It is not my business," she retorted dryly. "If we are told to prepare a meal, we serve it. Otherwise there is nothing."

I left the hotel (or whatever it was) and drove down to the gate. I looked skeptically at the piece of paper in my hand with Igor's telephone number. Was it even his real name? Or if I called the number would I be told that there was no Igor around? After all, it still remained unclear who owned Stalin's dacha, who managed the hotel (or whatever it was), or even to whom I had spoken.

*　　*　　*

The circumstance of my visits to the dachas of the other party bosses was quite different. I went with a few colleagues on invitation of the UNOMIG's Deputy Special Representative of the Secretary-General (SRSG) in Sukhumi, Roza Otunbayeva (in April 2010 she became the interim government leader of Kyrgyzstan). Roza, the former minister of foreign affairs of Kyrgyzstan and its ambassador to key world capitals, enjoyed high prestige among Abkhaz leaders. Without her personal involvement and contacts, we would have not stood a chance for such a tour. We received the security clearance necessary to go to the more secluded, off-the-beaten-track areas and were provided with a guide to assist us during the trip. We were also assured that all the dachas we planned to visit would be made accessible.

We began with one of Stalin's dachas in Coldstream (Kholodnaya Rechka). It is located close to Gagra, on a cliff with breathtaking views of the sea, surrounded by hills and dense subtropical forest. It had been one of the best protected of Stalin's residences and had become his favorite in his later years. Invisible from land and sea, it was accessible only through a narrow serpentine road lined with numerous security and observation posts, allowing for surveillance of the road connecting Sukhumi and Sochi unseen.

The house itself was an old, wooden structure sunken into the green foliage of its surroundings. Though spacious, it was far from extravagant even by the standards of Stalin's time. Its interior was elegant, however, carefully crafted in wood of impressive quality. It was dark, even on sunny days, because of its low construction: the surrounding tree-lined verandas and windows, the latter narrowly built, did not allow in too much light. Stalin, allegedly, did not like light. He preferred semidarkness, the curtains drawn.

Our guide, a middle-aged local man, shared with us a few stories told to him by his parents, who, he said, had lived in the area during Stalin's days. He did not have his own memories. He was a child in the postwar years, too small to understand or really remember. A few things stuck in his mind, however. He recalled that the mere mention of Stalin's name evoked a visceral, almost physical sense of fear. He said he could remember the feeling even today. He also remembered vividly his parents' instructions not to get close to Stalin or any of his companions and never get in their way. He had been aware (though he could not recall how) of local people befriended by Stalin later disappearing under suspicious circumstances. He never asked his parents for an explanation but had followed their orders to the letter. And he never mentioned Stalin's name, nor did his friends he said.

Standing in front of Stalin's house on a bright sunny day, over fifty years after his death, our guide still unconsciously looked around and lowered his voice.

"He always received visitors in this room," he said as we entered a large sitting room sparsely furnished with some big armchairs and a few other pieces.

"At the beginning of a visit, Stalin would remain invisible, hidden in one of the big armchairs in the darkness. Because of his extremely small size, a visitor would be under the impression that there was no one in the room. The pervading darkness further increased this impression. He could watch the person for a while, himself unseen. That gave Stalin a feeling of security and strategic advantage. He believed that in the case of new contacts, the arrangement gave him an opportunity to examine his visitor and form an opinion about his personality. In the case of people with whom he had already been acquainted, Stalin thought it gave him a chance to confirm or dismiss a suspicion and better assess the acquaintance's intentions."

We also visited a small house that had belonged to Stalin's daughter, Svetlana. "Even she, his daughter, could not visit him unannounced," the guide said. "So imagine the demands put on the others."

In Miusera, our next destination, we were not so lucky. Stalin's dacha was closed. There was nobody around. Although our visit was announced in advance and blessed by the Abkhaz authorities, the dacha could not be entered. Nobody knew exactly why, the building was simply locked up. We could see it only from the outside, a low, modest building overshadowed by trees and subtropical plants. We waited around for a while in the surrounding garden and were even told that someone was coming to solve the problem.

"Somebody was supposed to be here and let us in," our guide kept repeating.

He made a few frantic phone calls, but in vain. Most likely, there was no clarity as to who this "somebody" was. After a while, we gave up and went on to visit Khrushchev's dacha.

Khrushchev's and Shevardnadze's Dachas

The Miusera scenario repeated itself at Khrushchev's villa in Pitsunda, the only difference being that we could not see into the house even from the outside. Our guide brought in someone who informed us that the dacha was occupied by people from Putin's close protection and was therefore off limits to us.

"So is Putin here in Abkhazia?" somebody asked.

"No, he is in Krasnaja Polyana, close to Sochi."

"Not yet," someone else corrected. "He will come to Sochi shortly. They are waiting for his arrival."

"But why here, so far away? It does not make sense. Aren't there enough houses in Sochi?" one of my colleagues persisted.

Our guide was looking increasingly uncomfortable. He took me aside and whispered that I should convince my colleagues to stop asking questions.

"What's wrong with the questions?" I replied. "We came here from other countries and want to learn as much as possible about your history. People ask questions because they want to understand."

"But it is not good," he said in a weak voice. "*Eto nielzia.*"

We gave up. Whatever the logic or truth of the matter, we had to accept that Khrushchev's dacha was not available to us.

In the end, of the three dachas we were to see in the Pitsunda area, only one, Shevardnadze's, was open to us. It was a typical Soviet-era monument: cheaply constructed, it was built with large cement blocks in a pseudo-modern design. The building was also badly maintained, visibly rundown by the effects of rain, mud, and neglect. It looked more like one of the Soviet "people's houses of culture," common and impersonal, rather than the residence of a dignitary. Devoid as it was of personality, it was difficult to imagine what it was like when inhabited. Not much remained of the old days except for some dusty hunting trophies and Georgian goblins hanging on the walls and a chipped crystal chandelier that still managed to command the center of attention.

Gorbachev's Dacha

We proceeded to Agudzera where Gorbachev had built a modern dacha on a vast land estate on the coast. It was clearly the biggest, most extravagant, and expensive of all the dachas.

"He built it because he refused to take over a dacha from Stalin," the local guide explained. "He could not stay in the same house. He was a man of *perestroika*. And his wife was horrified by the very idea and refused to move in."

A local man listening to this explanation interrupted. "It is true that she had refused to move in, but it was probably because of the quality of the house, not the ghost of Stalin. It was too poor and not sufficiently elegant for her taste.

"So look what they did," he said, gesturing to a building not far from us. "They built this thing. It cost millions of dollars out of public money. They did not pay for it, we did. And look around at this huge piece of land. They just took it for themselves and made it inaccessible to the people from the neighborhood. Many lost access to the sea. They had to walk for miles to go to the beach or fish. But they built for themselves a harbor. Look there."

He pointed ahead to a small, manmade bay extending the length of the house.

"Raisa Gorbacheva personally supervised the construction. She kept coming, interfering with the architects and changing her mind every few months. They had to undo the construction and introduce major changes on a few occasions. She could not figure out what she wanted until she saw it. Only then could she decide if she liked it or not. The same happened with the furniture. The concepts kept changing so did the procurement orders. There was a lot of waste as she did not care what would happen to the goods she ordered. She did not have to pay for them.

"It took her five years to finish the construction. By the time the house was ready, Gorbachev was ousted from office. They never lived there. He has never even visited the place.

"So there is some justice in this world sometimes," he said, wrapping up. "Today, she is dead, and he is in the USA. He is not much in his own country. It is not surprising that nobody wanted to vote for him to be the president of Russia."

And the outburst ended. I, however, wondered why I had never heard any comparable condemnation of Stalin. Why did the mere mention of his name not evoke similar emotions?

We walked around the dacha, which looked like a poor replica of a German medieval castle. Had it not been new and so obviously fake, it may have made for a better fit somewhere in Austria, Hungary, or the Bavaria. Along the Black Sea coast, on the beach, it looked truly ridiculous. The interior, at least what we could see of it, was similarly garish. The hallway was covered with custom-made Turkish carpets. Their size and composition of colors had caused problems with their design, we were told, leading to numerous remakes. The colored glass windows rather belonged in a church than a summer home. Their colors, which carefully reflected those of the carpets, were echoed further in the huge crystal chandelier hanging over the staircase.

Our tour, however, had to stop there. It was suddenly interrupted by an agitated woman who told us plainly that we should not have been there and that we should leave instantly.

"You are disturbing people," she said. "The house is rented, and we have some important visitors."

"We thought that this house belonged to Abkhazia, and we got a permission to visit it from the authorities in Sukhumi," we explained.

"This house is rented," she repeated. "People paid a lot of money to be here. They do not like to see anybody around."

"But isn't this house the residence of the 'president' of Abkhazia?"

"Yes, but now it is rented." She was getting confused, worried that she had said too much or that what she did say was not politically correct. "You should understand that these are the president's guests. The president can invite whomever he wants. Now, please, go."

We left. I noticed that our security guard, assigned to us by the authorities in Sukhumi to facilitate our excursion, had remained conspicuously quiet.

As soon as we left the villa, we were met by a guard who reminded us that we were on private property and not welcome. "We have guests here," he stated.

"And who are the guests?"

"Some people from Moscow," he advised. "They pay a lot of money. All is arranged by a tourist office."

While we were talking, we saw two teenage girls approaching the house on bicycles. They obviously lived there.

"Look," the guard continued. "Have you ever seen such bicycles? They are thousands of dollars each. They can bike up hills, over grass, and on the beach, no problem. These girls have everything. These people have a lot of money. I tell you," he said, shaking his head. "Go back to your bus. Good-bye."

The excursion was over. It was instructive in many ways, in ways that I had not originally anticipated. I reminded myself that we were among the privileged. Otherwise, I could have felt mistreated.

Chapter 7

Of Peacocks and Swans

The compound at the Aitar Hotel was a place of neglect: lawns were overgrown, buildings in disrepair, water fountains left dry, and benches broken. It was a depressing place, contrasting sharply with the overwhelming natural beauty surrounding it—the brilliant blue sea, the crystal clear air, the massive subtropical plants, and tall mountains lining the horizon. The gloom reached the compound's inhabitants as well. The people appeared tired and resigned, UN staff included; the cats and dogs fearful; and the multitude of peacocks restless, strutting about quite noisily.

Peacocks must have carried some symbolic importance and been a highly valued market commodity. Extensive measures were undertaken by the Aitar administration to guard them. The small ones were kept in special cages. Several staff were tasked exclusively with caring for their needs, feeding, and tailing after them around the compound to ensure the birds neither escaped nor were stolen.

The Aitar flock was largely populated with unimpressive females. The males, distinguished by their colorful brilliance and easily spotted, were, consequently, more vulnerable to theft. The few that remained paraded proudly around the compound spreading their trains and sitting atop trees and the roofs and balconies of the hotel apartments.

The peacocks often woke the compound during the night. This occurred mainly in the spring, but not only. Their piercing screech could be heard echoing across the grounds for months at a time. It was a strange, unpleasant sound, sharp and metallic. Some took it for a bad omen, others for the wondering ghost of Beria. But would a bad omen keep returning every spring? Those who knew the birds' habits claimed that it was the deficient selection of females that caused the male peacocks to cry, not nasty spirits. Others, unpersuaded, believed that it signified Abkhazia's state of misfortune. Once the situation gets better, they reasoned, the peacocks will correct their behavior in view of the change in fortune.

Those who remembered the good old days in Sukhumi, and at the Aitar in particular, claimed that in those days the peacocks had been less boisterous and appeared less confused and more decorative and dignified. It was as if they had understood their privileged place in the community and their high worth. The war changed everything, including the behavior of peacocks. They broke order, stepped out of rank, and became wild and insubordinate. They developed loud, unruly mating habits, started disappearing into the tree crowns, neglecting their eggs and nests, forgetting their small ones, and wandering about the compound with reckless abandon.

Despite the special protective measures, there were occasional cases of peacock disappearances. On each such occasion, the incident of the missing peacock (or peacocks) was accompanied with a lot of excitement: cries of apologies from the wardens, loud insults and accusations hurdled by the authorities, shouting matches amongst witnesses defending their own stories and testimonies, often implicating each other in the (apparent) theft. At other times, the blame was put on the Aitar's defenseless cats or dogs, encouraging a wave of repression aimed at ousting them from the compound. They made for convenient scapegoats, absolving the humans of wrongdoing and allowing the authorities to bring investigations to a stop and a share in the spoils.

The story of the swans was even more mysterious. They had disappeared from the Aitar altogether. They had vanished together with the last of the tourists, among the first losses of the war.

"We had everything before the war," Galina told me in a dreamy voice. "We had speedboats, beach cafés, discos, restaurants, supermarkets, rest houses—everything, even swans. People from all over the Soviet Union used to come to Abkhazia for summer. All the prominent people—the party leaders—had their dachas here. It was a good life. There were many tourists from abroad. It was our Riviera, like in France."

It had all gone suddenly and quickly. No one had expected it. No one had thought that the Georgians, that Shevardnadze, would do it. But it happened. When Georgia invaded, they destroyed it all. Said Galina, "They even ate up the swans."

Sofiko had similar memories. She had been too young to understand what was happening, but she could recall the joy of her vacations, walks along the seashore, the colors of sunsets, first kisses in the botanical garden, the seagulls and flowers, the posh crowds strolling along the sea promenade, and the swans. The swans constituted an indelible part of her fondest memories. They were graceful and dignified as stunning as the world around them on the Black Sea Riviera.

And then, suddenly, the area was completely destroyed—its beautiful houses, cafés, and promenades had ceased to exist. Sukhumi and the other Abkhazian cities have never recovered. Neither has Sofiko, though she persevered and never left her beloved coast.

"The Abkhaz destroyed everything," she whispered to me. "They got Russian support and erased our cities with their historical buildings, piers, theaters, and parks.

"They even ate up the swans."

Chapter 8

Sochi

I was quite eager to see Sochi. Though a world traveler, I had never before had an opportunity to travel through the former Soviet empire, except for a few official visits to Moscow and the Baltic countries in the 1990s. My posting in Sukhumi and its proximity to Sochi presented the first opportunity of the kind.

I had read and heard a lot about the Soviet Riviera and its most attractive part, the Black Sea shore stretching from Sukhumi to Sochi. Georgians loved pointing out that the whole stretch once belonged to Georgia. Now Sochi was a part of Russia; and Sukhumi, New Athos, and Gagra—the other main resorts along the coast—were treasures of the Abkhaz. While the Abkhaz shore had been destroyed beyond recognition and did not resemble much of its former grandeur, I was most excited to see Sochi. It was a top vacation destination of well-to-do Russians, including President Putin, and the only place on the southern shore of the Black Sea that remained Russia's after the collapse of the USSR. It was also a mecca for UN colleagues working in Sukhumi. Easily accessible by road and just two hours from Sukhumi, it was their choice place for recreation and shopping.

Indeed, Sochi was a big city with a landscape and climate similar to that of Sukhumi's. It had long sandy beaches and seaside boardwalks and beautiful, though unattended, parks overgrown with oleanders and subtropical plants. The tourism trade seemed to me rather poor: overpriced restaurants with terrible service, unfriendly shopkeepers, crowded hotels, and noisy discos. I was surprised by its nearly exclusive Russian clientele, unusual to see in today's global world. There were no guidebooks or menus in languages other than Russian, except in a few international hotels. Nor were there quality post cards, tourist leaflets or maps—even in Russian—to be found, a problem common in former socialist countries. There was not even a shopping mall or a proper bookstore.

I was told at the hotel, however, that there existed a big shopping center. I tried to find it. After a few months in Sukhumi where we had very limited access to basic consumer products, I was looking forward to the opportunity to do some normal shopping and renew my supplies. I walked back and forth in search of the "big shopping center," anticipating a shopping mall or at least a supermarket. I could not find it despite directions from a number of pedestrians and vendors on the street. I finally realized that I was already there. Rather than a mall, the "big shopping center" was, in fact, a big street market, the kind typical for post-Soviet and developing countries. It consisted of a combination of small shops, street stands, and vendors offering all kinds of goods: pots, furniture, detergents, videos and music CDs, food products, cosmetics, toys, and all manner of clothes—everything from swimming suits and underwear to leather goods and fur coats to evening gowns. You name it, you could probably find it there. It was not much different, except in size, from the markets in Tbilisi, Tskhinvali in South Ossetia, and Sukhumi, with Tskhinvali being the biggest and Sukhumi the smallest.

All these markets operated without any quality control. The vendors were essentially running open-air fencing operations, passing off goods smuggled in from the region's black market. So apart from some local variations—like Russian-made leather clothes in Sochi or the wide availability of petrol in Tskhinvali—the choices were similar.

Service was unfriendly across the board, in the restaurants, shops, cafés, banks, pharmacies, everywhere. People took the attitude that proper service was a matter of personal favor, rather than an offering expected in return for payment, not to mention just good business decorum. Even the mildest complaint about the quality of food, the waiting time, or cleanliness of the cutlery was met with raised brows, surprised looks, and defensive comments such as the following:

"You should be grateful for what you get."

"If you do not like it, what are you doing here?"

These sharp retorts capture the general sentiment.

My hotel was no exception. It took forever to register upon arrival. There were a lot of formalities, including a thorough checking and photocopying of passports. Getting information was equally time consuming: either nobody was available or there were long lines of hotel guests patiently waiting.

Breakfast was an experience unto itself. The restaurant was always overcrowded, the table cloths stained, and the service chaotic. Guests were ushered to the tables and placed there as soon as a free seat was available. It did not matter how many people were in a party, as soon as a single seat at any table came free, someone was plucked from the party to sit there. Sharing a table with one's party generally was not permitted, or at least not a priority. And once seated, the waiting began to have the dirty dishes removed and the food allotment delivered. The breakfast was generally limited to a few pieces of bread, margarine (not butter), and *tvorog* (a Russian version of cottage cheese) accompanied by some colorless liquid brewed in large pots, euphemistically called coffee or tea. Additional requests were not appreciated and met with general hostility or, if you were lucky, simple indifference.

"Can I get a knife, please?"

"Don't you see that I am busy?"

"Can I pick it up myself?"

"*Nyet, nielzia*. When your time comes, you will get it."

"Can we sit together, at the same table, please?"

"Don't you see that I have only one place free?"

"Can we wait until you have a free table?"

"There is never a free table, there are only seats. Follow me or get out of the way. Other people want to eat as well."

In the hotels and around the main tourist sites, there were numerous ads for sexual services. The signs were typically handwritten on small pieces of paper or cheaply printed. Nobody seemed to care. They were displayed next to guest rooms, stuck on corridor walls, and sometimes slipped under apartment doors. Similar ads were posted around restaurants, at bus stops, and by money-exchange counters. At some top hotels, the approach was more direct: the hotel staff simply inquired into the needs and tastes of their guests, male guests that is.

"Would you like to have company tonight?"

"Some of my friends would be happy to show you Sochi. They are very beautiful. Just tell me, do you prefer blonde women or brunettes?"

"You can't get acquainted with the real Russia without Russian women."

Mark, the UNOMIG consultant, told me about such an experience in Sochi: "As soon as I entered my room, I got a call from somebody proposing to send a woman up. I did not even have time to open my suitcase. I reacted angrily. One hour later, I got another call. They wanted to know if I had managed to settle down and if I had any special preference. I threatened to talk to the manager and leave the hotel. Only then did they leave me in peace."

*   *   *

My best memory of Sochi is of my visit to the art museum, located in the middle of a park overlooking the sea. It was housed in a dark, battered old building, which must have known better times. Its collection included paintings from the early postrevolutionary days through the 1950s. While in poor shape and obviously depleted, the collection nonetheless offered an interesting glimpse into the early years of the Soviet Empire, better known for the political terror and revolutionary zeal of the time than art. The paintings documented that, through it all, there persisted some normality of life: scenes of pale-faced men debating under a tree, women going about their daily household chores, children playing in the fields, and displays of everyday joys and fears captured against the backdrop of rivers, small huts, flowers, and country landscapes. These images, encased in the silence and darkness of the museum's hushed interior, made the experience all the more unique.

The building was almost empty as I was its only tourist. Its custodians were as serious and bland as the museum itself, making the sunny and noisy streets of Sochi seem even more distant. I tried to engage them in conversation—there was at least one woman per two exhibition rooms—but in vain. They were polite, attentive, and ready to answer basic questions about the museum but not inclined to chat. My attempts at informal talk appeared to make them tense and uneasy. They watched me carefully from their assigned posts. I tried to figure out how many people visited the museum and whether there were times it was better attended, possibly by schools or organized tourist groups. I could not get an answer.

The Sochi beach was crowded, loud, and divided into three sections: guarded and "more guarded," both requiring paid entry, and public.

The beach and the boulevard along the coastline served, like at many other seashore resorts, as a promenade to meet friends, wine and dine, display the latest summer fashions, and take photos. There were scores of picture-making opportunities: camels, crocodiles, monkeys, parrots, and other exotic animals lined up next to stands with Russian food and works of local artisans. I was puzzled, however, by the groups of young, athletic black African men standing and sitting along the promenade, seemingly without purpose. They were barely dressed, wearing only decorative, colorful African bands around their hips, arm bands and impressive head arrangements. They looked like bodybuilders and spoke Russian. They were waiting for somebody or something. They did not look like tourists there to enjoy the beach.

After a few rounds along the coast, I finally solved the mystery: they were models. I watched in disbelief how young blonde women paid for photos in more or less intimate positions with one or a few of them. Its purpose escaped me. Where the pictures meant to create the impression of being in an exotic land or intended to make husbands or boyfriends back home jealous? Or was it just something to do, the start of a holiday adventure? Probably all. I could only guess. I also wondered about the men and where they were from. Was this only a seasonal job? Were the young men from African countries with friendly relations with Russia and present or former students of Lumumba University (now the People's Friendship University of Russia) in Moscow?

* * *

At popular tourist spots in Sochi, I noted special stands advertising tourism in Abkhazia. Knowing the disastrous condition of the Abkhazian infrastructure, I gave it a closer look. There were quite a few options: daily bus excursions, mainly to New Athos, and longer holidays to the best-known resorts in Pitsunda, Gagra, and Sukhumi. As Abkhazia had no functioning traditional hotels and only a few restaurants, which met even the most minimal of sanitary standards, I wondered what kind of arrangements were being offered.

I had recently traveled to New Athos. There I had come across several tourists and tour buses from Russia, themselves there for the main attractions: the caves and waterfalls, a depleted old monastery, and of course, the long sandy coastline. The area was surrounded by an endless green park with a café on the lake with swans, connected by a charming white wooden bridge to the main land. At the entrance to the caves, there was a small market with souvenirs and local products, such as honey with nuts, wines, homemade cheeses, and bottled drinks. It was rather unusual for Abkhazia where the market economy was still in its infancy.

This tourist area lacked basic services, however, like functioning toilets. I remember the following exchange I had with a waitress at the café on the lake:

"Could you tell me please, where is a toilet?"

"Over there," she said, pointing in the direction of the park.

I followed and looked around but saw no indication of a restroom. I returned and asked again.

"Over there," she repeated, again pointing toward the park.

"But I could not find any toilet there," I explained.

She looked at me surprised. "Just go there. I am telling you to go to the park."

"But—"

"Go to the bush."

With this experience in mind, I was curious about the arrangements being offered to tourists contemplating a trip to Abkhazia. I tried talking to a few women at the stands. They were polite, but reserved, almost suspicious. I was clearly a foreigner and did not look like a potential client. So what was my purpose?

Looking at the poor-quality photos in the brochures displayed at one stand, I asked, "Could you tell me please about the arrangements? What kind of accommodation is available?"

"So when do you want to go?" the woman asked.

"I do not know yet. I would appreciate receiving more specific information as to what is available, when, and the cost. Once I have that, I will think about it, make my plans, and get back to you to make a reservation."

"OK. So go home and think about it. Once you know what you want, tell me, then I will see what I can do for you."

That was typical of the exchanges I had, the refusal sometimes softened with a smile or more elaborate explanation, but mainly, the responses to my inquiry were crude and definite.

*   *   *

What I did manage to learn from these conversations, later corroborated back in Abkhazia, was the following: For most Russians, the southern coast of the Black Sea remained a top destination for summer vacation. It was a long-standing tradition, never changing in fashion, the place to be. Those with sufficient money and connections could rent space in advance at one of the few compounds that existed, such as the Aitar Hotel in Sukhumi or the Sanatorium in Gagra. Officials and others with connections to the Russian military stationed in Abkhazia used their facilities. In Sukhumi, for example, there was a huge complex in the city center occupied by the Russian peacekeeping force. The complex, known as the Russian Compound, was used to house the families and friends of the peacekeepers and Abkhaz and Russian officials and others with military connections who could make the proper arrangements in Moscow.

The Russian Compound consumed a large part of the seashore. The office and living quarters on its grounds were typical of Soviet-era buildings: large and built with concrete blocks. The compound had a few restaurants and cafés, a recreation area, and a beach. Summer nights were loud with the noise of music and voices dominating the neighborhood. The compound was closed to the public, accessible only to its inhabitants, invited guests, and individuals comprising the international community living in Sukhumi. The latter's entry, however, was subject to shifting interpretations. Occasionally, when relations between the Russians and certain international organizations—the UN in particular—got tense or when the political situation in the area deteriorated, the compound was closed to all outsiders. In practice, that meant it was closed to those who had no friends among the Russians stationed in Sukhumi.

I never understood the significance or attraction of access to the Russian Compound. I was there probably twice and, on both occasions, faced some difficulties. The local Abkhaz, save a small elite, were generally not permitted on the premises and resented it. The compound represented the "high life" permanently beyond their reach and was not appreciated in a society destitute and poor. While it was generally accepted that there was a price to be paid for the Russian role as a peace guarantor and protector against Georgia, it was increasingly difficult for the Abkhaz to accept it indefinitely and unconditionally. The Russian Compound added to this increasing discontent.

Most Russian tourists, however, looked for vacation lodging in private homes. As the average Abkhaz house did not have a bathroom or toilet on the premises, I was curious about how it worked. It did, and it was a massive affair. The lodging was secured long in advance, either through travel agencies in Sochi or in other Russian towns, with Moscow at top of the list. More experienced Abkhaz often maintained direct contact with clients who either returned on an annual basis or recommended friends.

I wondered how many people had a cut in the home-lodging business—likely many. In a place with a stagnated economy and strong political control, such opportunities would not be missed. Fear of antagonizing anyone who could influence the business and the murky decision-making processes of the local bureaucracy made broad sharing of the spoils the safest way to survive. Because of the fragile situation in Abkhazia, it was also essential to ensure at least minimum security for the tourists. That generally required securing a political patron, an official in the local bureaucracy or a security agency. Such patronage was also indispensable protection against possible denunciation, harassment, and "reporting" by one's neighbors and associates.

The actual provision of lodging space to tourists seemed to be the easiest thing. The Russians who sought such lodging were not demanding and only interested in the lowest possible price. The Abkhaz who rented out space in their homes would vacate most of their living quarters in the summer, squeezing their own families into one room or sending them off to visit relatives, in order to accommodate as many tourists as possible.

Georgians deeply resented the flourishing Abkhazian-Russian tourism business. The reasons were many, among them the alleged further appropriation of the land and houses of Georgians who fled the region as a result of the war. This often provoked hostile rhetoric and threats from the Georgians. The rhetoric always intensified in the summer months. The Russian military was a favorite target of such campaigns, but the hostility never moved beyond rhetoric. The Abkhaz feared that such provocations could irreversibly destroy their business. It was a psychological game where perceptions often mattered more than the facts.

The business seemed to work and expand from year to year to the mutual satisfaction of the Russians and Abkhaz. The industry really began to flourish after the recognition of Abkhazian independence by Russia in 2008, with the influx of Russian capital into the Abkhaz tourist sector that followed. The number of Russians visiting and even residing in Abkhazia since is astonishing. The only question is, how much have the Abkhaz benefited?

Chapter 9

Gori and Stalin's Birthplace

I first visited Gori, Stalin's birthplace, in 2003. By then it had become a cult destination. All of my interlocutors, independent of their political views, recommended that I visit Gori and Stalin's museum while there. It was a "must" they said. It was meant as a first step toward gaining some clarity on Georgian attitudes about Stalin. I knew their views were complex, if not ambiguous, ranging from "Stalin the Hero" to "Stalin the Mass Murderer" but was unaware that the picture could be rendered even more opaque.

Gori is an unusual place. Visually unimpressive, it is small town about a two-hour's drive northwest of Tbilisi. It is a provincial city with low gray houses, drab concrete buildings typical of the communist era, dusty streets, and a sleepy atmosphere. It is dominated by a wide boulevard named for Stalin; a huge monument to him also stands at its center. The boulevard itself leads to the hut where Stalin was born and the adjoining museum. The hut (more a shack really) is surrounded by a white temple ordered by Beria in the 1930s as an expression of his devotion to Stalin.

Stalin was born Iosif Vissarionovich Dzhugashvili on December 6, 1878, or December 21, 1879, depending on whom you ask. He was born to Vissarion, a low-skilled shoemaker, and Ekaterina née Geladze. His father, known for his heavy drinking and bad temper, had difficulty staying employed. He took his misfortune out on the family, getting violent with both his wife and the young Stalin. His mother cleaned for their more affluent neighbors in order to make ends meet. It was rumored that she was a mistress to some of her employers and that one of them, Koba Egnatashvili, actually fathered Stalin. Stalin, being on the worst possible terms with his father, seemed pleased by the possibility.

Egnatashvili was his godfather, and "Koba" would be the nickname he would use during his revolutionary days.

A religious woman, Stalin's mother wanted him to be a priest. As she had a close relationship with the local clergy, she managed to place him in the Tbilisi Seminary. He was expelled in 1899, and embarked on his revolutionary career from there.

*   *   *

The museum exhibition at Gori chronicled all stages of Stalin's life. His early years were displayed through the museum's collection of his grade school papers and family photographs. His revolutionary and early party days were featured in official contemporaneous photos. The museum also exhibited memorabilia from his later years, after his rise to general secretary of the Communist Party and *generalissimos* (*Wozdz*) during the Second World War and his postwar years, marked by his attendance at international conferences in Teheran and Yalta, in 1943 and 1945, respectively.

The museum, however, made no mention of or had any exhibit detailing the gulags, mass executions, ethnic cleansings, forced evictions and resettlements of entire ethnic groups, execution of war prisoners, and systematic torture and oppression of Stalin's reign, nor his crimes against the Russian population and extermination of his closest political allies and enemies alike. There was also no trace of Stalin's murderous activities in Georgia and the terror generated under Beria's helm.

Our guide, a soft-spoken middle-aged woman, talked a lot about Stalin's years in Georgia and his role in Soviet politics as if the crimes of Stalinism had not occurred. Astonishingly, she was absolutely unwilling and unprepared to discuss these matters, acting as if she had never heard of them.

"All I know is what is presented in this museum," she insisted.

"Why won't you bring the other documents? There are a lot of them," we asked. "Would you like us to provide the museum with some?"

"We have more documents in storage," she persisted. "We cannot exhibit all of them. They are selected carefully and arranged with some logic by specialists. This is a professional exhibition."

"What about the omissions and distortions of basic historical facts? What about portraying one of the most cruel and brutal dictators known to history as a great politician of simple peasant origins? It makes a mockery of the entire place."

She did not respond. We wondered whether she was merely parroting the official policy line or steeped in individual denial and whether such aversion to the truth was common in Georgian society. I cannot say that I ever truly discovered the answer.

Despite having good friends in Georgia and enjoying frank, lively discussions with them on all manner of topics—local politics, culture, the world—I could never engage them on the subject of Stalin. While mere mention of Shevardnadze, Gamsakhurdia, Gorbachev, Saakashvili, or Putin would elicit strong reactions and set off heated debates, the name of Stalin was met with indifference, dismissed out of hand, or simply ignored. And the question of Stalin—or anything related to his reign of terror—certainly never sprung up spontaneously in the course of any of our conversations.

The question was why. Were the scars still too fresh for those who suffered through those decades of terror, or was the silence a learned behavior, a legacy passed on to successive generations? Or was it simply a product of ignorance? I wondered what they taught in the schools, wrote in the history books, reported in the mass media. What was conveyed through the oral history?

Georgians were among Stalin's chief victims. He had opposed Georgian independence in 1921, contrary to the great majority of Georgians, to include the Bolsheviks among them. Convinced that he could alter their decision, Stalin paid a visit to Tbilisi and demanded that Georgia voluntarily join the USSR and abandon her independence ambitions. He was emphatically rejected, a public humiliation Stalin never forgot. Georgia, his native land, would become a primary target of his brutal repression as a consequence. Lenin would later cite the episode as an example of Stalin's brutal character and disrespect for rights of nationalities when he confronted Stalin and attempted (unsuccessfully) to disqualify Stalin as his successor.

True to his nature, following Lenin's death, Stalin escalated his repression of the Georgian people. The persecution continued with the appointment of Lavrenti Beria as chief of party in Georgia, in 1931, particularly intensifying in the period from 1937 to 1938. That year was marked by mass deportations, politically motivated arrests, and torture widely perpetrated against intellectuals, artists, and Georgian communists opposed to Stalin's ideas and unwilling to conform to the party line. The brutal oppression would continue on Stalin's orders, carried out by his willing executioner, Beria, in his capacity as head of the NKVD, the forerunner to the KGB, from 1938 until Stalin's death in 1953.

Georgia is a small country with the strong sense of tradition and national identity. The mass deportations, arrests, and killings that characterised Stalin's reign affected most Georgian families. One would expect that, with independence from the USSR, a national discussion and soul-searching reflecting on this difficult period would have commenced or, at least, that the issue would be discussed within families and among friends and that there would be a natural inclination to tell the current generation what had happened to their mothers and fathers, grandparents, and other relatives who simply perished and whose burial places often remain unknown. One would also expect an attempt to correct the record to clarify the fate of those Georgians who died as "enemies of the people," that steps would be taken to rehabilitate the names of those who remain defamed or erased in order to restore their reputations and proper place in history. Had such discussions taken place, the Gori museum in its present orientation would not have been possible.

I revisited Gori in 2009, exactly one year after the Russian invasion of the city. The shrines to Stalin had survived untouched: his birth home, his museum, the enormous monument to him dominating the avenue in his name. It seems that both parties to the conflict spared no effort to protect them. I was most interested in learning whether anything had changed in the official narrative concerning Stalin under Saakashvili, whose government was aggressively pursuing an anti-Soviet, anti-communist and nationalistic line.

On the main road to Gori, I noticed numerous advertisements inviting tourists to Stalin's birth place. The shack of his birth and the museum were clearly still attractions and drawing a cult following. Upon arriving, I found that the museum itself had been redesigned and equipped with a tourist shop selling souvenirs celebrating the *Wozdz*. All manner of T-shirts with his likeness, cognacs, commemorative books, and small statues were available for purchase.

I again joined the guided tour. The museum guides were well-dressed and professionally trained. However, their presentations were delivered monotonously and little time was left for questions or comments, and such were neither anticipated nor welcomed. The tour had a clearly set time and program—all rooms had to be visited and the main stages of Stalin's life explained. Notwithstanding, it began well enough. Our guide explained that many different perceptions of Stalin existed—from Stalin as a great leader and military strategist to Stalin as tyrant—and that the museum had chosen to focus on his life's story, his role in world history, and his "intellectual and psychological profile." After this brief introduction, we continued on to the exhibition.

"Here is Stalin as a boy with his parents. Look how similar he looks to his father," our guide commented.

"Yes," Devi, my colleague, interjected, "in this photo. But there is a strong belief that he was the son of Koba Egnatashvili and in other photos—"

"No, that is a rumor which by now is rejected by serious historical sources. Look at the photo. They look like each other. Let us move on," she said, cutting the conversation short. But controversy was bound to stay with us.

"This is Stalin's second wife, Nadya Alliluyeva, with whom he had two children, Svetlana and Vasily." The guide quickly gestured with her pointer to a black-and-white photograph of a dark-haired woman and turned to walk away.

"When did she commit suicide?" I asked. "In which year was it?"

"1942," she clipped, turning her back to me, rushing off to the next room.

"And when did Svetlana leave for the USA?"

"I do not know. She still lives there." It did not get any easier obtaining answers as we were raced through the exhibition.

"These are people who committed crimes," she said, pointing a tableau with the well-known photos of several Cheka, NKVD, and KGB leaders, among them: Felix Dzerzhinsky, Genrikh Yagoda, Nikolai Yezhov, and Beria. Khrushchev's photo was also included. Arranged in two rows, it gave the appearance of a most wanted poster. "They were very bad. They killed a lot of people behind Stalin's back. He did not know about it and now some try to blame him for it," our guide duly reported.

"What about the deportations, mass executions, and wave of great terror in the late 1930s that almost left Russia without a professional military on the eve of World War II? Do you have any documents from that period?" I asked.

"You will see them later in the special exhibition."

"Oh, so that is new. It did not exist six years ago," I noted. She did not react.

We pushed on to another room documenting Stalin's military and political honors and displaying his medals. It was not new but much better exhibited. Various *generalissimo* decorations, gifts, declarations of gratitude and loyalty from foreign leaders, and photos from Teheran and Yalta adorned the walls.

We concluded our tour and our guide thanked us for our interest and wished us a good day. She quickly turned to return to the reception area.

"Just a moment," I said as I ran after her. "Where are the exhibits documenting the gulags and other atrocities? You promised to show them to us, and we have not seen them yet."

"You have to ask. Please follow me."

I followed, completely disoriented. We were brought to an office at the back of the museum, and our guide disappeared. The woman behind the desk viewed me with suspicion and asked who I was.

"Does it matter? I'm just a tourist visiting the museum."

"Are you a journalist?"

"No, but why is that important?"

"We want to know who is visiting our museum."

I introduced myself, and she produced a key to the "Repression Room." Our guide re-emerged. After a lengthy struggle with the lock, we finally managed to open it and entered the room. It was small and sparsely furnished with a desk and chair, a few photos, some clothes, and a few personal effects, items which could have come from anywhere. There was no sign or explanation as to their origin or significance.

In the corridor leading to the room, there were excerpts from documents citing the numbers of those executed or deported along the wall, but they did not provide any additional details or explanation as to who, what, when, and why. Farther on, we saw again the photo tableau of the "bad people" who had supposedly misled Stalin, the same one we had seen earlier in another part of the museum.

"But why is Khrushchev's photo here?" I asked. "He was not a chief of the NKVD."

"No, but he was responsible for massacres in Ukraine," the guide replied as my friends nodded.

"Yes, but without diminishing his responsibility, there were many other high-ranking party members responsible for similar atrocities. I do not excuse his actions. I am just surprised that he is included in this group. It looks rather like revenge for his statement at the Twentieth Party Congress in 1956, and his disclosure of the atrocities committed under Stalin's helm."

Silence.

I stopped querying and began thinking of possible reasons behind Khrushchev's "special place" in Stalin's museum. In March of 1956, in his speech before the Twentieth Congress, Khrushchev quite deliberately referred to Stalin as "the greatest son of Georgia." He did so being aware that knowledge of Stalin's crimes was widespread. Georgian national pride was wounded by both, Khrushchev's revelations and his attribution of Stalin's character to his Georgian roots. The speech incited strong anti-Russian sentiment among Georgians, leading to mass demonstrations in Tbilisi. The crowds demanded rehabilitation of Stalin's name and independence for Georgia. The demonstrations, though peaceful, were brutally put down by Soviet troops, on Khrushchev's orders.

My thoughts were interrupted, and I was brought back to present by the guide. She was discussing a framed document on exhibit citing Beria's decision to release over one thousand people from the prisons and gulags after Stalin's death. It probably meant that Beria was somehow not as bad as Khrushchev, who shortly after had him eliminated. After all, Khrushchev was a Ukrainian peasant and Beria an educated, intelligent Georgian. On this note, we concluded our visit.

After leaving the museum, we were approached by an elderly woman. We were plainly the only tourists in the area. She wanted to know if we had liked the museum and was visibly proud that her city offered such an international attraction. I wondered if she had ever been inside. My guess was she had not. I carefully mentioned the omissions and historical distortions in the museum's exhibitions, alluding to the gulags and Stalin's victims, particularly the Georgians.

"Yes, he executed many people," she agreed. "We know that some Georgians were killed. But he killed many more Russians. We would need him today," she said, smiled, and walked away.

*　　*　　*

For lunch, we went to a hotel nearby. The building, which stood not far from Stalin's monument along the boulevard in his name, looked as it did six years ago; there were no signs of war. I asked about the events of the previous summer, but the young waitress obviously did not want to discuss it. That was new. Usually, Georgians enjoyed talking with foreigners, even more so to complain about Russians. It was possible that she was still traumatized by the recent memories of the war or simply afraid to make a political statement that could be overheard by Georgian or Russian security forces. Or was it a reflection of the new political climate?

Over lunch (which was delicious) we discussed our visit to Stalin's museum. One of my Georgian friends, Kaha, believed that the system should be blamed, not people. "What difference does it make if it was Stalin or Lenin or Beria?" he argued.

Living in Austria, I thought about the essential differences in attitudes, education, and laws.

"Can you imagine a similar museum to Hitler in Braunau, the place of his birth, omitting the holocaust and crimes against humanity and depicting him as a friendly man and great political leader?"

"It was not only Hitler," Kaha insisted. "He was armed by the West, and there were many others who were involved. It should not all be put on him."

"People in this region love Stalin," Devi explained. "I do not share this view, but for them, he is still a hero. They believe that despite the crimes and costs to the society, he changed the course of history, created a world empire, destroyed Hitler's Germany, and asserted the Soviet Union's position in the world. It gives them a great sense of dignity and pride because, after all, he was Georgian. Therefore, they do not take kindly to any criticism of him and want Gori to be a place of reverence to him rather than the site of a historically accurate museum."

So who was Stalin to Georgians? Is he Georgian, the favorite son, the source of national pride? Or is he the Russian, representing Russian imperialism and tyranny against Georgia and her people? I had not become any wiser by my visits to Gori. Except, I did come to realize that amid the ongoing bitterness and animosity between Georgia and Russia, their shared admiration for Stalin seemed to be the only commonality linking the two societies. In opinion polls conducted in Russia in 2008, Stalin was ranked second among the greatest Russians of all time. Maybe that too is something Georgians take pride in.

Chapter 10

Kodori Gorge

The image of the Kodori Gorge that I saw as part of a documentary presentation on the Caucasus many years ago in New York stayed with me and continued to fascinate me long before I knew that I would ever go to Georgia. Beautiful, remote, mysterious, and distant—the Kodori Gorge seemed to me to embody the essence of the Caucasus. You can get close, but never truly possess it. You can admire, but not quite conquer it. It is always there—hidden behind the clouds, changing colors and moods in the sun and mist.

Kodori geographically belonged to Abkhazia. Although it was formally under the authority of the Georgian government, it was ruled by the leader of the local militia, Emzar Kvitsiani. Barely accessible most of the year and practically cut off completely in the winter, the Kodori Gorge was in reality a no-man's-land—a convenient hideout for rebels and criminals from neighboring territories, a passage for smuggling contraband.

Owing to its strategic position and importance to the parties in conflict, a thorough monitoring of the Kodori Gorge was critical for the implementation of the UN Mission's mandate and preservation of peace. Any unrest in Kodori could potentially be explosive. Thus, timely information could provide an early warning against threats of renewed hostilities.

Monitoring and reporting of the area was mainly performed by UN military observers through patrols, local visits, and other forms of surveillance. The observers, who were all unarmed, were recruited by the United Nations from a number of contributing countries and acted under a joint UN command. Their area of operation was strictly defined by the mission's mandate and included, in addition to Sukhumi, the capital of the separatist Republic of Abkhazia, the Gali region and

Kodori Gorge. They were also present on the Georgian side of the separation line in the Zugdidi area.

Patrolling the Kodori Gorge was a difficult issue. Foot patrols could only be carried out in certain months because the harshness of the winter rendered most of the area inaccessible. Rapid fluctuations in the weather, the rough terrain of the high, uninhabited mountains, and the constant danger of kidnappings and attacks by roving criminal gangs exposed the observer missions to additional risks. It was known that UN observers were not armed and that their security depended on the presence of the CIS (Russian) peacekeepers.

There had been a few cases of kidnapping of UN patrols in the past. Fortunately, there had been no casualties, and the kidnapped observers were always, sooner or later, released. The details of the rescue operations securing their release were never clear. Neither the UN nor Caucasus authorities—whether Abkhaz, Georgian, or Russian—revealed their secrets. So there were rumors, tales, and legends instead. It also remained a mystery who was behind the kidnappings, what their objectives were, what benefits they sought to derive, and for whom. I guess that most people, at least among UN employees, did not know and the few who did could not (or would not) share their knowledge.

Members of the local population were equally evasive. Some would say that they did not know. Others would not even react to the question but show through body language—an empty gaze, a shrug of the shoulders, dismissive wave of a hand—that it was not a topic they wished to engage. There were also recurrent questions among the UN staff: Why is it that the hostages have always been released unharmed without ransom payment? If there was no money involved (which was the official UN policy and that of the Georgian government), why did the kidnappings continue? To demonstrate power? To intimidate?

Soon after my arrival in Sukhumi in the spring of 2003, UN authorities decided to renew the patrolling in the Kodori Gorge. It had been suspended after the last round of kidnappings and because of harsh weather. A new team was appointed, and preparations for a mission began. They would be deployed as soon as the political, security, and weather conditions permitted.

I met the team members in the Staff Club at the Aitar Hotel. We spent a pleasant evening discussing the situation in Abkhazia, their military experiences, and preparations for patrolling. As a newcomer to the mission and the area, I listened attentively to their conversation, positively envying their work experiences and familiarity with the region. Finally, I made a suggestion, "Would it be possible for me to join one of your patrols?"

There was silence. Then, some took it as a joke, others seriously. I assured them that I was serious and my intention sincere, but only if my presence would not in any way hamper their mission. I was pretty certain, however, that the mission's security and administrative departments would not be particularly inclined to entertain such a bold idea.

The team leader, a sporty Dane called Jorg, asked me, "Aren't you worried about being kidnapped? It can happen."

"Not if I'm in pleasant company," I replied. Everybody laughed.

"I am not joking," he continued. "It is not nice. They normally keep people blindfolded in a basement. You lose the sense of time and reality. You freeze, stink of dirt and fear, and you cannot see your captors."

"Are you sure you want it?" Greg, another military observer, questioned.

"And, moreover," Jorg continued, "your and others lives may depend on your physical condition, on how fast and far you can run, how long you can walk without food, water, and sleep and how quickly you can climb."

He suddenly became serious and gave me a critical look—my high-heeled shoes, tight skirt, and jewelry.

"Jorg," I told him, "I do not want to hamper your mission or put anybody at risk. Although I am not a sports champion, I can walk for hours, climb, and stay at high altitudes. And I do not go hiking dressed like this, do not worry."

I looked around the table, my gaze stopping at some of the members of his team: one slightly overweight, another too looking far from fit.

"Do not worry. I'm sure I would do as well as some of your team members here, if necessary," I added.

We continued our relaxed conversation over beer, considering all the options. I learned a lot not only about the area and the role of observers, but also about my military colleagues as professionals and human beings. Although divided on the question of whether or not I should try to get permission to join them, we parted as friends.

Jorg and the others promised to share with me the plans for Kodori, at least those not classified: the preliminary dates for the mission, logistics and security requirements, and other such matters. Jorg would also assess the propriety of my inclusion in the exercise. On my end, I planned to test the reaction of the mission authorities. I felt that in my capacity as a senior political advisor, I should have the option of visiting Kodori to get a better idea of what was happening there and to gain a better understanding of the geo-political ramifications of the peace process.

Shortly thereafter, I was told by Jorg that it would not be advisable for me to join the next patrol as it would be the first after a long break. If everything worked out and the patrols resumed a regular schedule in the summer months, as they should, I could join one of them, he said.

"Providing we are not kidnapped in the meantime," he added and laughed.

We went on with our respective work and daily routines. I had not seen the Kodori team for weeks. I put the idea of going there on the backburner as I was quite busy with other matters. Then one sunny day in June, I got news that the team of UN military observers had been kidnapped in the Kodori Gorge. I thought that I had misunderstood, that it was a joke of some kind. Not at all. It turned out to be the plain truth.

I got confirmation from the mission observer in charge of the operation. Yes, these were our colleagues, our Kodori team, the same which had been preparing for the first patrol since April. Yes, all four were taken. I left without a word. It was not the time for queries and disturbing questions. I thanked the operational group for their confirmation and quickly withdrew.

I went to the Staff Club—there were not many places to go on the Aitar compound. I could not absorb the news. I just sat there without uttering a word to anyone. I could not guess from the behavior of those around me whether the news had already reached them. The club was half empty. It was early afternoon, still too early for a crowd. Most of those present were local UN staff, along with some club employees. Suddenly, a military observer entered the club, a Dane and friend of Jorg. I ran straight to him.

"Is it true?" I asked.

"Yes." He looked exhausted and distraught.

"We do not know anything yet. It happened just a few hours ago. They are strong, they are well-trained. Jorg is a top security man and an excellent team leader. The kidnappers never harmed anybody in the past, so why should they do it now?"

He kept talking as if trying to convince me and himself.

"We are taking action on all fronts—diplomatic, security, militarily—directly and indirectly. We are also beginning to talk to their families. This is one of the toughest parts, but we have to do it as quickly as possible. They have to get the news from us, not the media, and be prepared on how to react if the kidnappers get hold of them. They should also be aware of the press."

"I can't believe it," I repeated.

"Me neither," he sighed.

The days that followed were full of tension, speculation, and concern. A hush fell over the compound. Both clubs were almost silent. People whispered over coffee and dinner alike as if they were afraid to awake a monster or conjure bad news. With voices low and faces sad, most staff kept to themselves, only cautiously inquiring of new developments. The mission leadership was fully and confidentially engaged with the Georgian authorities and the other parties, the Abkhaz and Russian peacekeepers (CIS-PKF). As the incident took place in Georgian territory, Georgian authorities were ultimately responsible. The CIS-PKF also bore a share of the responsibility. Their soldiers had accompanied the UN observers to the Kodori Gorge, ostensibly to ensure their security. Unlike the UN monitors, they were armed. But when it came to the ambush by an armed group, they did not resist and gave up their weapons. Some military colleagues, however, understood such a reaction. They believed that any resistance could have seriously endangered the lives of all concerned.

For a few days, there was no news except general information from unnamed sources shared with us at daily staff meetings. From private conversations with military colleagues, I knew that the hostages were alive and well, at least as well as they could be under the circumstances. Finally word came around that a team of Georgian officials were in Kodori and that a breakthrough was anticipated at any time. Indeed, the hostages were soon released and met by the Georgian officials in Kodori. They were then transferred to Tbilisi where they received a hero's welcome and a lot of press attention. Each underwent a thorough medical examination, de-briefing, and after some days of rest, returned to Sukhumi.

When the team finally reached Sukhumi, we were all relieved and overjoyed by their safe return. Gradually, life began to take on its normal routine, and we started frequenting the clubs and socializing again. We waited, however, until our colleagues felt like telling us their stories.

One day, I had a chance meeting with Jorg. He had been jogging around the compound.

"You know, when I realized that we were kidnapped, I thought of our conversation in the club. It was the first thing to come to my mind."

"That was my first thought when I heard the news," I responded. "I thought it was somebody's joke."

"But they did not keep us in a basement as I had anticipated. They kept us out under the sky, handcuffed and blindfolded. It was freezing cold, but at least, we had a lot of fresh air. Later on, they even allowed us to look around. There were three of them, but only one was a real pro. The others were amateurs.

"I was racking my head, what to do? Risk an assault on them and escape, or wait, hoping for a negotiated solution? Had I been alone, I would have quickly decided on the first option. But there were four of us, and some were already deeply affected by the ordeal.

"The worse was that we could not know what would happen next, how our captors would react to further developments, especially if they felt threatened or betrayed. What were their objectives? Who were their counterparts? These questions were constantly on our minds especially since we had no confidence in the parties involved, except the UN.

"Another disturbing part was the gradual loss of sense of time. How long have we been here, in the mountains, in captivity? The sequence of nights and days was difficult to follow. Each of us was individually going through a crisis, experiencing feelings of desperation, anger, and anxiety. If we had not controlled these emotions, the situation could have been worse. We watched each other closely and could see it coming. It was surprising how sensitive we became to such manifestations and how effectively, without words, we managed to encourage each other to stay calm.

"I remember one occasion, it was windy and about dusk. I felt that I could not take it anymore and was brooding over how to go about incapacitating the gang's leader. Tensed up, my concentration and body language were noticed by my friends, and I was suddenly brought back to reality by a strong cough from Anton. I looked at him and read it in his eyes and in the movement of his head. He warned me against taking any irresponsible step. I accepted."

Later on, in the Staff Club, I joined a noisy table with two other Kodori heroes, Anton, German, and Jules, French. I heard Anton saying, "I thought of my daughter and worried how she would receive the news. I suddenly realized how much I wanted to see her and make sure that she was safe. I started to recall stories of kidnappers contacting the families of their captives to negotiate a ransom, hoping that it would not be the case and that Germany was too far away from the perspective of the Caucasus."

Jules spoke little. He admitted that for him the experience was still too fresh and traumatizing to speak of lightly. He could not yet sleep normally and needed more time to come to terms with what had happened.

The chain of kidnappings in the Kodori Gorge remained a Caucasus mystery. The routine was the same each time. Officially, neither the UN nor the Georgian government negotiated with kidnappers any payments. Thus, allegedly, there was no financial gain. Nobody ever claimed responsibility for the kidnappings; they remained anonymous and therefore politically useless. Some Georgians, however, insisted that the abductions were carried out with the collaboration of all parties to the conflict—to include some members of the Georgian political establishment—in cooperation with the criminal gangs.

"Criminal groups do not worry about political and ideological divisions, and they have no problems with ethnicity. They simply do business. I am convinced that all of them had a hand in it—the Abkhaz, Russians, Georgians, and whatever 'locals,'" Marc, a French military observer, told me.

It rang a bell. I thought of my experiences in the Balkans during the war where—although ethnicity, religion, and historical grievances drove the ideological rhetoric and hate policies—it never affected the lucrative commercial operations of criminal groups.

*   *   *

With time and the Saakashvili government's consolidation of power, tensions between Georgian central authorities and Kvitsiani, the local warlord, heightened. In the summer of 2007, Kvitsiani finally threatened to separate from Georgia by force and formally impose his own rule. The Georgian army stepped in in response, and the region became subordinated to Georgian central authority. Soon afterward, the Abkhaz government-in-exile was resettled to Kodori from Tbilisi.

This arrangement did not last long. In the midst of the Russian-Georgian war over South Ossetia in August of 2008, Russian troops moved in and seized the Kodori Gorge and incorporated it into the Abkhaz state, in violation of existing agreements. The UN was asked to stay out and not interfere, and it complied.

Thus, the Kodori Gorge today is a part of Abkhazia. The land, however, has not changed. It remains as majestic, magical, and distant as ever.

Chapter 11

Smiling Faces

On the wall of the UNOMIG's so-called "military container," a building housing the offices of the mission's military observers in Sukhumi, there was a collection of photographs of several young, good-looking people. They were smiling, radiating energy and optimism. Placed in front of one of the main conference rooms, the pictures stood in sharp contrast to the often grim mood of the staff meetings and bleak spirit of the colorless, prefabricated walls of the corridors.

I looked at these photos almost every day while waiting for our meetings to start. I cannot explain what attracted me to them. They were black and white, regular in size, and displayed as in a traditional photoshop. I knew that all those portrayed were dead and that they had died within the last few years in the line of duty; all but one were men. Most were victims of a helicopter crash, the cause of which was extensively investigated but never satisfactorily explained.

The helicopter crashed on October 8, 2001. It was on its way to patrol the Kodori Gorge, an area about twenty kilometers east of Sukhumi. The situation had been tense due to resumed fighting between Abkhaz forces and pro-Georgian armed groups, but both parties—the Abkhaz and Georgians alike—had assured the mission that there was no risk to renewed patrolling of the area. The Abkhaz, who claimed that the armed bands had been driven away from the area, cleared the flight. The helicopter was shot down shortly after it took off. All nine people on board were killed.

"Look, it's Greg, a Swiss team leader of the helicopter," one of his colleagues, also a military observer, told me. I looked at the young, handsome face, smiling and open.

"He was with us two years ago. We talked as we talk now. Sometimes I feel that it is a bad dream, that I will enter the club and see him at the bar calling me to join him.

"On that terrible morning, I had breakfast with him and two others and saw him off for the patrol. I saw him climbing into the UN car and leaving the gates of the Aitar waving to us."

"They were such nice kids," Galina, a local receptionist, recalled, her eyes filling with tears. "Young, kind, and friendly. They always said hello, joked, and chatted with us.

"Why is it so that God takes away the best people and leaves us on earth with all these bastards? Look around. There are so many who would not be missed. It is as if God picks the best goods. I do not understand it. It is beyond me."

"It is the law of nature," commented Lavrenti, a local electrician. "What is solid and has its weight goes down, what is light stays at the surface. It goes for people as well."

Two of the victims were local staff members, interpreters.

"They were so happy and proud to have jobs with the UN," Galina continued. "They were among the best and therefore had been selected for this mission. Their families shared in their pride. After all, it was the first patrol after two months of hostilities. You can imagine the reaction of their families. Unlike the others who were far away—in Switzerland, Ukraine, or Turkey—they were here, on the spot, and knew instantly what had happened and who had gone patrolling that morning."

It had been a beautiful October morning, they said. Most mission employees were around, starting their daily routines. Some had even taken the helicopter departure as a positive sign that the most serious hostilities were over. "The worst is behind us," they surmised, "otherwise nobody would authorize the flight."

"Hopefully, after days of increased tensions, frequent curfews, and restrictions on movement, which has basically kept us confined within the walls of the Aitar, there will be a breakthrough" was a predominant feeling.

Some people in the mission remembered not only this fateful day, but also the uncertainty that had preceded it. Should the flight be authorized in such a highly volatile area? The fighting on the ground in the conflict zone had been ongoing since August 2001. The UNOMIG had managed to monitor the situation in all areas, to include along the cease-fire line, except in the Georgian-controlled upper region of the

Kodori. As some of the hostilities were taking place there and it was not amenable, under the circumstances, to ground patrolling, there was an operational need for a helicopter. The issue was obviously highly controversial, subject to lengthy consultations and assessments. Finally, the decision was taken and the team of nine—four military observers, two local staff, and three members of the crew—took off.

The crash had been under investigation ever since with no conclusive results or satisfactory explanation. A special investigation committee led by Ukraine (the country where the helicopter was registered), comprised of UN representatives and representatives of Georgian and Abkhaz authorities, was established. While the committee kept meeting and writing reports, debating and quarreling about technical details and responsibilities, and the matter of how and who authorized the fatal flight, they never reached a basic question—who did it?

Despite the shock to those around and the tragedy to the victims, their friends, families, and colleagues, and strong words from the UN Secretary-General—who called the shooting "an outrage" and stated later the same month, at the UN Security Council, that the perpetrators of the criminal acts against the UNOMIG must be brought to justice—nothing happened. The perpetrators remain unknown and, thus, unapprehended. None of the parties that gave security assurances ahead of the flight have faced any consequences for their "mistake" either.

The sad, gray stone, which laid in the middle of the Aitar compound where the crash victims lived during the last months of their lives, was another reminder of the tragedy. Placed close to the Staff Club and decorated with an artificial flower arrangement, it gave a decidedly different impression than the photos. It was unimaginative, impersonal, and cold, reflective of life at the Aitar rather than the vibrant lives of the victims it was to commemorate.

The gray stone, the black-and-white photographs on display in the UNOMIG headquarters, and the Memory Book on its Web site were all reminders of the nine young lives lost that day, the result of somebody's barbarian act and another's irresponsible promise. Their sacrifice and memories, although vivid among families and friends in this distant and obscure place, were never brought to the public's attention. The world was still in the shock of the September 11 attacks on New York and Washington, and such a "small" act of terrorism did not make the news. It may not have been deemed newsworthy in any case. It was crime perpetuated against the UN, in a distant land, far from the main political scene, the details of which were not sufficiently controversial or sexed up to command the world's attention. And who knows anything about Abkhazia? Even Georgia is generally associated with Atlanta, not the Georgia of the Caucasus.

The UN, for its part, traditionally refrains from publicizing these types of incidents too broadly, especially when they have obvious political ramifications. The peace process must go on; the mandate must be implemented and that requires cooperation of all parties. Antagonizing some of them is never in the cards.

"So who did it? What do you think?" I asked of some colleagues.

"Well, we will probably never know officially, but I believe that the Abkhaz were responsible. After all, it happened in their territorial space, close to Sukhumi. The only question is whether it was a deliberate act or a mistake.

"It is difficult to see how it could have been a mistake. It was a bright day. They were asked for a security clearance, so they knew to whom the helicopter belonged."

Others intimated that it was the Georgian side, either through its own officials or one of the criminal groups in the area acting on its behalf. "It was a provocation. They wanted to put the blame on the Abkhaz."

There was also the third suggestion: "The Russians were behind it. They are pulling the strings and running the show in the region. And it is in the KGB tradition. In the Caucasus, if you do not know who is behind something, be sure that it is the KGB. It has never been different."

As nothing has been officially clarified, the gap continues to be filled with rumors and speculation. It remains one of the many mysteries of the Caucasus.

Chapter 12

Maria

One of the smiling faces belonged to a young, blonde Polish woman called Maria. Some years ago, prior to my arrival in Georgia, I had seen the name at the UN Office in Vienna. There had been a photo accompanied with an obituary. It had said she died in service of the United Nations while serving with the peacekeeping mission in Georgia.

During my months in Sukhumi with the UNOMIG, I heard a lot about Maria, her vibrant personality, enthusiasm, and shocking death. She was a strong woman and particularly popular with the local women at the UN compound, the Aitar women. They remembered her youth, her generosity, her indiscriminating friendship.

"She did not differentiate among people," they said. "As you can see, we are just washing and cleaning ladies, doing dirty work, and are treated as such by many, but she treated us as equals. She would come by, sit with us on a bench, joke, and smile. Once, she brought in a big basket of cherries and put them next to the reception for all who were around. We all enjoyed the cherries. They were quite good. You have to taste our cherries when the season comes—big, sweet, and dark. There are no such cherries anywhere else in the world."

"Maria was very happy in Abkhazia," Marina recalled. "She liked the country and liked us. She worked hard but also enjoyed life. She had a nice boyfriend from Denmark, or maybe Sweden—I do not know—but they were very happy. She worked as a secretary to one of the military commanders. We often saw her in the club, dancing and drinking beer. She was very sociable. All seemed to be good and working for her until some problem in the office started up."

"Her boss had some problems, so he tried to blame it on her," Vika stated.

"No, it had nothing to do with her," Marina interjected. "He had some problems, it is true, messed up something or made some high-level enemies, but it did not destroy their relationship. He simply had to face up to his problems and reorganize the office. It was clear that he would not last long at the mission. Under the circumstances, they decided that she should be reassigned somewhere else, that it would be better for her to be out of this mess."

"No, it was Maria who did not like to work in this office," Vika corrected. "She did not like the changes. Besides, her boyfriend also had some problems because all these things were connected. Nobody knew exactly what has going on, but then, a lot of personnel and organizational changes were taking place. Some people left, others came. We got a clean up by the new broom. Still, we never expected that Maria would leave Sukhumi. After all, most of the mission's staff works here, only some in Tbilisi.

"When she got the news about her reassignment, she changed. She was not herself anymore. She got depressed, she cried often and tried by all means to delay her departure. But there was a lot of pressure to send her there.

"Somebody was in a hurry," Vika continued. "Either they did not want to have her here or something was cooking in Tbilisi. Her boyfriend was also very unhappy. I will never forget the day she left. She was so resigned that she did not even take care to pack her belongings. We helped her to bring some loose items to the car. She burst into tears."

"I tried to cheer her up," said Marina. "I told her that she would be back in no time, that she would come for a visit or be reassigned back to Sukhumi after a while. I also told her that Tbilisi was a very nice city, that she would enjoy it. We do not like Georgians, and they hate us, but it would be different for her. She would like the city's cafés, restaurants, broad avenues, and historical buildings. And she could shop and eat as she wished."

Marina stopped and shook her head.

"I will never forget it," she continued. "Maria looked at me through the tears and said, 'I will never be back. I will never see you again. I know it. I am saying good-bye to you and Sukhumi.'"

She then embarked into one of the white four-wheel UN cars and was gone. They said she did not look back or wave. She just slammed the door, still weeping.

"We started crying after she was gone," Marina said after another pause. "I had tried to control myself to cheer her up, but deep down, I was devastated. When I went home, I told my family how I felt. They could see it. That day was a quiet evening. My daughter tried to tell me the next day at breakfast that things may go well for Maria, that it was all about the boyfriend, that he would visit her soon, and that she may be happy again. I was grateful for her sincere attempt to console me, but at the Aitar, the mood was quite grim. The other women shared my despair. They too were shaken by the deep unhappiness and the sense of hopelessness of that otherwise positive young woman. It was so unlike Maria."

They tried to phone her, but it was impossible. The lines between Sukhumi and Tbilisi remained inexcusably bad, even during my time there. The reason was not technological—after all there were willing investors prepared to repair the lines—but political. Isolation, separation, and lack of direct communication helped to preserve stereotypes and the very idea of the other as "enemy" and ensured continued circulation of misinformation and rumors. People who communicate directly—talk and argue—people who develop economic relations and commercial exchanges are less inclined to fall victim to vicious propaganda and provocations.

If phone communication between Sukhumi and Tbilisi was difficult for the international community in the region, it was close to impossible for the local population. Marina had tried to get hold of Maria from her boyfriend's office, but they could not get through. He told her later that he had managed to speak to her, but only briefly, and that she was still terribly depressed. He had promised to visit her as soon as possible, but he needed time to arrange it. It would require a leave authorization from his superiors, a helicopter connection, and completion of some urgent assignments. So he could not make the trip to Tbilisi in earlier than four or five weeks.

Marina nor any of the Aitar women ever heard directly from Maria. They knew from others that she was adjusting, had found a good flat in the city center, and had began working in the Tbilisi UN office, a smaller but much better-equipped facility than the one in Sukhumi. So maybe all will be fine, they thought. She would have a new life there, visit Sukhumi from time to time, and one day reunite with her boyfriend.

"I was still very sad," Marina said, "but I tried to convince myself that it would go that way. I could not wait until her boyfriend went there so we could know more, be sure that things were OK. We also started collecting things that Maria liked—honey with nuts, homemade wine, oranges. Nowhere are there such good oranges as in Abkhazia. And we prayed for her. We could not forget her pale and tearful face, desperate and resigned."

"I will never forget the day when the news struck: Maria was dead. She had been killed," Vika recalled. "It reached us first as an incredible rumor and only later was conveyed to us officially. I will never forget that evening. I was working at the hotel, cleaning rooms and washing laundry for private clients. It was getting late and already dark. I was nervously looking at my watch worrying about how to get home. It was not safe to walk or wait for a bus in the darkness, they were not regular. However, I had to finish my work, and I had a lot to do on that day.

"I decided to ask around to see who else was still there so we could travel home together. Some of the girls had relatives with cars, others were met by their men—grown sons, husbands, or fathers. There was also the possibility of hiring a taxi, or rather, a car working as a taxi. If a few of us got together, it was worth paying for it. I walked around the compound and entered the Staff Club. That is when I heard it. Our girl at the bar was crying, the few others around were silent. There was no music, no talking. It was like a graveyard. I had felt that something was very wrong, but I had not expected that.

"I do not remember anymore what happened next. It was a shock. I did not want to believe it. On the other hand, I knew in my heart of hearts that this was the truth. My fears, my premonition, Maria's image. Suddenly, all fell into place. I could not utter a word, I could not breathe, I lost sense of time and place. All I remember is the silence and crying. Then I began to hear the whispers, the voices, and then finally discussions. The club was filling up, and people were learning the bad news."

With time, some facts emerged but they were never fully convincing. None of the various versions circulated were coherent. The investigation ran by the Georgian authorities had obvious gaps and the degree of UN involvement was limited. It is the role of the host country to carry out criminal investigations; the UN only has monitoring and access to data rights. Considering the high level of criminality in Georgia in those days and the notorious dysfunction of the Georgian judiciary and law enforcement agencies, it could hardly have been more different. The Georgian authorities had no credibility.

There were only a few facts which seemed to be established beyond doubt. Maria was killed in her own apartment in the center of Tbilisi after returning from work and daily shopping. There were no traces of forced entry into the flat. The apartment was not looted, nothing valuable was stolen. Was she followed by her murderer? Did she know him and open the door? Was he already waiting for her in the apartment? Nothing pointed to a crime of passion or planned robbery. If not that, then, what was the reason? What happened and why?

According to official sources, it was a robbery. The thief was in the apartment before her or entered it together with Maria, who was not aware of being followed. Or he could have hidden somewhere in the dark corridor next to her apartment and forced himself inside. In good shape and brave, Maria confronted him and tried to defend herself. Taken by surprise and not anticipating resistance, he hit back. As there must have been some commotion such that he did not feel secure, he quickly grabbed a few small items which were at hand and ran away. More attractive objects, like money, were not stolen.

In the months that followed, the lengthy court proceedings supported this version. A suspect admitted to her murder and was sentenced by the court in Tbilisi. But the proceedings left many questions unanswered. Because the victim was a foreigner and UN employee, the case was high profile and widely reported in the local media. It nonetheless concluded without a satisfactory outcome. If Tbilisi swirled in rumor and speculation about Maria's murder, Sukhumi—the place where she had spent the last two years of her life, deprived of access to even Tbilisi media—remained in denial.

"It is not possible, nobody believes it," one of the Aitar women told me.

"It was a conspiracy. She went there to be killed. It would have never happen in Abkhazia. Everybody here loved and respected her."

So who did it and why?

"Some evil people," said some.

"She was too honest to live there. She could not be bought or manipulated" was another sentiment.

"But who were these people? What did they want from her?"

"Don't you know? We all know how bad things are over there. They wanted to corrupt her, but she was pure."

Marina made a cross and asked God to protect Maria's soul.

"And her boyfriend," she went on, "he resigned from his UN job here in Sukhumi and went home. He was completely devastated. He did not believe one word of the official version."

Chapter 13

Sergio: Death in Baghdad

On the evening of August 19, 2003, at the Hotel Kartli, a friendly small pension in the center of Tbilisi, I got the news about a bombing of the UN Headquarters in Baghdad. I will never forget that moment. I was having dinner in the courtyard with some newly met colleagues. It was already dark, though still warm, and the food good as was the Georgian wine. Suddenly, I heard the report across the radio. I would not have paid attention if not for the repeated mention of "Baghdad," "United Nations," and "de Mello." I started listening intently and could not believe what I heard.

A lorry full of explosives had entered the UN compound unabated and slammed against the wall of an office building. It was not yet possible to assess the degree of damage, according to the report, but numerous were known to be dead and wounded. The head of the mission and Special Representative of the UN Secretary-General in Iraq, Sergio Vieira de Mello, was still trapped under the debris, fighting for his life. Efforts were ongoing to save him. Someone had even established phone contact with him as his mobile worked, but the rescue operation was lengthy and his condition critical.

I left the table and went to the hotel reception to verify the news, hoping against all logic that I had misunderstood. I had not. The news was still fresh, and we followed the developments in silence. I returned to my room to watch on TV, but it took a while before I could summon the nerve to turn it on. The facts were becoming clear. The unimaginable happened: the UN had been the direct target of a terrorist attack. The blue flag had not helped. Sergio Vieira de Mello, one of the most respected, charismatic, and well-liked of UN officials, was trapped; and other colleagues were dead or seriously wounded. We did not know at that point who the others were. I started thinking of who among my friends was currently serving in Iraq. There were four. I stayed hypnotized in front of the TV waiting for updates and getting desperate about Sergio.

Late in the night, the dreaded news came: Sergio Vieira de Mello was dead. They had failed to recover him from the crater created by the explosion. Efforts were continuing to save the others, but prospects were declining by the hour. I tried to call New York, but it was August, and most of the people I knew were still on holiday leave. I had to rely on media reports until the morning when I could receive more concrete information from New York at the mission office.

The questions—*Why did it happen? How could it happen?*—were turning in my head. And why of all people Sergio? It was impossible to understand or make sense of it. I thought of the colleagues in Sukhumi that I never met, the ones who had died over a year before my arrival while in service of the UN. I only knew of them from the black-and-white photos hanging from the office walls and the memories of them their colleagues shared with me. I recalled the words of one of the Abkhaz women, Galina: "Always the best and the brightest."

So it seems, I thought.

Highly popular and among the most visible of UN officials, Sergio was known for his impeccable dress and high degree of professionalism. "The best dressed and the best informed man in the organization," it was said. He also genuinely believed in the principles of the UN and its role in the international community and tried to apply them throughout his career in the organization, a career which exceeded three decades.

He died on the eve of his scheduled departure from Baghdad. He was about to reassume his position as the UN High Commissioner for Human Rights in Geneva; he had taken temporary leave from the position in order to go to Iraq. The mission had been concluded, and he was preparing the final report with his team when the terror struck.

With time, further details were reconstructed. It was confirmed that the blast had been caused by a lorry full of explosives, one which had entered the UN premises undisturbed. It had been driven into the wall just below Sergio's office. In addition to Sergio, there were twenty-one dead. The attack had occurred during his meeting with senior staff from other UN agencies, some of whom had come to Baghdad only a few days earlier. Of all those present at the meeting, only one, Henrik Karsrup, a Dane working for the UNDP, survived. He, however, would be in a coma for several months and his health seriously affected. I had known Henrik from his previous assignment in Bosnia and Herzegovina where we had occasionally worked together on the Srebrenica project. I soon found out that among the seriously wounded, there were two others who had worked with me at the UN mission in Bosnia and Herzegovina. Both underwent numerous surgeries but managed to recover fully.

*   *   *

The August 19 attack on the UN compound in Baghdad belongs in the annals of events that are not forgotten. Like the death of JFK and the September 11 attack on the World Trade Center in New York, for me and my colleagues, we will always associate it with the place where we were when we first heard the news. For me, it will be Hotel Kartli, on a warm summer's night, in Tbilisi.

Sukhumi

Black Sea coast

The author at Aitar hotel, with Tonya

Kitty at Aitar hotel, on the air-conditioner, Sukhumi

Kitty playing in our apartment at Aitar hotel (*Vasha koshka huliganka*—your cat is a hooligan—the Aitar women used to say)

UNOMIG colleagues in the Staff Club at Aitar hotel, Sukhumi
(Roza Otunbayeva, then Deputy SRSG on the left)

The author with colleagues and D/SRSG, Roza Otunbayeva in
front of the Gali UN compound

Lake Ritza, the author with UNOMIG military observers

The author at the picnic with UNOMIG colleagues and
Abkhazians

Sukhumi, the author with the UN colleague at UNOMIG
office in Beria's villa

Stalin's dacha in Cold Stream

Gorbachev's dacha in Agudzera

The author in Gobrachev's dacha in Agudzera

The author with international staff of UNOMIG and the D/
SRSG Roza Otunbayeva (second on the right) at the lunch
break during the trip to dachas of party bosses

Peacocks at Aitar hotel, Sukhumi

The author in New Athos (Novi Afon)

Chapter 14

The Caucasian Roulette

The developments in Georgia can also be seen in the broader context of the increasing instability in the Caucasus where relations between Russia and most nations of the North Caucasus have drastically deteriorated in the past fifteen years. The brutal war in Chechnya and Russia's increasingly violent relations with the Caucasian nations in her various republics—namely in Dagestan, Ingushetia, North Ossetia, Kabardino-Balkaria, and Karachaevo-Cherkesia—often carried out by Moscow-appointed rulers backed by Russian security forces is the cause for the fractured relations.

Moscow's attempts to suppress these independent impulses by force have failed to produce the desired political results. To the contrary, they have strengthened the resolve and determination of various forces in these societies, helping to sustain their resistance against Russia. The series of attacks against Russian-appointed politicians and Russian police and security forces and installations in Dagestan, Ingushetia, and North Ossetia over the last two years is confirmation that the war is far from over; that Putin's violent campaign against local populations has not only been counterproductive, but it has also played into the hands of local political and Islamic leaders and made these societies vulnerable to the influence of radical Islam, now perceived by many as their only source of support.

The story of Jamila, a refugee from Dagestan living with relatives in Tbilisi, illustrates the tragedy of the situation, one that is common to many families in Russia's conflict-ridden Caucasian republics.

"When Shamil called one of the local bosses corrupt, he was immediately thrown into prison and accused of terrorism. He was labelled an Islamic terrorist, beaten, and tortured. But he was lucky. Our brothers managed to bribe one of the local guards who helped him to escape."

Jamila lowered her head and continued.

"He is somewhere in the mountains with our people. He did not carry arms before, but now, he will fight. Where else could he go? My other brothers have gone to the mountains as well. We could not stay there after what happened. They would have come and destroyed us. I ran away from Dagestan myself."

"Who are 'they'?" I asked.

"Everybody knows that they are either local militias or the military acting on the orders of our leaders or members of the Russian military or security forces or ordinary criminal gangs. Normally they come during the night in masks. They use cars with no registration plates or false ones, so nobody can officially trace them afterward. They kidnap people. I know many cases of villagers who have disappeared that way. They were normal people, hardworking and simple, but they tried to preserve our culture and religion or defend their meager possessions.

"Some started asking questions or opposing acts of crime or injustice. For example, they tried to press money from a teacher in our village. He refused so they took him away and accused him of embezzlement. The school director was informed and rushed to his defense and testified that he was a good citizen. So they immediately removed the school director from his position, intimidated his family, and confiscated his car."

"And what happened to the teacher?"

"He vanished. Allegedly the money arrived, paid by his friends from Vladikavkaz, but it was too late for him. His wife ran away to her family somewhere in the Urals."

After a moment of silence, Jamila added: "In our case, they could have come for us officially during the day. After all, my brother had already been arrested, which meant that they took him for a criminal. After his escape, we all would have been officially implicated so we had to flee. I am concerned about my brothers, but they are at least among our own people."

Then she looked directly into my eyes.

"Do not believe that they are terrorists. They want to live in peace in the place of our ancestors. They were pushed to fight. The people who forced them out are the real terrorists, but nobody can say it."

Jamila was also concerned about her own future. She did not have an official status in Georgia. She just came to Tbilisi, fleeing the immediate danger. Here she learned that with the thousands displaced from South Ossetia and the economic problems in Georgia, her chances of obtaining refugee status were poor. Moreover, her case was not well documented; she feared endangering her family or falling under suspicion herself by giving actual names. Jamila also felt that she was not welcome, that she was just one of many desperate people seeking refuge from the violent discord in the Caucasus, trying to survive in Georgia. And she had heard on a few occasions that Russia often accused Georgia of "harboring terrorists," probably meaning people like herself.

Moscow lost the hearts and minds of the people of the Caucasus long ago. The case of Jamila illustrates how corrupt local regimes have become, blindly representing the interests of Moscow in disregard of their local populations, turning these societies against both Moscow and the local authorities. The abuse of power, terror, corruption, and destruction has only lead to more terror and violence with no winners. Islam has increasingly filled the gap, constituting the only way the disaffected may express identity and seek solidarity and defense.

That, however, works mainly to the disadvantage of the cause. While the first Chechen war (1994-1996) with its gross human rights violations provoked serious criticism from European governments, human rights organizations, and public figures, the second war, launched by Putin in 1999, was later declared to be part of the "war on terror" proclaimed by US President George W. Bush and, as such, has been increasingly perceived in Russia and abroad as a struggle against criminal gangs, Islamist jihads, and terrorists. The intensity of attacks on Russian forces and local pro-Russian leaders throughout the Caucasus and beyond more than ever targeting civilians and public infrastructures over the last two years increases this perception and suggests the emergence of some cross-border networks of rebel groups. The recent attacks in central Russia on the Moscow-St. Petersburg train and Moscow metro were large-scale terrorist operations attributed to Doku Umarov, the Chechen leader who declared the establishment of a Caucasus-wide network of "freedom fighters" in 2007. As the spiral of terror escalates, the world turns its back on the region considering it a battleground of radical Islam and people like Jamila are lost between the fronts.

I wonder how this situation will impact on the 2014 Winter Olympics in Sochi. That the city is close to the war-torn parts of the Caucasus raises serious security concerns. The city will become, no doubt, another showcase like Moscow and St. Petersburg. The preparatory work has already begun. To make space for new constructions, many houses and apartment dwellings around the city have already been levelled and people evicted. Where to and on what terms, we do not know. But could the authorities guarantee people's safety? The few incidents of explosions make these fears even more justified. The Russian president, Dmitri Medvedev, has ordered special security measures. However, as the Russian experience in the North Caucasus over the last decade has shown, they should not be overestimated.

It is yet to be seen how the recognition of South Ossetia and Abkhazia by Russia will influence the regional dynamics. Not only was it done in violation of all the existing international agreements promulgated over the past fifteen years regarding the status of the embattled enclaves, many of which Russia was either party to or sanctioned, it was against the will of the state whose territory the two entities were a part. If South Ossetia and Abkhazia can be independent, why not Russia's Caucasian republics?

Of course, it was never about the right of self-determination. It has always been about Russian control. It is well understood in the region that the two "independent states" are (and have long been) practically run by Russia through local political elites. The miserable living conditions, oppression, and lack of political freedom suffered by their inhabitants have been watched with increasing concern in neighboring territories. Most Caucasian nations fear this imperialist model. They do not want to be left to local corrupt rulers and governed from Moscow. They want true independence, not the "Abkhaz model" of sovereignty.

Indeed, this model, similar to the "chechenization" of war by the young Kadyrov, may constitute Moscow's emerging policy line in the North Caucasus: to rely heavily on local war lords and elites—whatever their ideological, religious, or political nature—as long as they are totally loyal to Russia and ensure security and relative stability in the republics. The human and economic costs do not count. The local rulers can continue with their lucrative contraband, gross human rights violations, and dictatorial rule and rely on the most generous influx of resources from Moscow.

With this focus, the situation in Abkhazia and South Ossetia is closely watched across the Caucasus and stories like that of Khamzat Gitsba quickly circulate throughout the region and do not increase confidence in Abkhaz authorities. During the Georgian-Abkhaz war, Khamzat Gitsba fought with the Abkhaz and had close contacts with Chechen organizations and other Muslims in Russia. From his return in 2000, Gitsba served as the informal leader of the Spiritual Directorate of Abkhaz Muslims and the first imam of the mosque in Gudauta. Although devout Muslims in Abkhazia constitute a small group, they have been in contact with Muslims in neighboring countries and regions, in particular Turkey. In August 2007, Gitsba was killed by an unknown gunman. Following his death, Abkhaz Islamic leaders stated that they believed he had been killed by Russian or Abkhaz security forces and expressed concern about their own security. They reiterated that they had no contacts with extremists but believed that they were nonetheless regarded with suspicion by Abkhaz authorities and their Russian allies.

This incident illustrates shifting loyalties in the region where the developments have been beset with outside influence. Initially, there was strong solidarity with both the Abkhaz and South Ossetian struggle for self-determination against Georgia. Chechen, Kazak, and other volunteers from neighboring republics fought along the Abkhaz in the 1992 war. It is difficult to pinpoint precisely when alliances began to change or establish with any clarity or how the patterns of foreign involvement have shifted in the midst of these conflicts. It is equally difficult to anticipate how alliances may develop in the future. However, the impact of the increasing rift between Russia and other Caucasian nations on those conflicts could, early on, already be observed. For example, in 1992, the Chechen Shamil Basaev began his career as a Caucasian volunteer fighting on the same side as Russia in support of the Abkhaz against Georgia. By 1995, he was already fighting on the other side. In 2006, he was killed by Russians as one of its most-wanted terrorists.

During the 2008 war over South Ossetia, there were no volunteers from the Caucasus fighting against Georgia. Neither was the support for Russian-sponsored independence of the two territories. And while Russian forces included some Chechen troops, they constituted part of Russia's regular armed forces and thus had no say on their assignment.

"By recognizing the independence of South Ossetia and Abkhazia in the autumn of 2008, Russia made a cardinal mistake," said former Georgian president Eduard Shevardnadze during our discussion at his home in July 2009. "There are bigger and more important regions within Russian borders that demand independence. It may cause a chain reaction from Tatarstan, Chechnya, Ingushetia to Dagestan. They keep them in line now using traditional Soviet methods, not nice methods as we know. But how long can it work?"

Chapter 15

Tbilisi, Mon Amour

I landed in Tbilisi in April 2003. I was exhausted after a rushed departure from the Balkans, packing and closing of the office and my apartment in Sarajevo on spot notice. Tired and uncertain of my final destination—Sukhumi or Tbilisi—I started my day with a coffee at the Marriott hotel in the heart of the city. It was a wonderful hotel, old and stylish with excellent food. It remains today my favorite place in town.

It was a crisp spring morning. The sun was bright. The first of green leaves had began to appear on the trees, and fresh flowers sold at the street stands. I enjoyed these first glimpses of the city, regardless of the visible neglect. The scene was impressive. Although old decaying houses dotted the landscape, the open spaces and distant hills marking the horizon were majestic. I felt instantly at home.

I was finally assigned to Sukhumi, in Abkhazia, the main base of the UN Observer Mission in Georgia, for the next six months. However, I continued to visit Tbilisi as often as I could. Each visit reaffirmed my fascination with the city. I was attracted by its architecture, its expansive layout and open views, its streets lined up with trees, its spread over the surrounding hills, its resonate energy and multiculturalism. Old Georgian Orthodox churches stood next to synagogues and mosques. All manner of Christian churches were accounted for: Catholic, Protestant, Armenian, Georgian, and Russian Orthodox. A Turkish bath in the middle of the old city was next to the small shopping center offering carpets from Iran, Turkey, and Azerbaijan. Then, there were small streets filled with art galleries and souvenir shops. The city's many restaurants offered not only Georgian cuisine, but also a variety of ethnic foods from around the world. There were cafés, pubs, and wine-tasting bars, and the everpresent street vendors peddling a broad assortment of goods.

I was not discouraged by some of the troublesome aspects of life in Tbilisi. In summer, the city was hot, dusty, and dirty with piles of garbage stacked along the streets. The underground passages were dark and smelled of urine, stairs were cracked and falling apart, and walls were covered in grime and graffiti. The hotels warned of pickpocketing, theft, and assaults on the streets, especially after dusk when most of the city was dark due to frequent blackouts. UN security also advised caution. Despite it all, I loved Tbilisi. I cannot fully explain why, except to say that when feelings are involved, sometimes no rational reason can be given.

I was eventually transferred to Tbilisi on November 2, 2003, the day of the fateful elections that led to the Rose Revolution. After months in Sukhumi, it felt like a liberation; I could enjoy freedom of movement, I could walk, I could drive, I could breathe, and I could choose my own accommodation. I did not have to report "Charlie, Charlie" every half hour to UN security. I could enjoy a variety of restaurants, good wine, the famous Georgian hospitality, and the infectious joy of living.

Unlike in Abkhazia, people in Tbilisi were not easily intimidated. I never heard *nielzia* there. They spoke freely and openly expressed their views, especially the critical ones. They had managed to preserve their national culture and traditions and maintain their strong national pride, despite the years of Soviet rule and attempted Sovietization. Georgian intelligentsia followed the traditional European *savoir vivre* and table manners. They were well-read and informed, had relatives and friends in all parts of the world, and spoke multiple languages. The foreign cultural institutes—the Goethe Institut, British Council, and Alliance Française—were all highly popular, their libraries and events well attended. So too were the concerts, opera performances, and many art gallery and painting exhibitions.

I rented a modern, beautifully furnished apartment at Vake, in one of the best quarters in town, close to Mziuri Park whose design was based on the idea of the famous Georgian writer, Nodar Dumbadze. The building itself, however, was in total disrepair. The staircase was usually not lit, windows were partly broken and never washed, and the walls gritty with dirt. Although there were a lot of wires sticking out from the walls, the lamps were long gone and the bulbs did not last either. Behind the building, a concrete high-rise was being hastily erected, consuming the entire view of the park and converting the courtyard into somewhat of a muddy, dark quarry packed with lorries and cranes.

"It will be impossible to live here in the future once these monstrous buildings are finished," Eka, my landlady and art historian, complained. "And I love this apartment so much. You see how much effort I put into its decoration."

"How is it possible? Isn't this construction too close to your windows?" I asked. "There must be some regulations."

"This is Shevardnadze's Georgia. All is corrupt. We do not even know to whom these buildings belong or who authorized the construction. Somebody simply paid."

"Why isn't the building renovated inside? Not even the stairs or windows. The entrance door does not close, so anybody can come in. There is no light, and there could be a disaster if anyone touches the electrical wires in the darkness."

"There is nobody to pay for it," Eka informed me. "There are very few people in the building who own the apartments. The majority got them practically for free, and their rights and responsibilities were never clearly stated. Most people are poor. They have meager incomes, if any at all. That is the communist culture—no one cares for the collective good. People would rather try to take advantage of one another. That is why there are no bulbs. Whatever is of any value is instantly dismantled."

Regardless of the challenges, I loved the apartment and felt fine there. I learned to carry a flashlight, always have candles and matches at hand, and how to push through the construction to park my car. Kitty, my little Georgian cat, also enjoyed it. She would climb into the fireplace, stretch out on the antique couch, and wash herself in the bathtub. It was her first home, the apartment where she grew up. We would later have many homes in all manner of countries. But the place at Vake, on Chavchavadze Avenue, was our first real home; so it holds a special place in my memories. I wonder how Kitty feels about it.

Our peace at Vake, however, was disturbed on one occasion. It was soon after the triumph of the Rose Revolution, on my return from a short vacation home in Vienna. I was welcomed back by an unknown neighbor from above: "Thank God that nothing happened to you."

I was rather surprised by this as Vienna was (*is*) definitely a safer city than Tbilisi.

"And nothing happened to your apartment," he continued. "One of my windows was cracked but still stays in the frame, so I do not have to change it.

"Your neighbors on the left were badly affected," he added. "All their windows are gone, and the glass is all over the place. They moved to their in-laws, but there is always somebody in the flat so it will not be looted. They also paid a policeman from the district to keep an eye on it, but he cannot be trusted."

"So what happened?" I finally managed to ask.

"Oh, so you don't know? Somebody blew up the office of MagtiCom, the company of Shevardnadze's son-in-law. It was a strong blast. Fortunately, nobody was hurt. It was done after office hours."

I realized that I did not know who my neighbors were. MagtiCom? Jokhtaberidze's company, just next door, in the same building?

"Who did it?" The moment I asked the question, I realized how ridiculous it was.

"Nobody knows," he stated plainly, "and nobody will know. The police will come to investigate, but they will not find out anything. Probably they did not pay their dues to some influential people, or somebody had a grudge against them, and it was time to avenge."

The next morning, I noticed that the pavement in front of the building was full of debris and inaccessible, blocked by the police. Some windows on the ground floor apartments were missing. The blast made the news and was broadly reported in the local media. Some colleagues at the office who knew where I resided were quite intrigued. However, once the dust settled, literally and figuratively, public interest vanished. An investigation was initiated but never conclusively resolved. The MagtiCom office reopened, and the building's inhabitants were left to repair the damage to their apartments by their own means.

* * *

Upon my return to Tbilisi in 2009, I noted a number of positive changes: beautiful flower beds, clean streets, refurbished historical monuments, normally functioning traffic as in any other big city, polite and properly equipped traffic police, and a lot of fountains.

I shared my observations with my friends Ana, a student, and Alyena, a real-estate broker, while having coffee at the Prospero, a book café on Rustaveli Avenue. The shop carried a decent selection of books, including publications about Georgia, the Caucasus, and other parts of the region. The choice of coffees and pastries called to mind more a café in Vienna than a coffee shop in a former Soviet republic. The Prospero was therefore one of the most popular meeting places in Tbilisi.

Ana seemed irritated by my praise for the city, the fountains in particular. She was not a Saakashvili supporter by any measure.

"We need hospitals, not fountains," she told me. "They are all over the place, and people do not have enough to eat.

"Personally, I am glad that our city looks so nice, but my neighbors are scared about their future. They have no jobs and two children to bring up," she continued. "I also do not have a job so my parents support me. It is embarrassing, I am twenty-two. I would like to earn at least pocket money."

"I understand your sentiments, but I am happy to see this beautiful city in much better shape than five years ago," I commented.

I was, however, disappointed that no more had been done to refurbish the dilapidated wooden houses which dotted the city or properly rehabilitate the old city and better protect its unique historical character and architectural style.

New buildings were appearing in all corners of the city, often in complete disregard for the community. These mammoth constructs were sometimes "growing up" on tree-lined streets amid old wooden homes with hand-carved balconies and verandas. Others were built on the land of such former houses, homes which had either fallen apart from neglect or were simply bulldozed to make space for the new buildings.

"This is a legacy from the old times, a leftover," Alyena told me. "Now the laws are very strict. It simply took time to clean up the regulations and the system for building permits and pass new laws. There is also shortage of money, so the authorities cannot renovate more than a few houses a year. Some historical monuments have priority.

"Moreover, they could not stop ongoing constructions, even if they were illegal. Many of them quickly provided much-needed hotels and comfortable apartments to accommodate the growing influx of foreigners. So the practical solution was to allow the construction to continue and fine those responsible."

"But not in proportion to the value of the investment," Ana clarified. "We should not forget that such wild constructions constitute a source of income for many in the local bureaucracy. Thus, the big developers have continued the destruction of the town.

"Moreover, some people, especially the elderly and uneducated owners and long-term occupants of such houses, have often found themselves at a disadvantage. The postcommunist legal system regulating property rights is confusing, and there is no functioning system of welfare, so they neither receive proper compensation for their properties nor comparable accommodation. For the poor and uneducated, a sum of a few hundred US dollars is sufficient to convince them to sign the papers and look for alternative accommodation with relatives or leave Tbilisi. Afterward it is too late to change the decision."

Spurred on by the beautification of the city and the controversy evoked by our discussion, I decided to visit my former apartment on Chavchavadze Avenue, in Vake, or rather look at the building and its surroundings. To my surprise, it looked as if time there had stopped: it had the same dark and dingy staircase, broken windows, and wires stretching out of the walls. Even half of the entrance door was still hanging by its hinges. The courtyard—or rather what remained of it squeezed between the tall, still unfinished concrete high-rises—was dusty, still muddy and full of vehicles, although the cranes and other construction equipment had gone. Nobody would guess that behind these buildings was a park. Perhaps the changes to the city were more superficial than it had seemed at first glance.

Did such superficial gloss extend to other aspects of Georgian reality?

Chapter 16

Kitty

She was tiny with beautiful green eyes, long shiny hair, and a lot of charm. She was scared and disoriented, just two months old. It was not a planned parenthood. It simply happened.

She was brought to the UN Mission in Tbilisi on a cold, gray December day. A stocky man from the neighborhood bounced her in front of me and mumbled, "It is a girl. She is healthy. She can eat anything. I wanted to bring her mother as well but the owner chose to keep her, she has been with them for a long time. They always seek good homes for the kittens. That is why I brought her here." He smiled proudly. "It is the UN."

He looked around self-assured. He had obviously found an excellent home for the kitten. The UN was considered a place of wealth and security—the best address in town, and not only for cats.

"She will be very useful," he continued, "you will see. Siberian cats are good hunters and very efficient. There will be no mice around."

With that, he placed the kitten in my hands and was gone.

I do not know which of us was more nervous, the kitten or me. The encounter had occurred in the middle of the UNOMIG's courtyard, without the least warning. I had been on my way to a meeting, one of those daily meetings standard to the UN routine. I could not appear with a cat. I looked around. The closest possible shelter was a security office. The guards did not seem surprised by my appearance with the cat. I began to think that they may have had a little something to do with the kitten's sudden arrival at the mission. I promised to buy provisions and left my living cargo with them.

The morning guards seemed genuinely enthused about having the kitten around and tried to take good care of her. However, when the second shift took over that evening, things changed. I heard a knock at the door, and one of the guards appeared in my office. In a rather confused and unsettled manner, in broken Russian, he tried to explain to me that the cat disturbed them (*ona nam mieszajet*), that she was dirty, and that their work and professional status were negatively affected by her presence. In sum, I was told, she should be removed from their office.

"If she disturbs you and if you consider her presence undermining to your professional status, please bring her to my office," I answered.

I was then a senior political adviser to the Special Representative of the UN Secretary-General, the head of the UNOMIG. It was Christmas season, and I was the most senior person on the grounds. Shortly, the other night guard appeared with the kitten. He expressed to me that he did not share the views of his colleague but nonetheless seemed quite relieved to have her out of his way. He placed her squarely on the carpet at my feet and departed.

I decided to take the cat home and keep her for a few days there where she could recover from the stress, eat, and sleep. Afterward, I thought I can find her a proper home. But after a few days, it became clear that she was already home and that it was up to me to learn how to accommodate her.

One of my first steps was to arrange a visit with a vet. His name was Waza. He had been recommended to me as an expert on dogs. As there were no cat experts on the horizon, I decided he would suffice and took the kitten to his office. The place was run down but full of waiting patients, mainly dogs with their owners.

When our turn came, the vet took the cat from my arms, turned her around, looked at her from various angles, and declared her OK. He confirmed that it was a girl about two months in age, of a Siberian breed. He prescribed some vitamins and advised where I could find pet shops. He also described for me how she would look in the future.

"She will be small, graceful with very long, strong hair, a big tale and hair collar around her neck. She will be nice," he told me, "but I have a real Siamese which will be even nicer. It is a boy, less trouble. Why won't you buy it? You can get it for $100."

"But why should I have a second cat?" *I have one, and I already feel overwhelmed*, I thought to myself. *And I am used to having dogs. I travel frequently. I spend long hours in the office.* All these thoughts were crossing my mind.

"It is a beautiful cat," he repeated. "Please let me know in case you reconsider."

As if understanding the hidden message, my little cat tried to dive into my sleeve. I left the consultation determined to learn as much as I could about cats and live up to this new challenge.

I surrounded myself with books—all imported as there was no proper literature in Georgia—and read as much as I could about felines. The rest was to be learned through trial and error. Soon I found myself immersed in the previously unknown world of pets and pet business in Tbilisi. I was surprised by the amount and variety of pet shops and pet products. They carried well-known international brands—Whiskas, Purina, Kit Kat—as well as local, cheaper products. The shops had cat cosmetics, shampoos, deodorants, brushes, and innumerable toys. Most also had live pets. One could find dogs and cats wandering around, hamsters, parrots and canaries, exotic fish, and sometimes even snakes and turtles.

Most shops also had veterinarian services and basic medications available on the premises. Indeed, it seemed to be easier to access medical services there than at the local hospitals and dispensaries, the latter too often overwrought with excessive bureaucracy and short on medicine supplies. I had not expected to find so many services for animals in a poor country like Georgia.

Kitty quickly realized what she had gotten into, that she had ended up in a household without regular cooking and where she would have a lot time to herself due to my long office hours and extensive travel. She used her freedom as she pleased. She was accorded the full status of a family member and, as such, moved about the apartment uninhibited. She explored it fully, getting into drawers, jumping all over the furniture, and climbing up the chimney above the fireplace.

She also instantly settled on store-bought cat food—the dry, canned variety—and completely disregarded all else. Ruzi, my housekeeper, tried to convince her that in her young age some other options, like fresh meat or fish, were advisable. Kitty ignored the offers, possibly sensing that her future life would take her to untold countries and, with the global market as it was, canned cat food would ensure continuity in her diet.

Another challenge ahead of me was naming the cat. I wanted a traditional, but simple Georgian name, an impossibility as it turned out. I asked my Georgian friends for help, but to no avail. Either they came up with complicated names like Ketavan or Gvantsa, or simple but (in my view) not particularly suitable names for a cat like Ruzi or Ana. So my kitten remained nameless. As I had to somehow communicate with her in the interim, I called her Kitty. So after the two months of fruitless efforts to find her name, she was registered as "Kitty."

Waza issued her a passport inscribed in four languages. It contained her official name (Kitty), her owner's (my) details, and a big photo. In the space reserved for "breed," Waza put "Métis" (mixed). I asked why he had changed his previous assessment that she was a Siberian cat.

"This is what is written in the passport," Waza stated.

"Because you wrote it. So what is she," I insisted, "a Métis or Siberian cat?" Not that I cared, but I was irritated by his attitude.

"It is a cat," he replied, "and that's all. Do you understand? All the information is written in the passport. Read it when you have time so you will learn."

I gave up. I grabbed Kitty, took the passport, and left his office.

My contacts with Waza continued as my new parental responsibilities required the services of a vet to ensure Kitty received proper medical supervision (vaccinations and vitamins) and that I was properly advised on matters of feeding and contraception. It was the latter that would bring our next disagreement. After two months in the house, Kitty began exhibiting strange behaviors. Instead of the active, curious, and people-friendly cat she usually was, she became moody and restless, lost her appetite, and would maul for no apparent reason. I phoned Waza who made a house call to examine the patient. He concluded that she was suffering from an unspecified minor stomach ailment possibly caused by hairballs or infection. He gave her an injection of antibiotics and left me the number to his newly acquired cell phone.

"By the way," I said as Waza prepared to depart, "don't you think that it could be the call of nature? That she might be in heat?"

Waza looked at me with surprise. "She is a girl, she is a child. She is only four months old. It is impossible."

"Well, as you know, there are cases of teenage pregnancy among humans, so why not among cats? Plus her diet and environment have changed since her arrival in my house. She gets more nutritious food and vitamins, and she has grown very fast. So why is it not possible?"

Waza became visibly annoyed. Not only had I challenged his medical judgment, but I had also developed this decadent theory. He looked at me with visible disapproval.

"I am trying to explain to you that she is a child. She is much too young for that," he insisted. "Such things do not happen to children. I know it. I have been a doctor for forty years, and I graduated in Moscow. I know what I am talking about." With that, he took his coat and, in a haste, left, still agitated.

Two days later, while at the office, I received a call from Ruzi. She was crying and asked me to return home immediately. Kitty was very sick. Ruzi feared that she was dying. In the background, I could hear the agonizing wails of my cat.

I was in shock. I asked Ruzi to call the vet and jumped in the car to rush home.

I do not know how I managed to cross town, which was jammed with the noon traffic, and reach the house. I was still in shock. At the staircase, I could already hear the cries of my cat. I ran. At the entrance to my apartment, I bumped into my neighbor, David, a graphic designer. Alerted by the noise, he had rushed over to find out what was wrong with Kitty, whom he adored. He would later admit to fearing that my housekeeper or an intruder was torturing her. As Ruzi was new in the house, he did not yet know her and was thus suspicious.

The whole scene was surreal. Kitty was rolling about the floor with glassy, transparent eyes, unconscious, in semiconvulsions. Her cries reverberated through the place, and the sound was truly awful. She could not slow down even for a minute. Ruzi, David, and I looked at one another, helpless and distressed. But suddenly, in the middle of this hell, I felt a sense of relief.

It must be the heat, I thought. *And if so, it is not deadly, she is not in danger. Think straight, do not panic.*

I shared my suspicion with Ruzi and David, and suddenly, we recognized the obvious. They agreed that that had to be the cause. At this point, Waza arrived and too concluded that—contrary to logic, his medical experience, and established knowledge of cats—it had to be "that." He was unusually quiet. He quickly gave her a tranquilizer and prescribed some contraceptives, even volunteering to fetch them for me.

He kept shaking his head in disbelief and talking to himself, "It is impossible. I have never seen anything like this."

And then he turned to me. "What kind of cat is it? What kind of girl? At this age? What will she do when she grows up? She will be all over the place. You better keep her at home.

"*Ona guliaszczaya*," she is a loose woman, he said as he left the apartment.

146

Chapter 17

Shevardnadze: Hero of Perestroika or "Silver Fox" of the Caucasus?

We sat with the former president in the main room of his residence, a room filled with memories. There were photographs of him, at the time foreign minister of the USSR, with James Baker, then US secretary of state, and Hans-Dietrich Genscher, the West German foreign minister; and at major summits with former US President Ronald Reagan and Soviet leader Mikhail Gorbachev in Geneva and at Reykjavik. Others were more personal, an assortment of family photos, most featuring his wife, Nanuli.

Looking back on this period, Shevardnadze was proud of his accomplishments. In those transformative years, he had been at the height of his powers, respected at home, and celebrated in the West. This pride manifested itself as he shared with me the story of his contribution to the release of *Repentance* (*Pokoianie*), the world-renown movie written and directed by the Georgian filmmaker, Tengiz Abuladze, a story he cherished.

Shevardnadze had been approached by Abuladze. At the time, he still held the post of first secretary of the Georgian Communist Party. Abuladze asked if Shevardnadze would read his script and help him get it past the censors. Without political clearance, he would not be able to produce it. Abuladze had already anticipated difficulties as the film dealt with the crimes of Stalinism. Shevardnadze read the script and found it to be quite good and compelling. He passed it on to his wife. The story reminded her of her own family's fate, in particular that of her father, who had been a victim of Stalin's terror. So moved was she that she could not sleep; she kept reading the script and crying throughout the night.

Shevardnadze had given a green light for the film's production, but its release was blocked by authorities in Moscow. At the first opportunity, in 1985, Shevardnadze said he brought the script to the attention of Gorbachev. Gorbachev read it together with his wife, Raisa, and both were impressed. "We need these types of films" Gorbachev is said to have assured him. Subsequently, Shevardnadze arranged for the film premiere in Tbilisi in 1986 and its submission to the Cannes Film Festival where it won a Special Jury Prize in 1987.

This was the man who would be hero of *perestroika*, the democrat. It was how he wanted to be remembered.

The Party Man

Eduard Ambrosievich Shevardnadze was born January 25, 1928, in the village of Mamati, in the province Guria, Georgia, the son of a Russian language teacher who taught in a local school. Both his parents wanted him to study medicine, but he ended up at the Teacher's Institute in Kutaisi, where he was quickly drawn into politics. There he progressed quickly through the ranks of the Young Communist League (*Komsomol*) and the Communist Party apparatus, which he had joined in 1948.

In 1965, after having held several party posts, he was appointed minister of Internal Affairs of the Georgian Soviet Republic. In this position, he declared war on corruption and carried it out in a very visible manner, leading to thousands of arrests and the successful case against Vasily Mzhavanadze, a long-time party dignitary and the first secretary of the central committee of the Georgian Communist Party (GCP). In 1972, he would replace him in this function. In that position, it was his job to champion communist ideology and ensure the unquestionable authority of the party. It implied rule with a heavy hand and suppression of any political opposition or expression of "anti-Sovietism and nationalism."

In his book *The Future Belongs to Freedom*, published in 1991, Shevardnadze admitted that the position of party leader required implementation of an all-Soviet policy across the republic. He had not resisted the job's demands nor been hindered by any political, psychological, or moral impediment in carrying out his duties. He was at heart a Soviet man and ruled with a cool efficiency. But then communism was, for Shevardnadze, both his religion and ideology.

Shevardnadze's rocketing political career was all the more unusual considering his youth, particularly by Soviet's geriatric standards, and familial background. He was named Georgia's first party secretary at the age of forty-four despite the fact that some of his relatives, to include his father, had been under suspicion. In the late 1930s, at the height of Beria's reign of terror across Georgia, his father was disappeared from their village. Owing to the support of former pupils, the elder Shevardnadze managed to return and clear his name. The father of Shevardnadze's future wife, Nanuli Tsagareishvili, was not as fortunate and perished during this time. Shevardnadze married her despite her original rejection of his marriage proposal. She had not wanted to destroy his promising political career.

Shevardnadze also had to navigate between the political minefield of local calls for independence and demands of loyalty from Moscow. Georgia was the most prosperous republic in the Soviet Union. Georgians knew it and were aware that their prosperity was owed in part to Shevardnadze's skillful political maneuvering and pragmatic use of the republic's superior economic position in its trade relations with Moscow. As long as Moscow detected no political discontent or separatist agitation and had no suspicion of disloyalty to the USSR, there was room for mutually beneficial exchanges. Georgians thus experienced relative flexibility and freedom within their republic. For its part, Moscow was able to cover some of its consumptive shortages through purchasing Georgian products—vegetables, fruits, and wines that Russians proudly featured in their otherwise empty shop windows. Georgians enjoyed an unusually high living standard as a result and suffered no shortage of basic goods as typically experienced elsewhere in the Soviet Union.

During his first twenty years as a party man, the years proceeding his rise to party boss in Georgia, Shevardnadze developed a governance approach that while not brutal by Soviet standards—he did not permanently eliminate his political opponents—it allowed him to effectively neutralize adversaries and remove them from political scene. His deft maneuvering also included a gift for remaining detached from controversy, particularly that of a politically sensitive nature. His approach—the *modus operandi* which came to characterize his political style—was to obfuscate when trouble arose and make seemingly unclear and inconsistent statements and policy decisions, leaving room to adjust (or escape) as circumstances may require. As he once told a Georgian Party Congress: "For us Georgians, the sun does not rise in the East, but in North—in Russia."

Shevardnadze's political convictions began to undergo gradual transformation in the 1970s. He became acutely aware of the prevailing gap between the promises of the system and the people's expectations on the one hand and Georgia's potential as a resource-filled, attractive nation and the straitjacket imposed on her by communist ideology and politics on the other. He was confronted daily with the criticisms of intellectuals, artists, and scientists challenging the system. This persistent agitation forced his recognition of the increasingly difficult living conditions of the Georgian people. He came to believe that without systemic changes not much could be done.

In the late 1970s, Gorbachev and Shevardnadze, one the future president of the Soviet Union and the other future president of an independent Georgia, developed a close friendship. Shevardnadze was first secretary of the Georgian Communist Party and Gorbachev the young and energetic first secretary of the party in Stavropol. They began to share experiences and exchange political and philosophical ideas and would visit one another, benefiting from the geographic closeness of their respective republics. Their informal meetings, in particular their talks during long walks away from the listening devices, enabled the consolidation of their friendship and clarification of many ideas.

In the 1980s, Shevardnadze came to be one of Gorbachev's closest associates. In 1985, after Gorbachev assumed leadership of the Soviet Union, Shevardnadze was appointed foreign minister, replacing Andrei Gromyko, who had led Soviet diplomacy since 1957. Shevardnadze strongly supported Gorbachev's policies of *glasnost* and *perestroika*, the process of democratization, and opening of the country to the outside world. He was also supportive of independence tendencies within the Soviet bloc. Shevardnadze's support of German unification was one of his most internationally respected and known acts. At home, it was one of his most contested moves. Aggressively opposed by the Soviet military and conservative party members, his position on the German question led to his eventual resignation in 1990. Gorbachev too was soon ousted by ideological adversaries and replaced in 1992 by Boris Yeltsin. The Soviet Union was formally dissolved and fourteen republics had gained their independence to include Shevardnadze's native Georgia.

*   *   *

Shevardnadze's precise role in Georgia's quest for independence is somewhat shrouded in mystery. In 1988, mass waves of proindependence demonstrations spread across the Caucasus and the Baltic republics. That autumn thousands of demonstrators, mainly students and young people, took to the streets of Tbilisi. After some delay, Gorbachev finally issued a statement confirming the Soviet constitution's guarantee of Georgia's right to secede. The demonstrations continued, reaching their apogee in April 1989. Crowds of people demanding independence demonstrated peacefully along Rustaveli Avenue. On April 9, however, they were brutally attacked by Soviet troops. Nineteen people were killed—most of them women and young people, and many others were injured and arrested. The casualties resulted mainly from the use of poisonous gas on the demonstrators. Its composition was unknown to the Georgian medical professionals, impairing their ability to properly assist the injured.

Shevardnadze, who had been in London with Gorbachev, arrived in Tbilisi twelve hours after the massacre. Why he had not come sooner and the exact details of his whereabouts in the hours immediately preceding the use of force remains unclear. One version lays the blame squarely on the Politburo, which, allegedly, took the decision to use troops against demonstrators. The decision was said to have been reached during an ad hoc meeting held in the airport's VIP lounge in Moscow with Gorbachev and Shevardnadze in attendance, having returned from London.

Another version places Shevardnadze in Georgia. It claims that Shevardnadze was ordered to Tbilisi by Gorbachev immediately upon their return from London and that a special plane was provided for this purpose. But Shevardnadze reportedly ignored Gorbachev's command. He is instead alleged to have received direct information from the republic's first secretary of the party, Dzhumber Patiashvili, that there was no need for such a rush. Some in Tbilisi, however, insist that he did arrive in Tbilisi as ordered by Gorbachev and just never left the airport; after some time, he simply turned around and returned to Moscow. Shevardnadze has consistently denied the veracity of these allegations as well as having any knowledge of the Politburo's decision to use troops against the demonstrators. Why he did not undertake timely intervention, Shevardnadze has never satisfactorily answered.

Demonstrating the political cunning that had propelled him throughout his career, Shevardnadze attempted to recast the events—or at least his role in them. On his first official return to Tbilisi, Shevardnadze publicly challenged the general under whose command the attacks had taken place, Igor Rodionov, and insisted that poisonous substances had been used against the demonstrators. Further parliamentary inquiry led by Anatoly Sobchak, the reform mayor of Leningrad, confirmed the allegations. Rodionov denied the accusations, but he was nonetheless found guilty by the parliamentary commission. The commission's report exonerated Shevardnadze and Gorbachev. However, when the report was submitted to the Congress of People's Deputies (Parliament), in December 1989, it was rebuffed by the military. Shevardnadze wanted to reply but, purportedly, was silenced by Gorbachev who refused his request for the floor. Shevardnadze, it is said, threatened to resign but was eventually persuaded by Gorbachev to stay. So there was no official closure. No one was ever held to account for the attacks on the demonstrators.

The shroud of mystery surrounding Shevardnadze's role in 1989 Tbilisi massacre, however, was not forgotten. Many attributed their support of Zviad Gamsakhurdia in 1990, and in subsequent Georgian presidential elections, and their participation in protests against Shevardnadze's return to Georgia to the events of April 9, 1989.

The Georgian President

The first free and independent parliamentary elections in Georgia took place on November 14, 1990. Gamsakhurdia, a well-known opponent and victim of the communist regime, from a family with strong intellectual and patriotic traditions, was elected president of Georgia and announced a period of transition to independence. Georgian independence from the USSR was decided in a nationwide referendum and declared on April 9, 1991, by the Georgian Parliament. Gamsakhurdia was re-elected as president the same year. His presidency, however, was as short-lived as it was disastrous. He was ousted in a coup by the so-called Military Council in 1992.

While effective in removing Gamsakhurdia, the Military Council had no solid credentials; it had neither structure nor program and no legal or political legitimacy. Its members, Tengiz Sigua, Tengiz

Kitovani, and Jaba Ioseliani were all of questionable character, each lacking in personal credibility and integrity. The country was on the brink of civil war, and its institutions were on the verge of collapse. To avoid complete state failure, Ioseliani convinced the other council members to ask Shevardnadze to return to Georgia to lead both a new state council, which would be responsible for governing the republic and the opposition against Gamsakhurdia.

Kitovani, a member of the Georgian Parliament, was a graduate of the Academy of Arts in Tbilisi. Ioseliani was a writer. Both were better known for their profiteering, trafficking in contraband, and other illegal activities than art or political enlightenment. Ioseliani was well-known in the criminal circles, in particular for bank robberies in Moscow and Leningrad and, according to some, was even popular among some of the Tbilisi inhabitants. After serving some time in prison, Ioseliani changed profession and became a doctor of philosophy. Both Ioseliani and Kitovani also commanded personal militias, which constituted their respective power bases. Ioseliani established and led the *Mkhedrioni*, a paramilitary force modeled after the Knights of Saint George of the Middle Ages. Kitovani led the National Guard.

The appointment of Shevardnadze to lead the state council was calculated to lend legitimacy to the council and prevent further disintegration of Georgia. Kitovani and Ioseliani had assumed that they could use Shevardnadze to gain international recognition of their government and generate inflows of foreign assistance. Believing Shevardnadze to be susceptible to political manipulation, they anticipated that he would serve only as a figure head and not constrain their activities and political ambitions. The opposite happened. Shevardnadze did, indeed, provide legitimacy to the new Georgian government and increase the flow of donor money but on his terms. He skillfully played on the existing animosities between Kitovani and Ioseliani, gradually maneuvering them out of power, again demonstrating his political mastery.

Shevardnadze formed a new federal government structure and re-established the post of president to which he was elected in 1992 and again in 1995. Both elections were considered by some to be rigged, but the results were nonetheless accepted. Shevardnadze was less successful in consolidating the state's authority and balancing a desired pro-Western orientation against Georgia's dependency on Russia. Though he prevented the total collapse of the Georgian state, he lost the 1992-93 war in Abkhazia. And in an ill-fated decision, he assented to a ceasefire agreement providing for Russian peacekeeping forces to guarantee it, a decision which led to the deployment of Russian troops in Georgia's separatist provinces. Shevardnadze again called on Russia for military assistance, this time to repel an attempted coup against his government by Gamsakhurdia, the opposition leader and former Georgian president in 1993.

These military defeats left thousands dead, wounded, and displaced and numerous cities and towns in ruins. The wars left deep scars in the psyches of many Georgians who felt betrayed and publicly humiliated by the defeats and let down by their own state. It also put Georgia at the mercy of Russia which, on the one hand, pulled the strings behind the scene and controlled the situation and, on the other, was indispensable to Shevardnadze's political survival and the cessation of hostilities.

Shevardnadze's reliance on Russia to quash the Gamsakhurdia coup was heavily criticized at home. Gamsakhurdia died on December 31, 1993, while being held in captivity. His death remains a mystery. According to some sources, he committed suicide. Others claim that he was murdered with the consent of Shevardnadze, an accusation that Shevardnadze has denied. He even launched an investigation into Gamsakhurdia's death; it went nowhere as with most such enquiries.

On the domestic front, the power struggle continued. Still formally allies, Shevardnadze, Kitovani, and Ioseliani were getting at odds. Having fulfilled their military roles in Abkhazia in 1992-93, and with the death of Gamsakhurdia, Kitovani and Ioseliani were increasingly becoming political liabilities to Shevardnadze. There was no further need for the National Guard or *Mkhedrioni*, and their continuing existence posed the risk that the militias could be used against Shevardnadze.

In the name of fighting corruption, Shevardnadze set out to politically eliminate his former allies, who simply miscalculated the situation. In October 1994, Kitovani established the National Liberation Front (NLF) with the aim of reclaiming Abkhazia on behalf of Georgia. Some months later, in January 1995, Kitovani led the NLF in an offensive against the province. The move was backed by Chechen soldiers with the support of the Chechen President, Dzhokhar Dudayev. Kitovani, who claimed that Shevardnadze had given his blessing for the maneuver, assembled hundreds of heavily armed volunteers and departed from the Iveria Hotel, a housing center for IDPs in Tbilisi, heading toward Senaki near the Abkhaz border. In Senaki, however, Kitovani was arrested and accused of violating the country's peace agreement.

Ioseliani faced a similar fate. After an assassination attempt on Shevardnadze in October 1995, Ioseliani's forces, then called the Georgian Salvation Corp, were disarmed and outlawed. After losing to Shevardnadze in the presidential election held the following month, Ioseliani was arrested and accused of participation in the assassination attempt. He was convicted and sentenced to a long prison term. Kitovani too was subsequently convicted and imprisoned. Thus, both adversaries were politically eliminated. Some years later, however, Kitovani and Ioseliani would be released on Shevardnadze's orders.

Shevardnadze proved again to be a master of the game, a skilled political survivor. He had perfected the art of divide and conquer and used the tactic skillfully. He astutely played various parties, groups, clans, and criminal gangs against each other, shifting the balance of their interests to allow him to have the last word. Successive governments and parliaments were formed under his helm, and although short-lived, they provided certain degree of stability or at least managed to prevent a complete collapse of the state.

* * *

Shevardnadze's human rights record in the period preceding *perestroika* was, like all else about him, rather uneven. During the years of his campaign against corruption while serving in the Ministry of Internal Affairs and later as the first secretary of the GCP, Shevardnadze was perceived as responsible for prosecution of many dissidents and using the crackdown on corruption as an opportunity to attack political opponents, the enemies of the system.

In the post-Gamsakhurdia years, Shevardnadze's government was accused of human rights abuses, particularly during a high-profile trial held in Tbilisi in 1995, against former supporters of Gamsakhurdia alleged to be terrorists. All of the accused were deprived of the right to a fair trial, and some were subjected to torture. In another instance, Shevardnadze signed emergency decrees allowing for the execution of looters on the spot. He defended the policies as necessary to combat rampant crime and corruption.

Later on, when conditions in Georgia began to stabilize, Shevardnadze's policy focus shifted toward ensuring traditional political rights and freedoms. Unlike in Azerbaijan, Turkmenistan, and Armenia, there were no restrictions on any form of political expression in Georgia, whether speech, art, media, or other public activity. Georgians did not live in fear of political persecution or reprisal. Criticism of political leaders, including Shevardnadze, was widespread. Civil society was active with several independent associations, NGOs, and political parties rapidly emerging during this time.

Little was done, however, to address social and economic rights and the general plight of the average Georgian. Georgia, like many postwar and postcommunist countries, had not done much to address the situation of the poor and marginalized who constituted the majority in the society; the situation remains dire even today. The economy remained in the hands of nefarious politicians, criminal groups, and ex-warlords who "privatized" the country and operated with impunity, taking all that was up for grabs. Government coffers were almost always empty, rendering budgetary allocations meaningless. Foreign assistance went into private hands as soon as it reached Georgia rather than to the poor and destitute. Corruption was pervasive and common at all levels of the society; it was part of the survival mechanism. This reality had no effect, however, on the West's perception of Shevardnadze as a "democrat," an image he would manage to preserve until the end of his political career.

Eventually, the rampant corruption, criminality, lack of even cursory scrutiny of financial records, and absence of reforms took its toll. It began to discourage inflows of foreign aid. Principal bilateral donors and international monetary institutions began recognizing that there had been no progress on implementing declared reforms and stopped providing further funds. I can recall some of the discussions in 2003 when highly irritated donors demanded explanations from the Shevardnadze government about what had happened to the projects and money allocated to implement them. They got nowhere.

It was obvious that no attempt had been made to develop many of the initiatives and that the funds had simply evaporated. The roads project was typical of such cases. After many years of appropriations, by the summer of 2003 it was apparent no investment had been made in the repair or development of the Georgian roads system in many years. The roads remained in a state of disrepair. Some queries about the status of the roads project were addressed directly to the president, who—deeply offended—stated that he had no money in the budget as it was obviously empty; that he, therefore, could not pay for the roads; and that even if some money had been allocated for the purpose by the donors, there was none at the moment.

But then Shevardnadze was a master at deflecting attention from himself for Georgia's problems. He claimed to have survived numerous coup and assignation attempts aimed at removing him from power, according to some sources nineteen. Two were grave assassination attempts that left behind some dead and wounded. Shevardnadze blamed the attacks on his political enemies, Russia in particular. I met some skeptics, however. While nobody denied that two of the assassination attempts had been genuine and serious, some of the less significant alleged plots were attributed to Shevardnadze himself.

"Nothing unites people more than a common enemy," my interlocutors advised.

"And you do not need much to increase the hatred against Russia, considered already our archenemy. Georgians are ready to believe the worse in this respect. So it is quite possible that on some occasions the alleged plots helped Shevardnadze to consolidate power," said another.

"The prospect of losing him in such an abrupt and violent manner would not only affect Georgians, but also our international partners. It was better to deal with the 'old fox' that they knew than to be exposed to the unknown—possible chaos, rivalry of competing gangs, further weakening of state institutions." So the old fox with the silver mane continued to survive.

In many ways, the secret to Shevardnadze's political longevity lies in his own words, words recounting not only the tactics, but also the manner of thinking, as he saw it, that had enabled his survival:

> My antagonists had taken everything into account, except for the way a person of my Georgian background operates. Since childhood, I have never allowed any encroachments upon my own notions of duty. Under the rules of the system's power monopoly over the individual, you must bear without a murmur all attacks upon yourself and [you] must accept as you're due the diktat of the political patriarchate, which arrogates to itself the right to decide your fate. While it decides what to do with you, sit tight, do your work, and take advantage of the privileges and benefits offered to you.

Don't try to yank the fish hook out of your mouth, or it will be certain death.

The Loser of the Rose Revolution

In the autumn of 2003, I was struck by the dissonance between the world's fascination with Shevardnadze and his poor image among Georgians. I was slowly discovering that, for the Georgian population, Shevardnadze had come to represent all that was wrong: the shame of dependency on Russia; the state dysfunction; the unchecked, rampant corruption; the poverty and helplessness; the inability of the country to modernize and integrate into the global community; the absence of effort to improve the lives of average Georgians. There were neither announced programs nor reforms. Access to basic services for most people was diminishing while private fortunes and unlimited financial opportunities flourished for a few. Salaries, even those of civil servants, were insufficient to provide for even minimal standards of nutrition and housing. The system forced, indeed expected, people to look to other sources for additional income to survive, legal and otherwise.

People at all strata of the society developed coping mechanisms. The few who were highly skilled and well connected could maintain through legal means; the rest either looked to illicit or semi-illicit means or gradually came to accept a life of exclusion and destitution. Begging children; decrepit, postcommunist city slums; prematurely aged women, still too proud to beg, trying to sell the last of their belongings along the city's main thoroughfares and streets (flowerpots, pillows, vases, whatever was left)—that was Shevardnadze's Georgia in 2003. This was not the image generally known to the West. There was neither sufficient interest, nor easily accessible information; but above all, there was the usual inertia serving to maintain the existing clichés. Shevardnadze was still seen as the hero of *perestroika* and a friend to many leading Western politicians; his deeds in Georgia, the condition of his own people as a result of his policies (or lack thereof), was of secondary importance. He was a "good guy" and that perception was not easily tarnished.

The corruption was ultimately Shevardnadze's undoing. His credibility was damaged by his cronies, the immediate beneficiaries of the transformation in Georgia. The list was rather long. It included the names of some well-known officials from previous and current regimes as well as members of the economic underworld. Shevardnadze's daughter and son-in-law, who own a cell phone company, were featured prominently on that list. Georgia is a small country with a small population, well less than five million. Everybody knew everybody, or at least of everybody in the capital. The same was true in the country's other towns and villages. Most people knew perfectly well how fortunes had been amassed, when, and under what circumstances. Thus, it was not merely the illegality of these transactions that increasingly upset Georgians. The Caucasus is known for its tolerance in this respect. It was the unfairness that angered many as well as the blatant indifference of the state to the misery and struggle of its people.

In Soviet times, some in Georgia had been quite rich while others had more modest means. However, all benefited from social and health services available across the USSR, and there had been no abject poverty or economic marginalization. That would come with the collapse of the old system and the disintegration of social services with it. With independence, the process of privatization was hijacked by party functionaries and their family members, criminal gangs and Mafia-types. The average Georgian could neither comprehended nor benefit from these processes. With time, people noticed that their traditional benefits were vanishing, that new opportunities were limited to a select few, and that independence did not translate into improved living standards, stability, and security. This knowledge hit the public at large at the turn of the century, and their discontent was tapped into by the opposition.

No area of society went unaffected. The Georgian state police had degenerated into a state of disrepair, a condition typical of government institutions during this period. There were thousands of them on the streets, by some estimates about seventy thousand, poorly dressed, often inebriated, and involved in bribes and extortion schemes. Indeed, admission into the police force itself required political connections, payment of bribes, or both. Officer salaries were low, and as with other civil servants, they were irregularly paid. Still, they had some privileges, like subsidies for housing and electricity, which made the job attractive. Most important, however, was the common understanding that in order to survive the police officers were expected to "help themselves" by all available means; hence their widespread involvement in illicit activities. Some bonded with criminal groups involved in smuggling, road robberies, and other criminal conduct; others restricted themselves to extorting payments from traffic tickets. Still others sustained themselves simply by collecting multiple meager salaries—their own and those of the fictitious employees they invented.

I remember a trip once to the airport one hour ahead of Shevardnadze. It was dark as all west-bound planes departed from Tbilisi around 4:00 or 5:00 a.m. I was astonished to see a series of strange silhouettes lined up along the road, emerging from the darkness. Every few kilometres, a shabby figure could be seen hovering behind a tree, sitting on the road bank, or laying against a street lamp. The driver explained that these were the police officers.

"Can you imagine? This is our police." He laughed. "They have not yet waken up. Some need many hours to get sober, but they hang around because they were ordered to come, to show that Shevardnadze is well protected. What a joke!"

* * *

I had an opportunity to watch closely Shevardnadze during his last days in power and in the immediate aftermath of his ouster. In my view, he was not aware of the enormity of the problems facing the society and the depth of the criticism that he faced and was even less prepared to cope with them. He belonged to a different era and could not find himself in the global world that had emerged. Even in daily politics, he kept making mistakes unworthy of the politician of his stature.

By 2003, the truth of this disconnect was painfully apparent and on display for all to witness. That summer, just ahead of elections, Nanuli Shevardnadze, the president's wife, was featured by mass media (ostensibly) to advise the audience on how to properly maintain a family on a pensioner's income. She presented herself as a role model and purported to explain how with 34 lari (US$17), the average pension, she was able to run her household, that is, prepare nutritious meals, buy detergents, medication, and other household needs (all still available at low prices because of the existing social support system, she said), dress properly, read books and newspapers, and enjoy cultural life. The Tbilisi intelligentsia, women in particular, were highly irritated; my Georgian interlocutors were furious.

"It is bad enough to be poor and have difficulty making ends meet," they told me, "but you do not have to add insult to injury."

The coverage also had an unintended consequence: it provoked angry reflections upon the finances of the Shevardnadze's family and his cronies. They were perceived as corrupt millionaires who had lost all sense of reality and decency. There was the criticism that they lived in a luxurious government villa surrounded by an enormous park and still enjoyed all the traditional party and state privileges of the Soviet system. They had never known different lives—never did they have had to pay for their living quarters, food, medical bills, or entertainment. It was always the party or the state footing the bills. Shevardnadze's children lived privileged lives as well. But with the change in the political climate, it was increasingly asked how the state, itself bankrupt, could keep providing for such a lifestyle.

It was obvious that Shevardnadze did not have much understanding for what was private property and what was public. Neither was it his particular concern where the money was coming from. It was ironic considering that his rocket political career from young political apparatchik to the first secretary of the GCP and member of the Politburo was inseparably linked to his spectacular and uncompromised campaign against corruption and acclaimed modesty so different from other party dignitaries. Obviously, people change with time . . . or is it merely their perceptions?

Chapter 18

Rose Revolution or Masquerade?

Georgian parliamentary elections took place on November 2, 2003. The results, which came in slowly and with high degree of uncertainty, were immediately challenged by the opposition. That, however, was not out of ordinary.

Since the collapse of the Soviet Union, the Caucasus had experienced a string of dubious elections, stretching from Georgia to Armenia to Azerbaijan, causing headaches for consecutive election observatory missions from the OSCE and other international organizations. The election results were always contested by some local groups. The observers' findings too were generally predictable: despite some imperfections, no major violations could be documented. The elections were thus always declared, in the end, fair and valid.

The political discontent brewing in Georgia in the autumn of 2003 appeared initially to fit perfectly this pattern. The opposition alleged fraud in the balloting for the parliament and called for a new vote. But there was the person of Shevardnadze, who, in the eyes of the outside world, should be supported in the name of stability and democracy. Admitting serious electoral irregularities committed by his party would have undermined his authority and reputation as a standard-bearer of democracy. Thus, it was anticipated that the election's observers would make a "responsible" judgment, which in turn would be accepted by the public, and uphold the reported results.

That was not to be the case. The protests were getting more visible and vocal by the day. Although dominated by young people at the beginning, with time, they became truly inclusive; old and young, men and women, people from all walks of life were joining forces to proclaim that it would not be business as usual. And the protests were gaining traction nationwide. Georgians from all parts of the country were making the journey to Tbilisi by any and all available means of transport—trains, cars, buses, motorbikes, even walking—to take part in the demonstrations. Soon, the international observers from the OSCE announced that the elections had been marred by irregularities and began discussing possible solutions.

The protests, however, continued. What was emerging was a social movement, mass protests against not only the alleged electoral fraud, but also the endemic of corruption, economic and social degradation, and poverty and exclusion as well. Their meaning was clear: "No, that is enough." Shevardnadze and his cronies were the main targets of the protests. So was discontent and frustration with Russia's continuing influence and interference, which the people blamed for many of Georgia's problems, to include her loss, in effect, of Abkhazia, South Ossetia, and Adjaria.

City Hall at Freedom Square in Tbilisi had become the center of operations. From its balconies, protest leaders spoke to the crowds and directed further actions. The political paroles—a host of signs, posters, leaflets, and other such materials bearing the movement's demands and slogans—were spread all over the city. Small groups of demonstrators kept gathering in front of parliament, city hall, and other locations. The traffic in the city center was paralyzed, but there were neither skirmishes nor accidents. The movement was becoming increasingly organized: its leadership had quickly consolidated and taken charge of developments. All actions were peaceful and demonstrators were friendly. They carried with them symbols of peace—paper pigeons, colorful ribbons and flowers, especially red roses, which would soon come to symbolize the movement, later called the Rose Revolution.

Three people emerged at the helm of the movement: Mikheil Saakashvili, a former minister of justice and chairman of the city council of Tbilisi; Nino Burjanadze, speaker of the outgoing parliament; and Zurab Zhvania, an experienced and shrewd politician and former leader of the Green Party. They were no strangers to Georgian politics or the public.

Saakashvili was young, just about to turn thirty-seven, and a lawyer with strong professional credentials from respectable Western European and American institutions. He had studied in Strasbourg and New York, where he graduated from Columbia Law School and worked for a respected Manhattan law firm in the 1990s. He had been involved in Georgian politics since the mid-1990s and was made minister of justice by Shevardnadze in 2000. He resigned from the post one year later over some disagreement with Shevardnadze concerning corruption charges against one of Shevardnadze's cronies, which he was not allowed to pursue. He went on to establish a new political party, the National Movement, which by the time of the 2003 parliamentary elections had become a base of support for the emerging protest movement and was in the center of opposition against the establishment.

Saakashvili was married to Sandra Roelofs, a Dutch and fellow student from the Strasbourg Institute of Human Rights. They had one son, Edward.

"You named your son after Shevardnadze?" people would ask Sandra.

"No, after my father."

They would later have a second son, born during Saakashvili's presidency. Young and confident, Sandra Saakashvili was active politically and highly visible. She commanded the Georgian language, participated in local development projects, and was perceived by many Georgian women as "one of them." During the electoral campaign, she was instrumental in gaining the support of female voters.

Nino Burjanadze was Shevardnadze's goddaughter. Her father was a wealthy businessman and one of Shevardnadze's closest friends from Kutaisi. She was an attorney by training and married to one, and the mother of two sons who sometimes accompanied her at political gatherings. In 2001, she became speaker of the parliament, a position she would not have attained without Shevardnadze's assistance. Although qualified and politically skilled, she would not have succeeded in navigating through the male-dominated politics of Georgia, particularly at her young age.

Zurab Zhvania had the strongest political credentials of the three. A biologist who had founded Georgia's Green Party in the late 1980s, he was elected to the first postindependent Georgian parliament in 1992. Shevardnadze later made him leader of the Union of Citizens of Georgia (SMK), Shevardnadze's power base, which had won an absolute majority in the 1995 parliamentary elections. Zhvania went on to become the speaker of the parliament.

Owing to his mastery at building alliances, reaching compromises, and persuading opponents to join the front, he helped Shevardnadze to survive politically and get things done on numerous occasions. With time, Zhvania gained the reputation of a skilful manipulator of

"Machiavellian" proportions. He was also dogged by rumors, though never confirmed, of being party to dubious business dealings and vulnerable to assassination.

In 1998, Zhvania's relations with Shevardnadze began to deteriorate over the government's failure to implement reforms and fight corruption. A faction of SMK in parliament, acting under Zhvania's influence, elected Saakashvili as its chairman and the two started to closely collaborate. The formal split between Shevardnadze and Zhvania took place in 2001 over a government crackdown on a popular independent TV station known as Rustavi 2. Zhvania resigned and, in 2002, formed the United Democrats, a party headed by Giorgi Baramidze. In the run-up to the 2003 elections, Zhvania's party allied not with Saakashvili but with the political block formed by his successor in parliament, Nino Burjanadze.

Zhvania's reputation as a shrewd and seasoned politician sometimes acted against him. In the first phase of the Rose Revolution, his involvement in the movement caused some to suspect that it would be business as usual, a mere reshuffling of posts among the political elite. He was also not charismatic and could not pull in the crowds on his own. That was Saakashvili's role. In the later stages, once the triumvirate had established itself and took off, his skill and contributions were priceless. Unlike the oft quick-tempered and impulsive Saakashvili, Zhvania represented calm and maturity. He started early building the institutional credibility of the new team and helped to bridge differences with its opponents. He worked well with the diplomatic community, conducted difficult negotiations aimed at easing tensions between the new team and outgoing officials, and was adept at handling the press.

*　　*　　*

All members of the new team were young, in their thirties, well-educated, and had extensive international exposure—unusual traits for people their age at that time in the former Soviet republics. And all were brought into politics by Shevardnadze and were supported by him at one time or another in the course of their respective political careers. They represented a new, postcommunist generation of Georgian leaders who came to the political arena with a much better sense of the global world and its requirements than their predecessors.

Their close political association with Shevardnadze, however, made some suspicious: Could Shevardnadze's former associates, individuals he mentored, truly turn against him? Could they bring about real change in Georgia and take on its main problems, in particular, corruption? After all, they came from well-established and politically connected families. Would they be prepared to clean up the political scene and introduce the rule of law and greater transparency and apply the law uniformly, even to their own associates and other members of the political elite?

The cohesiveness of the group was also questioned; some were skeptical as to whether the alliance could last. Each leader was ambitious and had his or her own agenda. In the past, they had appeared as if on a collision course, each standing directly in the way of the other. Their disagreements, known to the public, had been skillfully exploited by their political benefactor, Shevardnadze, to maintain the division between them and prevent any consolidated action, in typical Shevardnadze fashion.

The Rose Revolution, however, brought them together. They acted in a concerted manner and demonstrated unity. The most charismatic and aggressive of them, Saakashvili, emerged as the principal leader. Tall and forceful, he seemed to naturally dominate the scene and command authority. He mixed easily with the crowds and did not back away from skirmishes with the police. Wherever he appeared, he was greeted by calls of "Misha, Misha, Misha."

Every evening, after office hours, I wandered among the crowds, fascinated by the developments—the obvious unity of purpose, the friendly atmosphere, and confidence exuded that change was possible. During my evening rounds, I always met some Georgian colleague or colleagues from one of the international missions in the city and that gave us an opportunity to compare notes and speculate about what would come next.

One evening, I met two colleagues from the OSCE election observatory team, Rolf and Stein. We went to a café to chat.

"So it is over. The only question is if it will be tomorrow or a few days later," I remarked.

"And," they added, "what will come next and who will be in charge."

"Isn't it obvious?" I argued. "At this stage, the solution is rather clear. Shevardnadze will leave, the triumvirate will take over, the election results will be corrected one way or another, and Saakashvili be declared number one, the winner."

"But the international community will not allow the removal of Shevardnadze. After all, he is the only authority and guarantor of Georgia's stability. And what would Russia say to that? They could never accept Saakashvili and the bunch of pro-Western youngsters," replied Rolf.

As if in reaction to his statement, our conversation was interrupted by a spirited crowd chanting "Misha, Misha!" Some of the young demonstrators entered the café to warm up. They carried posters and wore T-shirts with slogans supporting the Rose Revolution, Saakashvili, and democracy and demanding the resignation of Shevardnadze, end of corruption and new elections.

"How can you imagine Shevardnadze continuing in these circumstances?" I asked my colleagues.

"It is sad," Rolf said as he gazed over the protesters, "that these young people, seemingly so spontaneous, are being paid by Soros. In addition to the posters, cars, and other tools of propaganda, they receive some per diem in US dollars for their activities."

"I am not sure about the details," I responded, "but I do not think that they are out here for a few US dollars per diem. It is a genuine social movement, and the young people are naturally enthusiastic about taking action and asserting themselves, fully aware of the absurd political reality in which they live, which has to be changed. As for the rest, unfortunately, every campaign has its costs, and there is no way this one can be free of charge. But I agree, the source of support can be legitimately questioned."

We drank some Georgian wine and continued our discussion.

"Moscow will never accept Saakashvili. It does not mean that they like Shevardnadze, but in a way, he is 'their' man and a great statesman. This one is totally pro-American, a product of Western influence and too young."

"Well, maybe they will settle for Abashidze," Stein suggested.

"What?" I could not believe my ears. It was truly an off-the-wall idea. "Who will settle on him and how?"

"He is a shrewd politician. He has all the confidence of Moscow. He has acted on their and Shevardnadze's behalf since the beginning of the trouble, traveling throughout the Caucasus, to Moscow, and a few Western European capitals. And he has highly placed friends in the West. His choice would ensure calm and stability."

Stability à la Adjaria, I thought. A "stability" built on oppression, terror, and the ruthless rule of a few over the impoverished and deprived many.

"You think that Georgians are fighting for that?" I asked.

"No, but somebody must be serious about the stability in this region where nothing can be achieved without Russian consent."

After this highly dispiriting conversation, I continued my walk and reached the Freedom Square. The speeches from the balcony of the Town Hall were ongoing amid the festive atmosphere. On one of the neighboring streets, I ran into Devi.

"You, here?" I was surprised. I knew of his political views but did not expect a career diplomat to attend anti-government demonstrations.

"Yes, I have been with them for a while, but discreetly. I told you last summer that it could not go on like this. This is our country, and we have to take responsibility."

"So I guess that you will have Saakashvili soon. I feel that there will be no bloodshed and that Russia will not intervene."

"No," he said, "not at this stage, but later. They will never leave us in peace."

And after a moment of silence, he continued.

"No, never. They will not allow us to breathe. They will get mixed up in all our matters. And what can we do, even if we modernize and have better leadership? We are a small country with a lot of problems. And the world will always consider maintaining good relations with Russia its priority. But you know, it is a pity because Georgia is such a beautiful country. I could never live permanently anywhere else."

"Let us hope that with the overall enthusiasm and international cooperation things will be better," I offered, watching his sad face. "Saakashvili spent enough time studying and working in the West to provide different managerial solutions. It will be a new generation of leaders—for good and bad—which should be free of the old communist mentality and ways of doing things."

"Yes, he is the best we can have at the moment or, rather, the only one. Nobody else less hotheaded and determined would be able to move the masses."

"Do you know him personally?"

"Yes, I know him," replied Devi. "I know him and his family." After a moment of silence, he added, "He is very young."

From the little I had seen of Saakashvili, I had never found him particularly sympathetic, but I was nonetheless puzzled by Devi's complete lack of enthusiasm. I had given Saakashvili the benefit of the doubt, impressed by his broad international experience and successful legal career in New York, traits unusual for leaders in this region. I was also aware of the financial and in-kind assistance from the West that would follow his election. Moreover, Georgia, as Devi rightly noted, needed a strong leader with the ability to appeal to the masses.

Soon, we finished our conversation under the chestnut tree. Devi left and I continued my walk. The Square was well lit, the crowds still growing, and there was an aura of joy and celebration permeating the air: no fear, no aggression, no revenge. I started moving toward Rustaveli Avenue planning to walk home. Soon somebody called out my name. I recognized Alyena, once upon a time a musicologist and currently a successful real-estate broker, one of the few solid professional ones in Tbilisi and popular with the IC.

She was happy, enjoying the moment, anticipating the long overdue change.

"Let us hope that we can finally live like human beings, have normal lives. It will not be easy, but it cannot be worse than what we have now. If only we could have some laws in place to end the corruption, to rationally use our resources. But as a society, we are not there yet. There has been too much Russian influence."

"Let us hope that the new authorities will manage," I continued my optimistic tone.

"Yes, let us hope," she echoed. "If they only listen to us and build on the current unity, we have a chance. But they have to be fair, abandon our traditional Caucasian spoils system, and establish the rule of law instead of this system of personal patronage.

"I am sure that this boy is the best bet under the circumstances," she continued, speaking of Saakashvili. "Actually, we do not know him. He has belonged to various political alliances in the past and he spent a lot of time abroad, which is good. We need someone with a broad, world perspective. But he will have a lot to learn. He needs good advisers, patience, and broad social consultation which includes his political enemies. Everyone is entitled to a voice."

"But you do not see many enemies nowadays," I noted.

"Yes, it is one of the main dangers," said Alyena. "In our tradition, people tend to read the minds of the rulers to get in their favor. Expressing dissenting opinions or pointing to alternatives that may be unpopular with the leader is not part of our political culture. Saakashvili's hero status will not help matters. But let us enjoy the evening," she said, brightening. "I did not expect that I would experience anything like it in my lifetime."

In the hours and days that followed, the enthusiasm for the Rose Revolution and anticipated prospects for radical change was visibly palpable. However, while there was unquestioned support for Saakashvili, the demonstrators' enthusiasm for the movement did not translate itself into equally warm feelings toward him. Some of my interlocutors were reserved and noncommittal on the question of Saakashvili. Others were would venture only short, careful remarks: "Yes, he is a good guy" or "It is good that we have him" or "We need somebody who knows the world."

There were also some substantive concerns expressed: "He is hotheaded, too impulsive," some worried. "He lacks experience and is too young," said the others. "He tends to be emotional, too self-centered. Let us hope that he will be able to listen and dialogue."

*　　*　　*

The performance of Shevardnadze's camp in those days was surprisingly poor and did not help his cause. The official, Soviet-style propaganda was not convincing: the disinformation campaign contradicting the reality and common knowledge of the people quickly discredited the pro-government media and rendered the contested elections even more suspicious in the eyes of many.

Shevardnadze's break with reality extended even to his diplomatic machinations. The incident involving a false press statement put out by the president's office following his meeting with the US Ambassador to Georgia, Richard Miles, was particularly telling. The statement, emphasizing the common position of the two officials, purported to claim that the American ambassador, like Shevardnadze, was against the demonstrations and believed them to be a threat not only to peaceful developments in Georgia, but also to stability in the region. This assertion was immediately rebuffed by the US Embassy, which issued its own statement explaining the American position. While the US government appealed for responsible conduct and respect for public order, it supported the right of free expression and the public's demand for speedy clarification of the election's outcome in accordance with international rules and principles. The United States' statement was broadly disseminated by the local and international media. It was also displayed on the embassy's Web site.

It was thus a puzzle as to why Shevardnadze's office had issued such a statement. Had he hoped against reason that the US would silently accept it and that the Georgian public would believe it? At that stage, there was no doubt where the United States stood. While originally its policy had been to support Shevardnadze for another term in office, the US position quickly changed as the circumstances on the ground changed. The electoral fraud could not now be ignored and had to be addressed. Shevardnadze's insistence on convening a new parliament notwithstanding, at all costs, further reflected his weakening grasp on reality. That jeopardized his political future.

The atmosphere in city was intensifying, and the demonstrations were increasing. Still the government continued to proceed as if it were fully in charge, preparing for the opening of the new parliament. The date was set for November 22. The alleged electoral infractions were to be rectified through minor corrections to the results in certain districts. Shevardnadze and his advisers appeared to be functioning in a parallel universe, as if by denying reality they could alter it. So they continued to ignore the events in the streets, the fact that the movement was expanding and the calls for change infusing the air.

As part of its campaign of disinformation, the state-run media and that friendly to the government (particularly in the Adjaria province) warned of possible bloodshed and confrontation with security forces loyal to Shevardnadze. While such claims were not taken seriously by the local population, some in the international community were concerned and feared potential street violence.

Most in the international community were totally unprepared for what was to come. For example, the security team led by United Nations Development Programme (UNDP), which was responsible for all UN staff stationed in Tbilisi, including the UNOMIG, advised us to stay "out of danger," go straight home from the office, and avoid the city center and the demonstrations. Fortunately, the Special Representative of the Secretary-General at the time, Heidi Tagliavini, a Swiss diplomat, left it to our discretion. Whenever a security advisory was announced, she would share it with us and ask that we take precautions, but she did not insist upon our staying home locked behind closed doors.

"Use your own judgment and do not take unnecessary risks," she told us. "After all, you are the ones who should know what the developments are. We, as the mission, assess the situation on a daily basis and report to headquarters in New York. I share with you the official security assessment, but I personally think it a bit exaggerated."

Some staff members, however, were truly scared. Such individuals had rarely ventured out into the city and did not have firsthand knowledge of the developments. They relied instead on local media reports (mainly Russian and Adjarian), UNDP security assessments, and office rumors. The Western media, per usual, had other priorities and rarely reported on Georgia. It was not until the breakthrough a few days before the Rose Revolution prevailed that the Western media turned its attention to the dramatically evolving events.

I was convinced that there would be no violence. I kept asking around who would fight against whom. I had not seen any evidence that any of the security forces—the Georgian military, state militia, or special troops—would be willing to attack the demonstrators. All indications were to the contrary. Further, the special security forces, whom many believed were paid a "fortune" by the state, still took home salaries far below those received by the private bodyguards of the local Mafiosi. Thus when the street protests started up in November of 2003, my Georgian interlocutors insisted that even the special troops would not move in defense of the authorities. I doubted as well that Shevardnadze would want to conclude his political career using force against peaceful demonstrators.

My thinking was confirmed by a conversation between two women, presumably wives of security officers, that I overheard in an exclusive, high-priced supermarket in Tbilisi:

"Why should my husband defend these people and risk his life?" a short, dark-haired woman declared. "They do not pay him well enough for that."

Her companion, a young, ponytailed woman carrying a Guess handbag, agreed, "Yes, you are right. We are getting more money than the others, but it is not sufficient. I am sure that my husband will try to help Shevardnadze stay out of trouble and not get mixed up with the crowds, but that's it. He should go home and let new people take over. He is old.

"My husband will never do anything against the demonstrators," she continued. "After all, they are Georgians like everybody else, like us."

"There will be shooting." It was the voice of an unseen woman calling out from behind the fruit stand. "People say that the security will shoot."

"Who will be shooting?" the first woman queried. "I am telling you, my husband nor any of these guys will shoot. They're not crazy. They want to live like anybody else. And these old apparatchiks did not even treat them nicely. Why should they protect them at all?"

"But aren't their bodyguards trained for this purpose?" the second woman asked, doubt creeping into her voice. "I'm afraid that my husband will consider it his job to provide close protection to the president, at least as long as it does not involve shooting the others. He is like this. He believes it to be his duty."

"Come on," the first woman interrupted. "My husband never took it seriously. It is a job like anything else, just better paid. So why not use it as long as it suits you?"

While I was convinced that Shevardnadze, in spite of his weakening contact with the society and understanding of its needs, would not be prepared to use force, I also doubted that he still commanded any. This view must have been shared by the Adjarian leader, Aslan Abashidze. While his television broadcasts obsessively reiterated the loyalty of the Georgian army to its leader and emphasised the capacity of pro-government forces to protect the president, he nonetheless dispatched lorries of "concerned Adjarians" to Tbilisi to defend the Georgian leadership, if necessary.

The lorries parked in the center of Tbilisi, and men in black leather jackets disembarked into the streets. They did not seek confrontation but situated themselves in the areas traditionally used by the demonstrators, particularly those in close proximity of the parliament. The protesters, however, quickly adapted, changing the frequency and venues of their meetings. It probably suited the Adjarians who must have felt a bit uncomfortable in a foreign city, facing controlled but determined crowds. They were not particularly active, staying only a few days to justify their mission. Some observers even claimed that the "concerned Adjarians" quietly admired the developments and watched them closely hoping that they would one day be able to replicate them at home. As it happened, that day came sooner than anticipated, in the spring of 2004.

* * *

The opposition called for mass demonstrations on the day of the first session of the new parliament, on November 22. "We will not allow it to happen" was the call. Massive crowds assembled at Freedom Square and from there started moving toward the parliament, the latter protected by barricades of old buses and cars and security forces. The day was sunny, the mood sober, and the determination indestructible. The three leaders led the crowd. They stopped in front of a barricade. As they were talking to the security officers, some demonstrators proceeded ahead, passing through the barriers and reaching the steps of the parliament unharmed. The crowd moved on. Some began greeting the security officers, handing them red roses, and calling on them to join. Some policemen did so instantly, in front of the TV cameras, others abandoned their posts and vanished. Access to the parliament became wide open, excepting one last obstacle, its massive doors which were locked and protected from the inside.

"Misha, Misha, Misha," the crowd chanted as Saakashvili moved toward the doors, which had begun to crack under the pressure of the demonstrators. After a short struggle, the doors finally gave way, and the crowd entered the parliament. Saakashvili, a red rose in hand, started slowly moving toward the podium, calling on Shevardnadze to step down. Others, hardly able to contain their excitement, jumped on the benches and tables and, using them as spring boards, moved too quickly toward the podium. The horrified members of the Shevardnadze-assembled parliament looked on in disbelief at the evolving scene. Some tried to block the passage between the rows of seats, others even tried to physically stop the intruders. All was in vain. They quickly came to understand that the game was over.

The demonstrators had entered parliament as Shevardnadze was delivering his opening address. He seemed not to see, hear, or be disturbed by the events unfolding before him in the hall. He did not take his eyes from the text—not when the doors broke, not in response to the increasing chaos and noise in the chamber as the demonstrators moved toward him. He briefly interrupted his speech once or twice, vacantly looking out over the parliamentary hall before continuing. The demonstrators continued to close in on the rostrum as Saakashvili kept calling on him to step down. Shevardnadze did not react. Finally, surrounded by his bodyguards, he was whisked from the room. He never once stopped reading and kept hold of the speech in both hands as he was carried away.

Saakashvili proceeded to the head table and, in a symbolic gesture, drank tea from the chalice. The hall was flooded with people. He made a short statement and then invited Burjanadze to take over—after all, she was the last parliamentary speaker and the new elections had not been recognized. All these events were followed intently by Georgian and international audiences. Local TV broadcasted them live that, by itself, constituted a unique political happening in Georgia.

The world was not prepared for Shevardnadze's rapid departure. Despite Saakashvili's assurances, some feared his persecution and many in the West expected Shevardnadze to leave the country. The German chancellor, Gerhard Schroeder, even invited him to live in Germany. Still today, I often hear the question where he lives. The assumption is that he must live abroad; it is a misconception. Shevardnadze is not and never has been politically persecuted. To have forced him to live in exile would have for him been a punishment and never his choice. I doubt that Shevardnadze would feel better anywhere else other than in his native Georgia. There he enjoys the respect afforded an old statesman and a former president. And while interest in his person and activities have, naturally, decreased with the passage of time, the overall assessment of his person and politics has been improving at a rate proportionate to Saakashvili's decline in reputation. By now, there is even nostalgic musing for the "good old times," the days of Shevardnadze.

Chapter 19

Shevardnadze: An Afterword

I am such a good Georgian as you.
— Eduard A. Shevardnadze

Shevardnadze's fall from power came as a surprise to many. The manner of his fall, his seeming break with reality and bizarre behavior in the days and months which followed, were equally stunning.

The story of Shevardnadze's alleged employment by the UN Secretary-General is telling of the time. A few weeks after he had entered private life, Shevardnadze gave a press interview announcing that he would soon take up a high-level UN job. "A representative of the United Nations recently visited Tbilisi, and he conveyed to me an invitation from Kofi Annan to be his adviser," Shevardnadze stated.

"I do not know yet the scope of my future portfolio," he continued. "It may be related to the peace process in the Caucasus but can be something else. After all, I have broad political experience and I am capable of assisting the secretary-general in many areas."

"Do you know where you will be posted?" one journalist asked.

"No. I guess it could be New York, at least periodically, but I can as well operate from Tbilisi or travel around the world on special assignments."

We knew that it was a fiction but could not figure out how it came about. It was clear that under the circumstances such an offer could not have been made, that Shevardnadze would not have been considered a suitable advisor in the aftermath of the Rose Revolution. The media, nonetheless, ran with the story and it generated a lot of excitement. At the UNOMIG office in Tbilisi, we would occasionally be on the receiving end of angry reactions from local NGOs and IDP organizations; we could only reply that we were not aware of the offer.

A few weeks later, in another interview—Shevardnadze was particularly fond of giving interviews after being ousted—he was asked if he was, in fact, going to take up an assignment with the UN.

"Yes, I am still waiting for a clarification from the secretary-general," he responded confidently.

"Are you sure that he actually wants you to work as his adviser?" a reporter inquired.

"Look, he was the one who invited me. He sent the message though his high-level envoy on a visit to Tbilisi. I recently asked New York for an urgent clarification so I can start preparations."

"And if he does not confirm it?"

"It is not possible. I am a serious person. I cannot be treated like this. They offered me a job, I accepted, and they cannot pull back on the promise."

The interview provoked an official intervention by the Georgian Ministry of Foreign Affairs, which, in a statement, explained that the former president was not their candidate for any UN function and that all high-level political appointments should, as customary, be preceded by consultations with concerned governments. "We will seek clarification from the office of the UN Secretary-General," the statement concluded.

It soon came. The UN Secretary-General's office finally broke its silence. Its spokesman, Fred Eckhard, addressed the issue at the press conference at UN headquarters in New York. He reported that the secretary-general regretted the misunderstanding and that he had enormous respect for the former president of Georgia, Eduard Shevardnadze, and his contributions to peace and international cooperation. He, however, wanted to clarify that the secretary-general had never made such an offer to Mr. Shevardnadze and that he would not have considered such an option in the circumstances.

There was no immediate reaction from Shevardnadze, but when asked about the matter at a subsequent press conference, he angrily dismissed the issue: "I do not understand it. They offered me the position through a special envoy and now they deny it. I am a serious and busy person, and I have better things to do."

So how did it all come about? Was it pure fiction or the product of a true misunderstanding? It is difficult to answer. As far as it is possible to trace the story, the following likely happened: A midranking employee of one of the UN's specialized agencies met with the former president during a visit to Tbilisi. It is not clear why he did so. Maybe they had met in the past, or he wanted to pay his respects to the internationally admired hero of *perestroika*. The content of this meeting remains unknown as well. The guest likely expressed his appreciation for Shevardnadze and alluded to his skills and contributions to the world affairs. He might have even, in order to seem more important, conveyed regards from the secretary-general or, most likely, from his superiors, the leaders of the agency. He could have stated how much the UN valued his host's skills and that such qualities were needed in the work of the organization.

I doubt that he went any further. The rest must have been Shevardnadze's own interpretation. I am also positive that the unfortunate midranking employee never expected that his private conversation with the ex-president would become the subject of worldwide debate and embarrassment to the UN.

There are some, however, who considered this and other seemingly unfortunate political moves, and even the ouster of Shevardnadze itself, as his continuing attempt to outmaneuver his opponents and stay in the game. Saakashvili's hasty promise of immunity and assurances to Shevardnadze that he would be allowed to keep his assets and use the government-owned villa, added to such suspicions.

"It is my villa," Shevardnadze claimed. "I bought it with my own money."

"When?" skeptics asked.

"Long ago. I worked very hard all my life. I wrote books, I gave lectures, so I had my own means. It is my villa," he insisted.

Similarly, some questioned the immunity granted to Shevardnadze and wished to see him held accountable for his actions while in office, particularly for the widespread corruption involving his family and close associates. Such views, however, were in the minority. The issue of his responsibility for the wars in Abkhazia and South Ossetia, and the crimes committed by Georgian forces there, were not the focus of the Georgian public, though in Abkhazia Shevardnadze was often perceived as a war criminal. In Georgia, only some IDPs blamed him for their destroyed lives and lost property.

Most Georgians accepted the fact that Shevardnadze would continue to live in the residence where he had spent most of his life.

There he writes and receives visitors from all over the world. His last book, *Als der Eiserne Vorhang zerriss* (How the Iron Curtain Was Torn) was translated into German, with the foreword written by his old friend, Hans-Dietrich Genscher, the former German foreign minister. The former president followed closely developments in Abkhazia and South Ossetia but refused to talk about the 2008 war until the Tagliavini report, commissioned by the European Union, was published. Neither would he discuss his successor—a noble gesture considering the circumstances of his ousting and the often disparaging comments Saakashvili is known to make of him.

Today, Shevardnadze lives in his memories, surrounded by the photos, art objects, books, and souvenirs from his many foreign trips. He cherishes the peace and his family. In the courtyard of his well-protected villa is the grave of his wife, Nanuli, who died a few years prior. That is where he wants to be buried one day.

In Georgia, Shevardnadze's reputation has already begun to benefit from the lapse of time and the misfortunes of his successor. The relative prosperity and political freedom that existed in Shevardnadze's Georgia, his less hostile dealings with Russia, the international respect he commanded, and the family-man image he projected have all contributed to the nostalgia taking hold in Georgia.

"So what do you think of Eduard Shevardnadze?" I asked my friends. The assessments were mixed.

"He is a typical, clever, and sly Caucasian man, a silver fox, very manipulative, tricky (*oj kakoj on szczvanyj*) and very corrupt," Dato, a driver told me. "He is one of us. That's why he knew how to survive."

"He listened to people, made a lot of common sense decisions, and tried to reason. I received his support on some occasions when I had an interesting proposal to make," said Kaha, an architect and former official in Shevardnadze's government.

"He was a Soviet man, apparatchik with dubious connections to the KGB, who governed Georgia in the communist tradition," snapped an opposition member.

For the outsider, it is difficult to reconcile the image of the "dove"—the hero of *perestroika* and darling of the West—with these internal, critical Georgian perceptions of Shevardnadze, who, undoubtedly, is one of the most influential politicians of our times. The story history writes will likely be as uneven and complex, stretching from his years as a party apparatchik, to his years as a world-renown democrat, helping to liberate Eastern Europe and the USSR from the dread of the communist system, to his last decade in politics serving as the Georgian president, succumbing peacefully to the Rose Revolution.

It is up to Georgians to evaluate his impact on their country. He did not stand up for dissidents and never put his neck on the line or offer public support in politically controversial cases; he would not have survived the Soviet system had he done so. On the other hand, he is not known to have personally ordered political prosecutions, and he did not brutally oppress his people or engaged in acts of terror as his predecessors. Undoubtedly, within the framework of Soviet communism, he was on the liberal wing; but he was nonetheless a master at playing intrigues and removing his enemies from political posts, but not, like most of his predecessors, from life.

The one-dimensional image of Shevardnadze as the hero of *perestroika* and friend of the West, as all portrayals in black and white, contributed greatly to the misreading of the situation in Georgia under his helm. Things are not so manifest in the Caucasus; one must engage in the complexities.

His fall should not have come as a surprise. Saakashvili (and the West) would be wise to heed the lesson.

Chapter 20

Russia, Georgia, and Their Leaders

The Countries: Georgia and Russia

The Georgian-Russian war over South Ossetia in the summer of 2008 came as a shock. But looking back, one must ask, should it have really been so surprising considering the strained and fragile status of relations between the countries, the long unresolved territorial issues, and the personal animosity between their two leaders?

Georgian-Russian relations have never been good, but in the years since Georgia gained her independence in 1991, they have only been aggravated. Relations took a particularly bad turn in 2003, after the Rose Revolution. Since then, dealings between the two countries have been dominated by mutually reinforcing enmity, mistrust, and conflicting views on Georgia's place in the world. Russia has always considered Georgia part and parcel of its sphere of influence. Georgia has, conversely, aimed at building political and military alliances with the West, where she has long had strong cultural ties.

The replacement of Shevardnadze, often irritating and rebellious but at his core a Soviet man, by a new generation of Western-oriented Georgians was, by itself, unwelcome news for Moscow. So was Georgia's assertion of control over Ajaria in the spring of 2004, which meant not only the loss of a loyal man, Aslan Abashidze, but also the loss of a strategically important Black Sea terminal and military base and share in the region's lucrative contraband.

Bilateral relations have also been perpetually strained over the status of Georgia's two breakaway territories, Abkhazia and South Ossetia. Russia has played a particularly important role in the conflicts, partly through sanction of the many multilateral and bilateral agreements drawn up over the years to mediate the disputes, and partly through imposition of its will on Georgia through a variety of coercive means, sometimes in breach of those same agreements.

Until 2008, Russia officially acknowledged the unquestionable principle of Georgian territorial integrity and repeatedly affirmed this position in the various accords and agreements to which it was party and in official statements. The conduct of its politicians toward the contested enclaves, however, belied its official position or at least gave rise to doubts about its seriousness. Prior to recognizing the two provinces, numerous Russian politicians visited Abkhazia and South Ossetia, received their separatist leaders in Russia as state dignitaries, and made public statements in clear support of the separatist position. Over time, Russia and various Russian institutions increased their economic support for both territories as well.

Another divisive measure was Russia's policy of granting Russian citizenship to the inhabitants of the separatist provinces. The process began in 2001 and by 2005 over 80 percent of the Abkhaz population held Russian passports. Most Abkhaz welcomed this opportunity. It allowed them to travel outside of their tiny territory where they had been practically confined since the 1992-93 war. Their original travel documents were good only for travel within Abkhazia and possibly travel to Russia. The frequent and bitter protests by Georgian authorities had no impact on this policy. The Georgians feared (and rightly) that with most of the population holding Russian citizenship, Russia might, either on its own initiative or upon request, assume new obligations toward their protection, economic well-being, education, and cultural development.

The role and conduct of Commonwealth of Independent States (CIS) peacekeepers—comprised almost entirely of Russians—constituted another source of friction. In 1993, Eduard Shevardnadze and Vladislav Ardzinba, Abkhazia's de facto president, agreed on deployment of a Russian-led peacekeeping force to monitor the separation of Georgian and Abkhaz forces along the Inguri River. Having lost the war and being at the mercy of Russia, Shevardnadze had reluctantly accepted the agreement. The United Nations quickly endorsed it and authorized deployment of 136 UN observers to monitor all actors, including the CIS peacekeeping force.

The latter provision was never truly implemented in practice by the UN observer mission. The assumption that a handful of unarmed UN observers could monitor the conduct of the Russian military and that a report of the mission to the UN Security Council could ever be critical of Russia, a permanent member on the council, was highly unrealistic, to say the least. As time passed without resolution of the conflicts, both Georgian presidents, Shevardnadze and Saakashvili, turned to their Western allies seeking through informal channels assistance in establishing a full-scale UN peacekeeping mission to replace the CIS force. They were, however, advised against it by consecutive American and European governments, in order not to antagonize Russia.

Another sticking point was the Georgian forces takeover of the Kodori Gorge, in the far northeast corner of Abkhazia, in 2006. Georgia had moved in to recapture the Gorge following accusations that some of the region's inhabitants, known as the Hunters, had collaborated with Russian and Abkhaz forces against Georgia. Russian protests against the action fell on the deaf ears.

Bilateral relations were further seriously aggravated in 2006 when a row erupted between Tbilisi and Moscow over alleged spying. On September 27, Georgian authorities detained, with much fanfare, four Russian officers along with ten other people. The alleged spies were paraded on TV while the Georgian Minister of Internal Affairs, Vano Merabishvili, released for public consumption a detailed record of their purported illegitimate activities. They were eventually handed over to the OSCE.

Moscow responded in kind with its own diplomatic overkill: it recalled its ambassador to Georgia and ordered a partial evacuation of Russian embassy personnel and their families, issued warnings advising Russian citizens against traveling to Georgia, and suspended issuing visas to Georgians traveling to Russia at its Tbilisi embassy. The Russian Defense Minister, Sergei Ivanov, called the Georgian action a provocation against Russia, "the type of hysteria typical of the Georgian authorities," and compared the arrests to Stalin's repressions in the 1930s, alluding to Stalin's Georgian origin. The Russian president, Vladimir Putin, struck a similar tone, releasing a statement proclaiming that the detentions were "a sign of succession of Lavrenti Beria both inside the country and in the international arena."

Russia then moved beyond the war of words and began to flex its political muscle, introducing a set of economic measures intended to remind Georgia of her dependency and vulnerability. Russia banned the import of Georgian wines and mineral water. Georgian wines were withdrawn from Russian shops and restaurants, purportedly because they constituted a serious health hazard. Millions of bottles of the famed mineral water from Borjomi (Georgia's top export) were similarly removed from Russian stores and destroyed in a countrywide action. The loss to shop owners and importers in Russia, and to producers and exporters in Georgia, was counted in millions of euros. Wines from Abkhazia—produced in vineyards surrounded by Georgia proper—were prominently displayed in Moscow supermarkets under the Abkhazian flag. Obviously, they did not pose a danger to the public's health.

Additional provocations took place, signaling Russia's intention to up the ante. In January 2007, in the middle of winter, the pipelines delivering gas and electricity to Georgia were blown up on Russian territory. The disruption set off a prolonged energy crisis in Georgia with painful consequences for the Georgian population and broader economic and political implications for the Saakashvili government. In the end, Georgia was forced to agree to higher energy prices than originally negotiated to end the crisis. The price increase, however, did not extend to her two breakaway republics.

In another move, the Russian government started imposing arduous visa requirements on Georgian citizens (except for the inhabitants of Abkhazia and South Ossetia), when none had existed before. Considering that roughly 700,000 Georgians worked in Russia and their remittances went into the millions of US dollars each year, it gave Russian authorities yet another powerful means of demonstrating their capacity to dominate and control the course of events inside and outside Georgia.

Georgia's increasingly open quest to shake off her remaining dependency on Russia and join Western alliances, NATO in particular, ostensibly supported by the Bush administration, was also not to Russia's liking. The Georgian desire to align with the West was understandable, particularly considering both her experiences of domination and occupation by Russia and the USSR and long-established cultural connections with Europe. However, implementation of this policy has often been misguided. Saakashvili's expectations of American assistance have been highly unrealistic; he entirely misread the extent to which his personal friendship with the then-sitting US president, George W. Bush, would influence American foreign policy. The statement of the

Georgian Minister of Defense, Davit Kezerashvili, during the dramatic events of the 2008 summer evidenced this naïveté or misplaced confidence: "We are now in a fight against the great Russia, and our hope is to receive assistance from the White House because Georgia cannot survive on its own."

*   *   *

Saakashvili's declaration that Georgia was the "Israel of the Caucasus" and his pursuit of a "special relationship" with Israel has antagonized Moscow. Georgian-Israeli military cooperation, which has included arms sales to Georgia, has been a particular point of contention. In a secret agreement between Israel and Georgia, two military airfields in southern Georgia were designated for use by the Israeli military in the event of pre-emptive attacks against Iranian nuclear installations. In the midst of 2008 South Ossetia conflict, Russian troops raided the fields and other facilities in the area, capturing some Israeli military equipment. The outcome of this expedition was reported by General Anatoly Nogovitsyn, the Russian military deputy chief of staff, at a press conference in Moscow in September 2008.

The 2008 war over South Ossetia led to the official breach in diplomatic relations between the two countries, and Russia's formal recognition of Abkhazia and South Ossetia as independent states. It closed the chapter on the standoff over the status of the breakaway enclaves, which had lasted nearly two decades. Given the circumstances, the governments of the new states considered the continuing presence of international missions on their respective territories redundant. Both the UNOMIG and the OSCE observatory mission in South Ossetia were closed soon thereafter. But with Russian forces still occupying parts of Georgia proper, and Russia's refusal, as a matter of policy, to engage in any form of dialogue with Georgia as long as Saakashvili remained in power, the stalemate in bilateral relations persisted.

"It is a pity that with the 2008 war Georgia broke off diplomatic relations with Russia," commented Shevardnadze, the former Georgian president. "The lack of diplomatic contacts prevents any kind of communication. If there is no exchange of views, there can be no progress. It was a serious mistake."

The Leaders: Putin and Saakashvili

The animosity between Putin and Saakashvili has further complicated the bilateral relations between the nations. Saakashvili passionately loathes Georgia's historical dependency on Russia and Russia's colonial attitude toward its former republics and their leaders. Putin has found equally contemptible Georgian demands to be treated as an equal, Saakashvili's arrogance and his demonstrative friendship with the (former) US President George W. Bush. Moreover, both leaders have been unable to refrain from direct personal attacks or mask their visible irritation with the other.

The bad chemistry between them seems to have resulted more from their shared personality traits than political differences and physical dis-similarities. The short, slim, and athletic Putin and the huge, heavy, and elephantlike Saakashvili are both arrogant egomaniacs resentful of any criticism or disagreement. They both demand total loyalty and blind obedience. They perceive any dissenting view or independent opinion as a personal attack, an act of disloyalty, or a challenge to their authority.

During meetings with politicians and the public alike, they deliver monologues rather than engage in dialogue. In the manner typical of Soviet apparatchiks, they talk to people rather than discuss matters with them as equals. In this way, Saakashvili, like Putin, is incapable of gracefully facing criticism and is more inclined to find himself in confrontations or having uncontrolled fits of anger.

With the 2008 war, the rhetoric and personal attacks became particularly vicious. Putin and his entourage questioned the mental capacity of Saakashvili and asserted that it was not possible to deal with such an insane leader. For his part, Saakashvili, during his many dramatic press conferences in August 2008, referred to the Russian leadership as "barbarians" and accused the Russians of attacking Georgia in a period "when all civilized people were enjoying vacations and the Olympic games in Beijing."

Back in Georgia after the war of 2008, I sought to look beyond this open hostility and personal animosity. Turning a more critical eye, I concluded that the similarities between the two leaders do, in fact, extend beyond their common personal characteristics to governance style and policy choices. It appears that Saakashvili has attempted to model his Georgia on Putin's Russia, albeit a milder, weaker form, rather than on a traditional, constitutional democracy as one would expect of the leader of the Rose Revolution.

The most striking similarities include the following:

- *Manipulation of the law to augment and consolidate power.* The changes to the Georgian Constitution in 2004 were effected in the Soviet/Russo hard-line tradition. Procedurally, the process was democratic in form only. Substantively, the amendments augmented the powers of the president at the expense of the parliament, consolidating Saakashvili's grip on power, not unlike the way in which legal reforms and changes to the Russian constitution where implemented during Putin's presidency to strengthen the executive's powers.
- *Lack of an independent judiciary.* There is no independent judiciary in Georgia. The entire judicial system is dependent on political patronage.
- *Absence of transparency and the rule of law.* There is no rule of law. Political dissenters, critics, and those simply pegged politically inconvenient can be thrown into jail for extended periods without a clearly stated reason and without access to a lawyer. They are often charged with criminal offences involving drugs, guns, or theft although they have no previous criminal record or known association with such criminal activities. Participants in public demonstrations are particularly vulnerable to such arbitrary use of state power.
- *Control by terror.* The number of people kidnapped, disappeared, beaten, and tortured is on the rise. The victims' relatives and associates are subjected to intimidation as well. The acts of violence are often committed by masked men and cannot officially be linked to any state-run institution. The perpetrators are hardly ever identified, and official investigations typically end inconclusively.
- *Elite corruption.* Saakashvili has used his police powers and the courts to suppress political dissent and exact revenge on perceived enemies. His so-called anticorruption campaign has not been in accord with the rule of law, and punishments have not been commensurate with the gravity of the crimes. Rather punishments (indeed the decision to prosecute) are usually determined by political connections and the financial utility

of the offender. Those politically and personally loyal to the Saakashvili government essentially operate outside the law and escape scrutiny. For others, the law is used as a weapon to force their submission or cause them financial or personal ruin. Thus, corruption has not been abated; rather, now it is more selective or, as some call it, an "elite corruption" that persists. In addition, bail is often used as a form of extortion, another means for corrupt officials to extract payments without risk of punishment.

- *Abuse of state powers.* There exists no transparency and many authorities, to include elected leaders, act with impunity and are not held accountable. Any serious political challenge or criticism is perceived as anti-state activity and, in extreme cases, treason. There is also the tendency of the Saakashvili government to deflect criticism by attributing it to a foreign (mainly Russian) influence, conspiracy, or attempted *coup d'état.*

- *Suppression of speech and political rights.* Freedom of the press and speech have been seriously constrained compared to Shevardnadze's time. The state media monopolizes access to and dissemination of key political information, mainly through the state-controlled TV channels. People increasingly fear engaging in critical political discourse and activities, particularly in the public sphere.

- *Exploitation of nationalism.* Excessive attention is given to the country's image and its history, past glories, symbols of power, and above all, to its leader. Tbilisi, like Moscow and St. Petersburg, is made a showcase. Political leaders fixate on the "enemy" to detract from and ignore the persistent poverty and misery of the general populace: out of sight, out of mind.

- *Creation of a police state.* Strength and power is manifested through the projection of military and police control over the society through the use of state security forces, as in Russia, and not through development of the civil society by increasing participatory democracy, cultural and political diversity, and transparency.

It took me a while to reach these conclusions, to separate the rhetoric from the hard facts of the reality on the ground. How did the "beacon of democracy" Saakashvili and the authoritarian Putin come to have so much in common? Is it possible that it is not merely perception and Saakashvili, as some suggest, has in fact attempted to model himself after Putin and follow in the footsteps of the Russian leader, the archenemy, the symbol of evil and oppression of Georgia? I shared my thoughts with my interlocutors in Tbilisi. They were not surprised by the basic premise.

"We live in a Putin-like country, viewed as democracy, schizophrenic, postmodern Stalinism, with elements of neoliberalism and economic crisis, strong involvement of foreign lobbies, increasing violation of human rights, subordination of the justice sector to politics, or rather to the political elite," Salome Zurabishvili tells me.

"You should know that after his first meeting with Putin in Moscow, early in his presidency, Saakashvili stated that that was the way to run the country, meaning Putin's way. He was deeply impressed by Putin. He shared this view with his closest associates," a Georgian friend, a former member of the government, told me.

The story was confirmed by some foreign diplomats with whom I spoke. They knew the story and, off the record, commented on Saakashvili's fascination with the Russian leader.

"He is obsessed with Putin. He would like to be like Putin, consciously or subconsciously, but will never be even a 'mini' Putin. Well, at least, the poor boy has some role model," remarked one Western diplomat.

"Yes, he is trying to copy the oppressive system that he knows best," Levan, a university professor, confirmed over a glass of whisky at the opposition club. "We thought that he had been influenced by the West, but he is a typical, nasty Soviet-style apparatchik. He never mentally and politically left the Komsomol to which he once belonged."

"He thinks that he is Putin," another opposition member sneered. "He is not Putin. Putin is clever, and he is a fucking Mickey Mouse."

"Don't complain about it," I remarked. "Had he been Putin, your street barricades would not have lasted even a day, and we would not have enjoyed this conversation. The opposition club would have been blown up by some 'Caucasian terrorists,' in this case, probably some Abkhaz or South Ossetians."

I also came across some conspiracy theories explaining Saakashvili's conduct. According to Gia, a former high-ranking civil servant, Saakashvili actually worked for Russia, not for Georgia. Noting my skepticism, he explained, "Look at the situation into which he maneuvered us. On the surface, he has always been aggressively anti-Russian. He has never missed an opportunity to insult them. Then he started this idiotic war last year, knowing that we would lose it. But nobody can touch him because the Russians refuse to deal with him and have requested his dismissal. Nobody wants to play into Russian hands and interfere in our internal matters. So in the end, because of Russia, he has to stay in power. What a masterpiece!"

"It is the ideal situation for Russia. He is messing Georgia up to their advantage and yet remains their proclaimed enemy," agreed another conspiracy theorist.

"And in the meantime, Russian business dominates our market. We are totally dependent on Russian energy. And Russians are aggressively buying up Georgian property and doing all the investing," Gia added.

What is the truth? Who is Saakashvili? A "beacon of democracy" and pro-Western leader, friend of the United States? A reformer and modernizer? Or is he at heart a *homo sovieticus*, the former Komsomol member consciously or subconsciously playing into the hands of Russia? Or a Russian agent as believed by some? Only the future may tell. As with most else in the Caucasus, nothing is as it seems.

Chapter 21

UNOMIG: Mission Impossible

The United Nations Observer Mission to Georgia (UNOMIG) was established in 1993 as part of the international effort to sustain the cease-fire brokered between Georgia and her breakaway province, Abkhazia. The agreement was subsequently expanded in 1994, as part of the new Agreement on Cease-fire and Separation of Forces, known as the Sochi agreement for the city where it was negotiated. The Sochi Agreement provided for the deployment of a Commonwealth of Independent States Peacekeeping Force (CIS-PKF) to maintain separation of the warring parties and to monitor compliance with the agreement. The UNOMIG's mandate was to monitor implementation of the agreement, observe the performance of the CIS-PKF and verify its compliance, and patrol the Kodori Gorge in the east of Abkhazia.

The mission was strictly observatory. Daily monitoring of the cease-fire and overall situation was carried out by unarmed military observers in the Gali and Zugdidi sectors and in Kodori whenever security conditions permitted. The UNOMIG's mandate also included regular reporting on the situation to the UN Security Council and facilitation of dialogue between the parties in conflict. The UNOMIG's mandate was limited to Abkhazia while the OSCE was entrusted with South Ossetia.

From its creation, the UNOMIG participated in the search for a lasting solution to the conflict. The UN led numerous efforts aimed at preventing the violence and increasing confidence between the adversaries to build a foundation for long-term peace. One of the most promising UN proposals was the so-called Boden Plan, named for the UN Special Representative of the Secretary-General at the time, Dieter Boden, drafted in 2001. The plan, as proposed, outlined a distribution of responsibilities and powers between the central Georgian government in Tbilisi and the Abkhaz government in Sukhumi within the framework of the Georgian federal state. The plan was rejected outright by the Abkhaz as it defined Abkhazia as an integral part of Georgia. A subsequent proposal submitted by Shevardnadze was rejected on the same grounds.

In early 2003, a new attempt was made to reach a comprehensive solution through tackling three critical aspects of the conflict: the security and political situation, the requirements for economic development, and the return of IDPs. Under the auspices of the UN, a working group known as the Friends of the UN Secretary-General—comprised of representatives from France, Germany, United Kingdom, United States, and Russia—was formed and tasked with developing proposals to address each of these critical issues.

At the same time, a similar agreement was reached between Shevardnadze and Putin, who were engaged in parallel negotiations in Sochi. The key areas that agreement addressed included: return of IDPs to Abkhazia, first to the Gali region and then later to other parts; creation of a mixed police force, consisting of Abkhaz and international police, to provide security in Gali; re-establishment of rail transport between Sochi and Tbilisi via Abkhazia; and repair of the Inguri hydroelectric power station in Abkhazia, which provided areas of Georgia, Russia, and Abkhazia with electricity.

Each proposal was rejected by the Abkhaz.

In response, the UNOMIG revised its approach and decided to attempt to undertake some incremental steps aimed at encouraging the parties to learn from the experiences of other countries in similar circumstances. It organized a study trip to Bosnia and Herzegovina and Kosovo to study the results of their respective police reforms, ongoing international police training and efforts to integrate minority returnees.

Having previous experience in the Balkans, I was entrusted with organizing this high-level tour of senior politicians and civil servants from Georgia and Abkhazia, to be led by the head of the UNOMIG, Heidi Tagliavini. The formalities related to the tour were unceasing and caused considerable headache to colleagues in the UN administration and elsewhere who had to deal with its diplomatic aspects. Abkhazia was not recognized as a state, and Abkhaz "passports" were therefore not valid internationally. Although all high-level Abkhaz politicians had Russian citizenship and carried Russian passports, the tour offered them an opportunity to press the point of Abkhaz nationality further and insist on traveling as Abkhaz citizens. As there were no direct flights from Tbilisi to Sarajevo or Pristina, and the only connecting flight between Sarajevo and Pristina was via Vienna, the trip required endless changes of planes and transits and related visa arrangements. Thus, the mission had to deal with absurd logistical arrangements and organize a trip around Europe for people without valid travel documents. But it was done.

The very act of having the adversaries together for over a week at all daily meetings and meals, and in the same hotels, buses and cars was unusual and provided a framework for their "forced socializing." In these informal settings, unlike in conference rooms, they seemed to be at ease with each other. They were also interested in the program that we had prepared but were not completely convinced that it was not staged for their benefit. They were particularly surprised at the level of security, which allowed them to walk around safely in the evening, along crowded streets and in shops.

"Can we walk around?" I was asked in Sarajevo and then in Pristina. "Do you think that we can go on our own shopping?"

They were also surprised by the new constructions, mainly of family houses, along the road to Banja Luka. "You see the millions invested by the West," one Abkhaz participant remarked. "We could also do well with such money."

They were equally impressed by the visit to the international police training center in Kosovo. The center was well-equipped and the mood friendly. We believed that the samples of good practices on display at the center, although applicable to both sides, would be particularly relevant to the situation in the Gali region in Abkhazia where, based on a previous agreement, a small contingent of international police was about to be deployed. Thus, it was anticipated that the "lessons learned" from the visit would encourage Abkhaz cooperation with the international police force there. Both sides were also invited to send some of their police cadets to the training center in Kosovo. The UN Security Council, in remarking on the report on the study tour submitted to it by the UNOMIG, noted that this innovative approach to the frozen conflict was appreciated.

Nonetheless, soon after our return to Tbilisi and the arrival of the first contingent of the international police force, comprised of officers from various European countries ready to take up their positions in the Gali region, the Abkhaz refused to allow their deployment. It was a total reversal of their previous position with no justification. And of course, there was no way to enforce the previous commitment. The foreign police officers were temporarily stationed in Sukhumi and Zugdidi, in Georgia proper, next to the cease-fire line. The assignments of those who had not yet arrived were cancelled.

* * *

In September 2004, Saakashvili proposed a new peace plan and a road map for resolving the conflicts in Abkhazia and South Ossetia to the UN General Assembly. It included a three-phase approach consisting of a set of confidence-building measures and calling for demilitarization of the conflict zone, deployment of impartial UN observers, and the fullest possible autonomy of both regions within Georgia. The plan was immediately rejected by the two entities.

Despite UN efforts, there had been no breakthrough in the situation in Abkhazia since the cease-fire in 1994. In spite of numerous diplomatic initiatives, the stalemate continued and other critical issues were left unattended. There had been no basic change in the situation of the IDPs who continued to live in inhumane conditions, whose human rights continued to be systematically violated, and for whom the possibility of return was not getting any closer. The security situation in Abkhazia, particularly the Gali region, remained precariously dangerous, affecting especially its Georgian population. Economic stagnation and isolation prevailed, and the unresolved political problems and lack of basic security and rule of law prevented any broader economic intervention by the international community. Small-scale projects aimed at providing immediate support for local housing or agriculture amounted to humanitarian assistance rather than development aid.

The various approaches and frameworks employed to address the problems of Abkhazia and South Ossetia turned out to be ineffective, or even counterproductive. According to Alexander Rondeli, head of the Georgian Foundation for Strategic and International Studies, neither the involvement of the OSCE nor the UN had been particularly helpful. The OSCE was "blackmailed by Russia," he said and could not perform its mandated role in South Ossetia. As for the UN, he was of the view that it practically contributed to the consolidation of the status quo in Abkhazia. This view was echoed by some experts on the Caucasus after the 2008 war and formal recognition of Abkhazia and South Ossetia by Russia.

But was the absence of progress and failure to achieve a solution satisfactory to all parties the fault of these intergovernmental organizations? Should the finger be pointed in their direction only? Before judgment is made, the following points should be considered:

The UN mandate was weak. It was strictly observatory, authorized under Chapter VI of the UN Charter, which required the consent of the parties involved for its implementation, and not Chapter VII, which would have allowed for enforcement measures upon UN Security Council authorization.

- In the early 1990s, Georgia agreed to various compromise solutions under Russian pressure, among them allowing the CIS (read Russia) to lead the peacekeeping force in the conflict zone. These preexisting bilateral agreements severely restricted the framework within which the UN could act. Both Shevardnadze and Saakashvili wanted the CIS-PKF to be replaced by a UN force, but they knew that it could not be achieved without the broad political support of key Western partners. Shevardnadze raised the issue with US leaders and the UN Secretary-General at the time, Boutros Boutros-Ghali. They advised him against such a move. Similarly, under Saakashvili's presidency, attempts were made to gain the support of the European Union. While high-ranking EU representatives acknowledged as legitimate Georgia's attempts to replace Russian peacekeepers on her territory with an international force, they also pointed to the "unnecessarily provocative" tone of Georgian statements and deeds toward Russia. Javier Solana, the EU high representative for Common Foreign and Security Policy, as well as others, made it clear that the EU would not respond positively to such a request, if ever made.
- Georgia, following the advice of her Western partners, did not make a formal request seeking an international peacekeeping force, to avoid antagonizing Russia. The issue of deploying a UN peacekeeping force to replace the CIS-PKF was therefore never formally put before the UN Security Council, and thus, never a subject of UN consideration.

Russia controlled and manipulated the peace process.

- Russia played multiple roles in the negotiations and actions on the ground. Russia's omnipresence and domination of the peace process was never challenged by any other state with the exception of Georgia on occasion. Russia's duplicity was instead silently accepted.
- Similarly, the fact of Abkhazia's total dependency on Russia was formally ignored. Russia, as a result, often played at both ends of the table. It presented itself as a facilitator of peace, taking part in international peace negotiations and task forces established to tackle the critical problems in the conflict areas (security, economic development, status of IDPs), and participating in confidence-building measures and then was behind the Abkhaz rejection of these same agreements and initiatives or obstruction of their implementation. Officially, such were accepted as Abkhaz decisions as it was the party controlling the disputed territory. Russia, formally, was not recognized as having anything to do with the decisions.
- Russia's duplicity, proseparatist position, and complete lack of neutrality in the conflicts were thus never challenged. Georgia was the only country to lodge an occasional protest against Russian actions. For example, she tried to stop the process of granting Russian passports to the inhabitants of Abkhazia. Nino Burjanadze, the speaker of the Georgian Parliament, argued in 2005 that "Russia has to make a choice. It can be either a peacekeeper and a civilized state or a state that supports separatism and terrorism." She called on the parliament to reconsider the role of Russia in the conflict zones and formally request withdrawal of Russian peacekeepers. Such a demand, of course, would not have been supported by the IC precisely because it would antagonize Russia.

The international community did not insist upon adherence to preexisting agreements and international law and was too accommodating of the Abkhaz.

- While there was very little that the IC could do given the embedded role of Russia and the various bilateral agreements that existed, the IC's often uncritical search for solutions to accommodate the ever-changing "Abkhaz" demands did not help. It resulted in a kind of cat-and-mouse game, leading politically nowhere, wasting time, and consolidating the status quo to the advantage of the Abkhaz and Russians.

- The search for new solutions—combined with the constant interruptions of negotiations due to provocations, military incidents, and violations of the ceasefire agreement—gave the priority to "keeping the peace-process alive," compromising substance for form. Typically, previously agreed-upon principles were quickly forgotten, and new negotiating forums created. No one bothered to keep the talks in line either with previous agreements or principles of international law and insist upon the principle of *pacta sunt servanda*.

The Abkhaz position was uncompromising, and they did not in good faith seek a negotiated solution acceptable to all parties.

- In all negotiations, declarations, and actions during all phases of the conflict, Abkhaz authorities insisted on sovereignty, rejecting anything less. This position was known to reflect the sentiments of the Abkhaz people. Occasionally, however, Abkhaz authorities would ask Russia to grant Abkhazia the status of an "associated member" of the Russian Federation. As both options were incompatible with the territorial integrity of Georgia, not to mention prior agreements, the negotiations, in terms of their long-term objectives, were bound to fail from the beginning.

The separation and isolation of the Georgian and Abkhaz people from the other diminished the potential for reconciliation.

- The Georgian and Abkhazian societies were increasingly becoming separated. There was no attempt to reconcile them and increase their contacts as part of the peace process. The isolation, the prevailing image of the other as "enemy" (perpetuated by the isolation), the hostile rhetoric and propaganda, and the extreme poverty suffered by both populations created the conditions for continued suspicion and animosity rather than dialogue.

The UN was unable to act independently given that it was tasked with supervising Russia's compliance and simultaneously reliant upon Russia to provide security for its observer missions in the conflict areas.

- The UNOMIG was put in an impossible position. The question should have been asked, how can the UN monitor the work of the CIS-PKF, dominated almost exclusively by Russians, as part of its mandate, when (a) it reported to the UN Security Council on which Russia was a permanent member, and (b) the mission had to rely on this same entity, Russia, to protect it in the conflict areas? Some UN observers were very much aware of abuses committed against the population in the Gali by Russian forces or forces under its helm, in collusion with the local authorities. While the observers managed on some occasions to provide assistance to the victims, there was no climate for official reporting of such incidents to the UN Security Council. Politically, it was not possible. In the prevailing climate, neither the UNOMIG's leadership nor UN Headquarters in New York was willing to take the political risk and provoke Russia, especially if the UN would not get political support of other states.
- The UNOMIG was dependent upon the CIS-PKF/Russia for its security. This point cannot be understated. The mission's military observers—of which there were only a handful and those few were unarmed—together with the UNOMIG's security team did not have the capacity to resist an attack on its premises or staff. This security situation rendered the directive calling for UN supervision of Russian forces even more ridiculous.

In reality, nobody was prepared to critically assess the role and performance of the CIS peacekeeping operation, which has been "appreciated" in virtually all (if not all) UN Security Council reports, year after year, since 1994, even in recent years although the "peacekeeping" operation was almost exclusively Russian and it lacked a CIS mandate. With Russia's unilateral recognition of Abkhaz independence, UN Security Council reports have been silent on the cause for the crisis. Similarly, nobody has attempted to analyse the UN role in Abkhazia from its commencement in 1993 and assess why it failed to implement its mandate, play a crisis-management role in the summer of 2008, and prevent the abandonment of the commitment to the territorial integrity as applied to Georgia.

It was not until the report to the UN Security Council on the events of August 2008 that it was admitted that the UNOMIG had been "denied freedom of movement, threatened with weapons, and intimidated on numerous occasions by Russian and Abkhaz forces." The report nonetheless concluded with the traditional note of thanks to the CIS-PKF. The report also continued to refer to the situation as the Georgian-Abkhazian conflict, despite the fact that Russian troops had advanced into Georgian territory. Old habits apparently die really hard.

*   *   *

Abkhazia was the only former Soviet zone where a UN presence was accepted by the Russians. The price of this acceptance, however, was politically very high and should serve as a lesson learned by the UN. It was during this period that the de facto integration of Abkhazia into Russia took place. It was also during this period that over 90 percent of Abkhazia's inhabitants acquired Russian passports, that the UNOMIG's freedom of movement and capacity to perform its mandate were seriously restricted, and that Russia assumed virtually complete control of the Abkhaz territory and its politics.

Ultimately, favoring form over substance undermined the process. Diplomatic efforts were too often, if not always, based on the false premise that all partners were equal and that Georgia and Abkhazia were the only parties to the conflict. Quiet acceptance of this fiction by the international community created a situation in which "activity" and "process" were given precedence over substance. With the recognition of Abkhazian statehood by Russia, such pretences were no longer necessary. The UN was asked to close down its observatory mission in Abkhazia as was the OSCE in the case of South Ossetia.

One year after the 2008 war, the UNOMIG ceased to exist. No international presence now exists in Abkhazia, except for Russian forces.[*]

---

[*]   While the UN Observer Mission in Georgia was formally and completely concluded, the OSCE's mandate was transferred to the EU Monitoring Mission in Georgia.

Chapter 22

Abashidze and the Council of Europe: An Odd Alliance

In the spring of 2004, Adjaria, its capital city of Batumi and the ruling Abashidze clan found themselves in the eye of the storm generated by the Rose Revolution. Adjaria, located in the southwestern corner of Georgia along the Turkish border, had developed into a separate, autonomous administrative entity. Unlike Abkhazia and South Ossetia, Adjaria had not demanded independence from Georgia, but it nonetheless enjoyed a high degree of economic and administrative independence. Shevardnadze and Aslan Abashidze, the leader of Adjaria, had quietly agreed to this so-called autonomy in exchange for Abashidze's neutrality during Georgia's political upheavals in the 1990s. As a result, Adjaria stopped paying revenues to the central budget, introduced its own system of customs and tax collection (all going to the Abashidze family), and installed road blocks at its borders to control the movement of people and goods and extract payments. Abashidze enjoyed unspecified and, in reality, dictatorial powers. He controlled Adjaria's economy, police and security forces, as well as its mass media, to include the television station.

Adjaria's traditional wealth came from its access to the Black Sea and possession of an oil terminal used for the transfer of oil coming from Azerbaijan to other parts of the world. Its position along the Turkish border also provided a unique opportunity for cross-border transactions, mainly illicit. A narrow coastal road connecting Adjaria with Turkey was easy to control and constituted one of the main contraband routes in the area.

Batumi and its surroundings, typical of Black Sea resorts, would make for an impressive tourist destination. However, the lack of proper infrastructures, development, and maintenance has gradually reduced Batumi to shambles. Neglected gray concrete buildings, overgrown sea promenades, and decaying villas marred the landscape of this potentially beautiful and prosperous city.

The Abashidze clan, however, prospered enormously. They enjoyed unchecked power and unlimited financial resources. They played a role comparable to that of feudal princes as if nothing had changed since the fifteenth century when their ancestors ruled Adjaria. The family treated the province as if it were their private property and had managed to maintain their dominant position over the centuries. They even survived Stalin's terror although Aslan's grandfather was executed on Stalin's orders, and his father sent to Siberia for long years.

Aslan Abashidze's lavish lifestyle was well-known. Villas with parks, swimming pools, and tennis courts, boats, fast cars, and private jets stood in sharp contrast to the impoverished condition of the Adjarian people and the daily hardship they experienced. At his estate in Batumi, Abashidze eagerly entertained foreign guests, politicians, and celebrities using such occasions to display his wealth and power. His grand parties and the expensive gifts he showered on his guests were themselves famous. In the years immediately following Georgian independence, Abashidze was, undoubtedly, the richest man in Georgia—and of that he was proud.

Abashidze skilfully played on the regional disagreements and conflicts. He also ingratiated himself with the Soviet Union and her successor, Russia. He was generally critical of the Georgian government as disorganized, arrogant, and incompetent and considered the Georgian political system too democratic and, therefore, ineffective. He never missed an opportunity to underscore that Adjaria, unlike Georgia, had no problems with street crime, theft, civil unrest, or insubordination. Indeed, he often liked to compare himself to Franz Josef Strauss and Adjaria to Bavaria.

A seasoned politician, Abashidze rightly assumed that the Rose Revolution would not stop at the road blocks at Adjaria's border and perceived the movement to be a threat to his own power. He undertook a number of actions to stop it. Although there was no love lost between him and Shevardnadze, Abashidze tried to build an alliance to prevent his dismissal. He also embarked on an extensive and widely publicised diplomatic tour across the region and to some European capitals seeking support and made every effort to prevent the spread of the protests. He presented himself as a leading statesman with the ability to turn the tide and ensure stability in the region. He visited Russia, neighboring Armenia and Azerbaijan, and the Council of Europe in Strasbourg.

He used his media monopoly to promote his nonstop campaign against the Georgian "hooligans" and "foreign agents" and actively spread misinformation about the developments in Tbilisi, falsely reporting the forthcoming end of the demonstrations, a military takeover by forces loyal to Shevardnadze, and protests by some "patriotic" Georgians and foreign diplomats against the "coup."

With time, Adjarian television was turned into one big show of support for Abashidze. As in the former Soviet Union, Ceausescu's Rumania and Mao's China, the government-controlled TV broadcasted daily workers' meetings in support of Abashidze, featuring workers expressing their gratitude for his generosity and leadership and threatening his enemies with the hell of consequences if they attacked the paradise of Adjaria. For a time, Abashidze and his entourage briefly joined such meetings to encourage broader participation. That led to an explosion of enthusiasm: women ran to embrace Abashidze to thank him for their secure lives and families, children greeted him with flowers, and some participants composed songs for him, others wrote poems. It was a picture of joy and happiness *à la* Adjaria.

With the subsequent victory of the opposition in Georgia, it became clear that the Abashidze regime's days were numbered. The Rose Revolution soon began to move toward Adjaria, infecting its inhabitants, who despite claims to the contrary by the government-controlled news outlets, were genuinely dissatisfied. They lived in economic conditions comparable to those of Shevardnadze's Georgia, were victims of rampant corruption and rapidly declining living standards, and had no prospects. But unlike Georgians, Adjarians still lived under a repressive, Soviet-type regime, one distinguished by its use of oppressive security forces, censorship, centrally controlled media, and brutal suppression of any criticism of or opposition to the Abashidze regime.

The substantial income earned from the Batumi oil terminal was stolen outright by the Abashidze clan and the Adjarian people benefited little, if at all, from its enormous profits. This was also the case with the receipts from the harbor and border controls, which Abashidze regime officials shared in part with those directly involved in the trafficking of contraband. There were broad accusations of other ongoing criminal activities, including involvement in the narco business and illicit arms trade.

Under Saakashvili, Georgia's demand that Adjaria integrate into its federal structure gained traction. Unlike Abkhazia and South Ossetia, there were no formal obstacles, and Georgia's actions received broad international support. Abashidze regime's obvious violations of the basic human rights of the Adjarian people who, significantly, were also Georgian citizens, further strengthened the Georgian position. Saakashvili cited existing legal regulations, according to which, *inter alia*: Adjaria was part and parcel of Georgia and, as such, could be legally integrated into Georgian structures; and the inhabitants of Adjaria, as Georgian citizens, could claim their legal rights under Georgian law on equal standing with Georgians in other parts of the country. Saakashvili also declared that the "privatization" of Adjaria by the Abashidze clan was not only unconstitutional, it was criminal. These statements were followed by calls from Georgian leaders (Saakashvili in particular) on the population of Adjaria to join in the Rose Revolution, throw out the Abashidze regime, and demand democratic elections.

The calls fell on sympathetic ears. Despite restrictions imposed by the Abashidze regime, the demand for free elections in Adjaria was getting stronger. They began initially with small peaceful protests in the streets of Batumi, at which the participants were treated harshly, beaten, and arrested. But the events in Adjaria were widely broadcast across Georgia in spite of the strict media restrictions, attracting public interest and support. And the Georgian government called on the Council of Europe (CoE) to assist in restoring democracy and human rights on its territory, namely in Adjaria.

The CoE responded. In February 2004, President Saakashvili and Walter Schwimmer, secretary-general of the council, traveled together to Adjaria. They were accompanied by other members of the Georgian government and Plamen Nikolov, the CoE's representative in Georgia. The meeting with Abashidze led nowhere, but the visit had encouraged mass demonstrations. Crowds of unprecedented size gathered in front of Abashidze's office where the delegations were meeting. The demonstration was peaceful and the demands, including calls for Abashidze's departure, were clearly articulated. In response, the Adjarian government dispatched a large security contingent to the scene, the officers of which soon turned on the demonstrators, brutally attacking the generally peaceful civilians. The protestors were beaten and arrested in front of TV cameras. The visiting dignitaries watched the events from the balcony of Abashidze's villa. Saakashvili was outraged. Walter Schwimmer quickly departed.

The push for democratic change in Adjaria continued; it had already reached the point of no return. Adjaria had been shaken by her own version of the Rose Revolution. Since the CoE's memorable visit, the unrest had continued to grow, and Abashidze started losing control of the situation. It seemed as if he believed the fiction of his own propaganda broadcast across Adjarian TV and could not face the reality: Were these demonstrations really against him? How could that be? His security agents, one by one, began to defect to Tbilisi. Some gave press interviews critical of Abashidze. It was obvious that the new government of Georgia was working behind the scenes to encourage and speed up the process. Abashidze looked for outside alliances, but there were none.

In late April, the Georgian parliament adopted a resolution condemning Abashidze's leadership as "an open attempt to encroach on the country's territorial integrity" and calling on authorities to "restore the rule of law and order within the constitutional borders of Georgia." Georgia then began large-scale military exercises in Poti, just north of Batumi. Abashidze responded by demolishing the three bridges connecting the province to the rest of Georgia. The move would trigger the final blow to his regime. Georgian security forces intervened in May 2004, arriving on the night of mass demonstrations, taking control of the remaining handful of security officers loyal to Abashidze. The security intervention was accompanied by the spectacular entry into Adjaria of Georgian government officials, lead by the president, who formally took over the province. There were no casualties.

Abashidze resigned and accepted an invitation to leave for Moscow, conveyed to him in person by the Russian foreign minister, Sergei Ivanov, who also appeared in Adjaria on that fateful night. For the second time in the span of a few months, Russia was assisting in the removal of a political ally from power in Georgia.

In the months leading to the intervention, particularly in late April to early May, both sides had aggressively attempted to mobilize broad international support. While there was clear political support for Georgia throughout most of the diplomatic community, the CoE took a "neutral" position. Schwimmer stated, "Just as the European Council is celebrating enlargement from 15 to 25 States, it is shocking to hear that in another CoE state, Georgia, bridges are exploded because the central and the local authorities have lost their ability to dialogue." The statement was reiterated by the Council's representative in Georgia, Plamen Nikolov. It provoked outrage in Georgia. Georgian authorities responded with an unprecedented diplomatic offensive against the CoE.

The strongest criticism came from the country's president, Saakashvili. During a meeting at the University of Batumi on May 9, he remarked, "We do not like it, [what] they said—as if both sides were equally to blame. That is not the position of a European. It is the position of an arrogant bureaucrat with a bloated salary with a careless attitude." Saakashvili pressed further and noted that "[w]hen [the] demonstration was broken up in Batumi before Schwimmer's eyes he just got up, put his hat on and left Batumi by plane . . . Georgians themselves can teach a lot to people who behave like Schwimmer and his cli[que]."

The next day, on May 10, Saakashvili continued in the same manner, stating, "I think that the Secretariat has adopted an extremely unconstructive position . . . It was completely at odds with the position of the Parliamentary Assembly of the CoE, it was completely at odds with the EU's position . . . and the American position. It was the position of a bureaucrat who had somehow been lured along by Aslan Abashidze—I do not know how[.]"

Nino Burjanadze, the parliamentary speaker, tried to smooth these statements, emphasizing, "We value relations with the CoE . . . That was probably the reason for our strong reaction . . . I am sure that the President's reaction [was] prompted precisely by the failure of an international organization—that had been most friendly to us—to make an appropriate and correct assessment of events."

Other members of the Georgian government went on the offensive as well. The country's foreign minister, Salome Zurabashvili, too objected to the CoE's statement as incorrect and not reflecting the real situation. She subsequently traveled to Strasburg to make the case against Schwimmer and Nikolov.

The controversy generated significant press, and the media started reporting stories aimed at explaining the CoE's bias. They implied that there had been a long-standing personal friendship between Abashidze and Nikolov who, allegedly, frequently visited Adjaria and enjoyed Abashidze's hospitality. Similar allegations were made against

Schwimmer. Some publications even alluded to financial corruption. Vano Merabishvili, secretary of the Georgian National Security Council, went so far as to publicly state, "The CoE secretary general should serve the CoE members' interests and not pay visits to a feudal lord (Abashidze) and receive expensive gifts from him."

The CoE did not respond directly to these accusations. Georgia demanded Schwimmer's replacement, whose term of office was about to end in any case, on grounds of pro-Abashidze bias and breach of the Council's mandate to support democracy and human rights. The scenes from the demonstration, including his speedy departure, were broadly circulated and self-explanatory. The Saakashvili government soon announced that the CoE ambassador was no longer welcome in Georgia, and should leave without unnecessary delay. "If Plamen Nikolov is not recalled from Georgia, if the CoE does not take him from here, the *persona non grata* procedure will be applied," stated the spokesman of the Georgian Ministry of Foreign Affairs.

Nikolov quietly left Georgia that June. Schwimmer, whose term was about to end, was replaced by Terry Davis, as the new secretary general of CoE.

Chapter 23

Democracy of the Fist:
The Georgian Crisis of 2007

Tbilisi, 2007. The same golden autumn; sunny, sometimes misty and melancholy. Dusty streets alive with crowds and lined with decaying buildings. Stylish cafés and well-dressed women. The city had been again overtaken by politics, infused with the energy of spontaneous gatherings, antigovernment demonstrations and high-spirited, bitter debates. There was a sense that the government, and Saakashvili personally, had failed to deliver on the promise of the Rose Revolution and that life had not become any better for most Georgians, except of course, the rich who, as usual, kept making fortunes.

Across the country, the poor continued to live in dehumanizing conditions and sizable parts of the city continued to decay, while historical monuments were renovated at substantial cost. Corruption prevailed, albeit in a new form, "elite corruption." The coalition that had so successfully defeated Shevardnadze just four years prior had fractured with the various factions publicly turning on each other. And the government that had assumed power with the promise of making a better life for Georgians and governing democratically was increasingly being accused of arrogance, repression, disrespect for the society, and inability to deliver.

Some official data contradicted the negative assessments: Georgia was one of the most attractive countries in which to invest, its GDP continued to rise, a new roads system had been built connecting all parts of the country, massive construction and investments projects in Tbilisi and in the surrounding areas were improving the quality of life, attracting foreign business and providing new employment opportunities. But the people were nonetheless disappointed and taking their grievances to the streets.

The increasing public criticism and street protests against the government in the autumn of 2007 called to mind similar scenes from November 2003. The demonstrations were organized by ten opposition parties who had joined together to establish the National Council. The National Council compiled a list of complaints addressed to the Saakashvili government. Corruption, abuse of power, disrespect for human rights, and lack of social and economic development were among the grievances cited. On November 2, the council organized large-scale demonstrations, which lasted five days before they were put down by Georgian security forces on orders of Saakashvili. Arrests, beatings, and a citywide curfew followed. Unlike his predecessor four years earlier, Saakashvili used brutal force against his political opponents, against the Georgian people.

Saakashvili's actions provoked outcry across Europe and in the United States and further antagonized discontented Georgians. The repression seriously shattered Saakashvili's image as a modern politician and "beacon of democracy." Although Saakashvili called for new elections, which he subsequently won in January 2008, the problems did not go away. Instead, the opposition pulled together, attracting broader support from people outraged by Saakashvili's actions.

Many of my interlocutors considered these events a turning point in the consolidation of the current political fronts. On one side was a broad, though loose, opposition convinced that Saakashvili had to go. On the other stood Saakashvili and his inner circle determined to stay in power, ruling the country by fist, if needed. Indeed, since the autumn of 2007, accusations of abuse of power and human rights violations were on increase, a system of repression was gradually being institutionalized, and a sense of fear had spread through the society. Under Saakashvili, violence and the use of force had become means of governance and problem solving.

Human rights organizations, lawyers, the public defender of Georgia (the ombudsman), and key opposition members were in agreement as to the main manifestations of this autocracy, this "democracy of the fist":

- *There were increasing restrictions on freedom of press in Georgia.* Independent media was silenced, and there was de facto censorship. No criticism of the president or his inner circle was permitted. The government adopted Soviet-era propaganda, referring to opponents as "subversive elements," "spies," and "foreign agents"—the only difference being that now "foreign" implied Russian, rather than American spies. The government also attempted to use the media and public relations stunts to improve the image of government officials.

- *People were deprived of basic rights related to access to justice.* Judges were not independent, court proceedings and procedures flagrantly violated, due process rights denied, and lawyers made "unavailable." Prosecutors were empowered with undue authority and interfered with law enforcement and judicial proceedings at all stages of the proceedings and beyond. Suspects, many who happened to belong to the opposition, were arrested and held *incommunicado* for weeks at a time, in blatant disregard of their basic rights, and without pronouncement of the legal grounds for the arrest or court order.

- *There were increasing incidents of torture, kidnapping, and disappearances.* Opposition members and demonstrators were followed, put under surveillance, intimidated (as were family members and associates), and in some cases, tortured, kidnapped, and disappeared. For example, it was commonly known that the black and silver jeeps circling opposition meetings were there to stake out the gatherings and target their participants on the way home, assaulting and kidnapping them. "We made photos of those cars," a human rights defender, told me, "with their registration numbers and took them to the Ministry of Internal Affairs. They simply told us that they had no knowledge of such cars and that even though the registration plates were Georgian, they could have been photographed anywhere in Europe. So it proved nothing, they said."

- *Police brutality and anonymity of actions were on the rise.* The photos on display in front of the parliament represented victims allegedly killed by the police. Many believed the actual list of victims to be much longer. There was a growing awareness that government security forces were perpetuators of severe beatings, arbitrary arrests, and detentions in inhumane conditions—in windowless cellars without access to water and toilet facilities—and that they used drugs, sleep deprivation, and other torture techniques to extract forced confessions and to increase the sense of fear in the society.

- *Political opponents were targeted by law enforcement and prosecutors and charged with trumped-up criminal offences.* In Georgia, there were few cases of alleged treason, subversion, or civil disturbance. Rather, demonstrators and political opposition members were targeted following demonstrations and later arrested for alleged involvement with drugs and gun trafficking or theft. "Can you imagine," one activist told me, "that in the few weeks since the demonstration over fifty participants have been arrested on such criminal charges? These were people with good reputation and no criminal record. So we have no political prisoners in Georgia, only criminals."

- *There were serious violations of property rights and cases of outright misappropriation of private property of citizens by government authorities.* Misappropriated goods ranged from cars and personal effects to houses, workshops, and other commercial enterprises. Such actions were ostensibly taken on behalf of the state, but often directly benefited the officials involved, who acted with impunity, without regard for the law or fear of repercussion. This "elite corruption" has continued unabated with most, though certainly not all, victims who happen to be political opponents or their associates.

I started to dwell further on these accusations. The sense of fear pervading the society as a result of these transgressions by the government was, perhaps, the most shocking change I noted compared to 2003. People did not want to discuss political matters over phones, in the car, or at the office; and they tended to whisper rather than talk. They dreaded being beaten, losing their jobs, or endangering their family.

"But how could it happen? How could things have evolved in this direction since the Rose Revolution?" I asked.

"I thought that with the Rose Revolution my troubles and activities would be over," Nana, the human right defender, told me. "I had joined the NGO's front against Shevardnadze to make the change. The government was weak and had no authority, and the opposition carried promise. Today, I have to admit that it was a mistake. The situation is now worse than ever.

"We have a sham democracy," another human rights lawyer stated. "Our president managed in a relatively short time to create a system of closed decision making. Gradually, he surrounded himself with a group of people who basically control the state unchecked. They take all basic decisions which suit them, and afterward legitimize them by implementing new laws or executive orders. Some of the laws are not bad as such but are abused and misused. For example, it is not wrong to confiscate a stolen car as long as the procedure is strictly regulated. The way it works in Georgia, however, is different.

"We already went through a period in which many new and expensive cars were confiscated by the Ministry of Internal Affairs presumably because they were stolen. Some owners received a notice and went there, usually during the night, to "negotiate" their release. Others, however, tried to document the vehicle's legitimacy. As the cars had been imported, the officials kept asking for papers from abroad, and the owner was forced to keep making appeals, paying lawyers and so on. In the end, most got their cars back, but usually only after the cars had been damaged in accidents and ceased to be attractive to the high-ranking employees of the ministry."

Dato, a driver, told a similar story. His relative, Sergo, had purchased a car in Germany from an authorized dealer and brought it to Georgia. After a few weeks, his car was confiscated by the police as "acquired from an illegal source," in short, stolen. Sergo had all the required papers, but their validity was questioned. He was asked to "pay" for the car again at an amount close to the original price. He refused. The proceedings and negotiations through his lawyer continued. The car, as one of many confiscated, was stored in the parking lot of the police.

Then, one day, Sergo saw his car being driven through the streets of Tbilisi. "He thought he was having a bad dream," Dato recalled. "He rushed to the parking lot and found his car was not there. Over the next days, he started discretely watching it. Indeed, some men in plain clothes were using it. Who were they? The police? Their friends? Family? Sergo had no clue."

After six months of the ordeal, Sergo was able to find a proper "connection" to the senior police officer. He indicated that the car might be released shortly. It happened two weeks later, but the car was missing the front seats and headlights, and it was damaged. "It must have been in an accident prior to the confiscation," the releasing officer said in response to his complaint. "You should be grateful to get it back," he continued. "If you do not like it, we can send it out for scrap metal. You will get the confirmation in writing."

Sergo quickly signed the receipt for the car, disappeared from the office, and called on friends to help him to transport the wreck back to his courtyard.

"These are just a few examples," they continued. "There is no security and no guarantees for private property. The same can happen to your house, your livelihood, your business. It has never been like this before."

"Under Shevardnadze, we had widespread corruption. But like everything under Shevardnadze, even the corruption was more democratic. Now it is an 'elite' brand of corruption."

The story of Kacha, a shop owner in the city of Rustavi, was even more shocking. He was lucky and had gradually expanded his business contacts beyond Georgia to Germany and Turkey. He did not make a fortune, but considering local conditions, he was doing much better than the others. One day, two men appeared at his house. He had been absent so they took away and terrorized his sixteen-year-old son. As soon as he returned, he rushed to the police and raised hell demanding his son's release. The boy-hostage was set free, but Kacha was confronted with accusations of dealing in drugs. He protested, argued, and proclaimed innocence as he had never been mixed up in the drug scene. All in vain. He obviously had not gotten the message. He was arrested on the spot, allegedly because drugs had been found in the containers he had personally brought from Germany.

In his anger and frustration, Kacha overlooked the possibility of a "compromise." Had he accepted his "mistake" and made a "contribution" to a proper "NGO" fund, the matter could have been resolved. He asked for a lawyer instead. He was told that the lawyer's cell was switched off. He then asked for access to a phone so he could try to call himself but was refused. He had wanted to contact his wife but was informed that it could compromise the investigation. In cases of such serious allegations, all precautions had to be taken to prevent a suspect from making contact with his alleged criminal network, he was told. In the meantime, his house was searched and additional drugs were allegedly found. Kacha was sentenced to six years and today still sits in prison.

"He got stubborn and lost his sense of reality," his brother told me. "It was all unnecessary. They just wanted money, even a child knows it. The amount could have been negotiated. His main mistake was being outraged at the idea of being accused of having anything to do with drugs. He also did not want to be implicated or blackmailed in the future. But it was stupid. We should worry about our today in Georgia, not tomorrow. If he dies in prison, there will be no tomorrow."

Listening to these stories brought to mind the sensational case of Gia Jokhtaberidze, Shevardnadze's son-in-law, in the early days of Saakashvili's presidency. Jokhtaberidze was apprehended in spectacular fashion at the airport while attempting to board a plane to Paris. He was handcuffed and arrested in front of the gathered press. He was accused of tax evasion and obstruction of justice. His was meant to be a showcase, a demonstration that under the new government things would be different. Jokhtaberidze's detention, however, did not last long. His wife, in an equally public and spectacular fashion, paid the bail in cash, possibly even exceeding it, and took her husband home. Bail had been set at about US$15 million. She insisted that they had not done anything illegal and that their company had complied with all existing rules. She further declared that in order to resolve the matter and gain the release of her husband, she paid the estimated fine, in cash, without questioning the assessment.

"My husband did not like the idea initially," she said. "He wanted to fight, to prove that he was innocent and that our activities were legitimate. But I convinced him that it was not worth it. Georgia needed money, and the family needed him back home. Isn't it what any Georgian woman would do for her husband?"

I had been shocked then by those first lessons in democracy and the rule of law under Saakashvili, which amounted to a mockery of justice. Soon after the Jokhtaberidze incident, the new government declared a kind of amnesty: Those guilty of economic crimes who voluntarily came forward, declared their assets, and paid back a required amount would not be prosecuted. Saakashvili argued that it would keep businesses going and prevent the outflow of money abroad. He also argued that it would save budgetary expenditures by reducing the number of prisoners. The idea, however, was most controversial. It provided an easy way out for those involved in corrupt business practices and created a double standard of justice, one for the rich and another for the poor. Moreover, the process was far from transparent. It was unclear, for example, how the estimates were calculated and by which offices within the government. Neither was the process subjected to public scrutiny.

Georgia's bail system was equally corrupted and vulnerable to manipulation. My friends advised me, "There is an NGO called the Fund for Development of Justice to which certain defendants or alleged criminals pay their bail. The fund's status is not accessible to the public. There is no transparency. It is supervised by a kind of board. The amount of the 'contributions' is determined based on a 'procedural agreement' (*procesual soglaszenie*) negotiated by the prosecution and defense or victim. The system has been applied to redress all kinds of alleged legal violations, including crimes. Critics call it 'state racketeering.' It is obvious that in a deeply impoverished country like Georgia, the system protects those who can afford 'bail.' For most people, however, it is the choice between going to prison or giving away their meager possessions. Moreover, there is a feeling that some of the alleged violations are staged solely for the purpose of extortion or politically motivated."

"You never know when the police will knock at your door and claim that they have found drugs in your car or in your office or when they will produce witnesses claiming that you attempted some theft or assault. Some of these police actions have even been broadly broadcasted on the main TV channels," Sozar Subari, the Georgian ombudsman, told me.

"The worst, however, is the increasing terror aimed at political opponents or individuals who are not submissive to the authorities," Subari continued. "It is a deliberate promotion of fear. I have written numerous letters to the Minister of Interior and other authorities, addressed the president and parliament, and informed the international community. But my efforts have been met with indifference. 'There is no time for the human rights, first we have to build the state' is the sentiment.

"Sometimes, there are some gestures to demonstrate that the president cares. For example, after I sent the president an open letter on January 14, 2008, providing an account of the ongoing human rights violations and raising the issue of the still-ignored abuses committed by security forces during the November 2007 demonstrations, I received an unexpected visit. Misha, the president, burst into my office unannounced. He said he was concerned about my letter and wanted to hear more and help. We sat in my office and talked. I gave him the full picture as I saw it and as I had presented it in writing. He also wanted to know why I had been beaten so severely by the police during the November demonstrations.

"My case is well-known and recorded on DVD," he noted.

I knew it and had seen it.

"I was attacked during the peaceful phase of the demonstration. People were about to disperse when the security forces arrived on the scene and began attacking them. They started hitting me with bludgeons. 'What are you doing? He is a public defender,' some called out. 'We know who he is,' they answered and kept beating me. I suffered twenty-five injuries.

"I told the president that I was bringing up the details of the ordeal not because of personal resentment but because it was an attack on my office and the values it represented. He wanted to know what police were involved, what kind of uniforms they wore, in short, who did it. I referred him to his own ministers. How could I know?"

"So what was the outcome?" I inquired.

"He seemed to be unhappy about the state of affairs. He promised to help, look into the matters I raised, and take appropriate action. After he left the office, he was surrounded by a crowd of journalists, which had gathered, so he held a press conference that allowed him to express his support for human rights and democracy."

"And then?"

"Nothing. Nothing has changed. None of my queries have been answered. All pending cases are stuck somewhere in various offices, and people continue to be harassed. Oh, maybe one thing has changed," he said, smiling. "I was called the worse ombudsman in the world by some of our politicians. But they will not be forced to put up with me for much longer. This autumn my term is up, and obviously, I will not be reappointed."

Echoes of this conversation were reverberating in my mind when I met Aslan, a student from the University of Tbilisi, recently released from detention. He showed me his half-paralyzed hand.

"They broke it while I was in prison," he explained. "It did not properly heal because there were no doctors around, and it was not put in a cast. I can move only some fingers, and I have no feeling in parts of my palm."

Aslan's damaged hand was only one of the consequences he suffered as a result of his participation in demonstrations in front of the presidential residence. Yes, he knew that the demonstration was not officially legal, but it was peaceful. They were not disturbing public order or even blocking traffic. They just wanted to show to the president how disgusted they were with the state of affairs in the country and his brand of politics.

They had stood in front of the presidential residence holding posters calling for Saakashvili's resignation. They chanted "Georgia, Georgia." When the police arrived, they were prepared to be arrested and did not put up any resistance. But they did not anticipate the brutality and torture that followed. They were attacked, beaten, handcuffed, and thrown into police vans. Afterward, they were thrown into dark, wet basements in some unspecified location. They were kept in the darkness, in the mud, without water or access to toilets or other sanitary facilities. They were regularly beaten by men wearing masks who called them traitors and Russian spies and chanted "Misha, Misha" throughout the ordeal. They were occasionally hit with hammers through sacks thrown over their heads. They were not permitted to contact their families or lawyers as they were cut off from the outside world.

Aslan was released after one month. Some of his friends were still there. He was sure he would join them again soon as he was determined to fight the regime with all available peaceful means.

"According to the West, Georgia is the model post-Soviet democracy," Aslan stated. "Nobody wants to see anything else. Diplomatic representatives in Tbilisi do not want to convey home bad news. As the media is suppressed, there is not sufficient information. Human rights reports are not broadly read and often easily dismissed as biased, especially given the politically sensitive context. They do not want to understand that Saakashvili is not Georgia and that the Georgian people should have voice in their own country."

Sergo, owner of a restaurant and active member of the opposition, recalled his own ordeal: "After one of the street demonstrations called for by the opposition, I walked home. It was a peaceful event, and we were dispersing in various directions. It was already dark. Suddenly I sensed that I was being followed and picked up my pace. I had reached the courtyard of my house when I was attacked by three masked men. They pushed me to the ground, started hitting and kicking me. I managed to scream, but then, I felt hands pressing against my throat, and I lost not only my voice, but also my consciousness. I regained consciousness when the iron hands wrapped around my neck slightly relieved the pressure. They asked me, 'What are you up to? What have you decided at your meeting?' Then I felt the iron grip tighten again and passed out.

"Fortunately, I was close to home. The neighbors heard the commotion and rushed in my direction. The *sonder-brigaden* ran away. I was lucky. I recovered after a few days. Otherwise I would have constituted one more mysterious death, one which could never be solved. I wrote a complaint to the Ministry of Interior but did not get any answer."

"That is typical," Nana confirmed. "They either ignore complaints and requests for action or routinely reply that they will investigate providing they get more details. And what details can we give them? Tell them how black the masks were? What the assailants said? After all the assailants are never uniformed police officers, but masked individuals without identification. Why should the Ministry of Interior be responsible for them? They know nothing, right?"

Chapter 24

The Summer of Olympics, 2008

Skirmishes along the line separating South Ossetia and Georgia proper and the trade of mutual accusations were daily phenomena. A few villages at the border zone were affected. Nobody, however, expected that these incidents—even with the sharp rhetoric accompanying them from Tbilisi, Tshingali, and Moscow—would lead to the most severe political and military crisis since 1992: the war of August 2008.

It was opening night of the Beijing Olympics, on August 7, and the world was tuned in. Ruzi, my former cleaning lady, was watching from the outskirts of Poti, on the Black Sea coast where she stayed with her children. Though the area housed key Georgian military installations, she did not expect that the next day she would be fleeing a Russian attack on the area.

"We were enjoying our vacation on the seashore. It was wonderful," she told me dreamily. "For years, we used to go there every summer. It was the only luxury we afforded ourselves. I always put some money aside so we could spend some time there.

"Suddenly, we heard the planes and the shooting. I had no idea what was going on, but the people around us knew right away that the Russians were attacking and that there was war in South Ossetia. Don't ask me how, they just knew. I was horrified. I cannot stand war and the killing. I've had enough of that in my life.

"I decided to run away as quickly as possible, but it was difficult. The main road, the only real road leading back to Tbilisi, was already clogged with military personnel. We had to find a passage through some small back country roads. I was desperate. I felt like I was in a trance. I wanted to protect my children and be as far as possible from the rockets and gunfire.

"We spent a few days in a remote village with some distant relatives. They were quite poor and lived in tough conditions, but at least, they were far from the wars, politics, and intrigues. We did not know exactly what was going on because they did not have a TV, only an old radio, but it seemed that the shooting had stopped. After three weeks, we returned to Tbilisi, again taking back roads. Only there did we learn that the Russians had stopped just forty kilometres away and that they had taken control of Gori and the main road.

"When we arrived home in Tbilisi, I found a note on my apartment door requesting that my son report to the military commission. They had began drafting young men. My heart sank. I started worrying about my son," she confided. "Fortunately, our neighbour's son of the same age told us that it was over. He had been there a few days before. They had examined him and told him to report the next day, which he did. Nobody, however, paid him any attention. He was given a uniform and that was it. He was sent from one place to another, and at the end of the day, he simply returned home. They did not need him anymore."

"Who was commanding Georgian forces?" I asked.

"Our president," Ruzi responded, seemingly surprised by the question.

"Personally?" I asked, equally astonished.

"Yes. I thought it was obvious, but now that you ask I am not so sure anymore."

The matter was confirmed during my further discussion with David, an employee in one of the government ministries: "Yes, indeed, he was our commander-in-chief. He was directly giving orders, like the president of the United States in war time."

"But that is not what US presidents do. Even George W. Bush did not directly command the troops in Iraq. There is a professional military for that," I protested.

"Not in Georgia. Misha was running the military operations. He was occasionally assisted by the mayor of Tbilisi, Gigi Ugulava. Sometimes they could be seen driving around in military vehicles together."

"Is Ugulava a military officer?"

"No, he is a civilian. But he is a close friend of our president."

It was hard to believe, but the story had been around, and I heard it on a few more occasions during my visit. Some even noted that Saakashvili's direct intervention in the war theater had led to his conflicts with some senior military brass. They had not been part of the decision-making process or strategic planning, were marginalized during the hostilities, and blamed in the end for the results.

Marina, an IDP from South Ossetia, remembered that night and the events of the following days vividly. We are sitting in her two-room shelter, located close to Gori. She offered us fruits, tea, and sweets.

"I am sixty," she told me. "I have lived long enough to learn how to cope with rumors, threats, and misunderstandings. But I believe in reason and common sense to prevent war and destruction that in the end will not help anybody."

Marina had lived with her family in a mainly Georgian village in South Ossetia, close to the separation line from Georgia.

"Our lives were not bad. We had a large family house, one big enough to accommodate a multigenerational family, and lived off the farm," she told us.

There were problems, she said, but the situation was slowly improving. They had no complaints about the South Ossetian authorities and lived in harmony with their neighbors, irrespective of their nationality. The main problem was difficulty reaching Georgia proper. Due to the political circumstances, they could not take the most direct route to Georgia; rather, Georgia could only be reached by taking the mountain roads around, which made each trip long and exhausting.

Their lives had changed dramatically with the war. They knew that summer that something was going on: skirmishes between South Ossetian and Georgian forces had become more frequent and violent than usual, and people talked about the concentration of Russian forces and the possibility of war. Their neighbors had even started stocking up on food and other basic goods. Marina, however, did not take it seriously.

"There was always some talk about the Russian threat, and we were used to the clashes and skirmishes in some of the surrounding villages, but not in our own. Suddenly, this night we heard explosions and saw lights across the sky. The next day we were warned by the authorities that the war had begun, and we better leave as quickly as possible. The message was soon repeated to us by the Russians who warned us that they could not guarantee our security. 'Get out of here for your own safety. Get out quickly, go quickly,' they kept repeating."

Marina rested her hands on her lap and shook her head as she looked at her two grown sons sitting silently in the room. They had fled, leaving everything.

During the war and beyond, the parties exchanged recriminations and used strong language in their war of words. The Russians made it clear that they would not deal with Saakashvili anymore and would be prepared to start a dialogue only with his successor. Such an ultimatum—implying regime change—was neither acceptable to the international community nor to the Georgian population. Despite serious reservations about Saakashvili's leadership, the attack on the country and his person by Russia mobilized the public in support of their president and prevented any rational discussion of his role in the crisis for months. Whatever Georgians' complaints about Saakashvili, the possibility of Russian occupation or direct interference in their internal affairs, which would have rendered the fragile nation a puppet state, was more unsettling and unacceptable.

The matter came before the UN Security Council where the Russian and Georgian ambassadors, Vitaly Churkin and Irakli Alasania, respectively, predictably traded accusations. On occasion, there were also unfriendly exchanges between the Russian and American ambassadors with the former vehemently rejecting American claims that Russia sought to remove Saakashvili from power, insisting that "'regime change' has not been the Russian policy." The EU, under the active presidency of the French, led by their president, Nicolas Sarkozy, was simultaneously undertaking intensive efforts to broker a cease-fire and stop Russian progression into Georgian territory. While the negotiations were ongoing, the Russians continued to press deeper into Georgia every day, destroying strategic military posts, training camps and installations, as well as roads and railways, ultimately occupying Poti and parts of the Georgian coast and territory along the South Ossetian "border." With Georgia's military destroyed, the Russians could have easily reach Tbilisi, if such a decision had been taken, without much effort.

Under the circumstances, most European leaders, among them German Chancellor Angela Merkel and French President Sarkozy, as well as the foreign ministers of the United States, France, and the United Kingdom, pressed Georgia to agree to a cease-fire and support the negotiations lead by France on behalf of the EU. Some countries from the former Soviet Bloc—Poland, Latvia, Lithuania, Estonia, and Ukraine—took a radical anti-Russian position. They joined in public solidarity meetings in Tbilisi in a show of support for Georgia and its president and lobbied the various diplomatic forums—the EU, OSCE, the UN—in support of Georgia.

The immediate result of these efforts was the successful conclusion of a cease-fire agreement, referred to as the Sarkozy agreement, mandating, *inter alia*, the withdrawal of all forces to their prewar positions and the appointment by the EU of an independent commission to investigate the events.

The consequences of the 2008 war have increasingly come under intense scrutiny at both the international and national levels. The four pro-Georgian EU members have strongly pushed for NATO membership for Georgia and Ukraine as necessary security guarantees against Russia and its expansionist policy. Most EU members, however, have drawn opposite conclusions. Had Georgia been a NATO member in August 2008, an Alliance confrontation with Russia would have been inevitable. Europe was not yet ready to extend such a security guarantee to Georgia (or Ukraine) as their policies were increasingly perceived as irresponsible and reckless and their internal affairs chaotic. Saakashvili's adventure in South Ossetia merely validated the criticism and further diminished international confidence in the country. And although Russia emerged from the affair politically damaged, its power position in the region was generally strengthened.

In Georgia, the mood on the fifth anniversary of the Rose Revolution, in November 2008, was therefore far from celebratory. The mounting opposition against Saakashvili as a result of declining international confidence in his leadership, and unanswered questions at home regarding his precise role in the events of August 2008, dampened spirits. International leaders, most of who had appeared in Tbilisi only a few months earlier, declined to come again. Only the Polish president, Lech Kaczynski, decided to demonstrate his support for Saakashvili by returning and attending the observances, despite opposition from some government officials and public figures in Poland.

The gathering of the two leaders resembled very little of the broad international support expressed in August. Rather it symbolized the increasing isolation of Saakashvili; it was telling that his only support came from Kaczynski, himself highly unpopular in his own country. The event had even less in common with the enthusiasm that had infected the city in 2003 as it celebrated the victory of democracy, the Rose Revolution, and Saakashvili.

As if the mooted celebration were not enough, the two presidents made an impromptu excursion to the South Ossetian cease-fire line. Somewhere, not far from Gori, the presidential convoy came under fire. At a subsequent press conference, the two heads of state voiced their outrage and attributed the action to the Russians. Russia, for its part, immediately denied the accusations. With time, disturbing facts emerged, generating more unanswered questions. For example, it was learned that the adventure was Saakashvili's idea and not envisaged in the original itinerary and that the trip was spontaneous and never fully planned out. It was also revealed that the Polish security detail obliged to accompany its president had been dismissed by the Georgians; they were made to stay behind. It was never established from which side of the cease-fire line the shooting originated either. And the incident, which initially commanded great visibility and attention in Georgia, quickly vanished from front pages.

"The Georgians were shooting into the air," Giga, a member of the opposition, told me. "Our president arranged this provocation. It is a shame."

"It shows Saakashvili's sense of humor," Levan, a university professor, remarked. "He likes such jokes. Once he took some ministers for a ride on a carousel. It was supposed to be a fun surprise."

"It was quite embarrassing to have the president of a friendly country, and a very important country like Poland, be subjected to this incident. It is incomprehensible and intolerable. Why were his security guards ordered to stay behind in Tbilisi? In a normal European country, it would have been enough for the president to resign," Salome Zurabishvili commented.

If I had had any doubts about the shooting incident, they were dispelled later on, in March 2010, when one of the main television stations, one controlled by the government, transmitted a hoax Russian invasion. The images were so realistic that they generated panic throughout Tbilisi. On the streets, there were some casualties, including one dead (of heart attack). The memories of the 2008 war were still fresh. Many people, including some opposition leaders, ran to the television station to clarify the matter. After a while, they were told that it was just a movie. Was it a conscious decision, another "joke" orchestrated by Saakashvili and his entourage? The incident was broadly reported across the world, but there was no viable clarification from the source as to how it had come about.

The 2008 war also generated mutual accusations of grave violations of human rights and international humanitarian law, including ethnic cleansing and war crimes. Both parties claimed to have collected sufficient evidence to present to the International Criminal Court to back up their respective assertions. There was little dispute that the city of Tskhinvali had been leveled, that its inhabitants had suffered the brunt of the consequences, and that Russian forces had been welcomed as saviors by most South Ossetians while the ethnic Georgian population was "cleansed away." In Gori, the city was shelled and some houses and roads were destroyed, but the damage there was more measured. Nothing happened to Stalin's museum although some surrounding areas were hit; apparently, both parties took care not to damage it, the Stalin's museum that is.

Amid the theater of mutual recriminations and continued Russian presence on Georgian soil, everyone awaited the independent report by the EU-appointed commission of international experts led by the senior Swiss diplomat and former head of the UN Observer Mission in Georgia from 2002 to 2006, Heidi Tagliavini. The report, which was released in September 2009, provided a thorough accounting of the events leading to the confrontation and, more importantly, a comprehensive analysis of the background of the conflict, which had been festering for the past fifteen years. Professionally and objectively, the report examined the conflict's root causes, to include the many declarations of international bodies that were never adhered to, and did not shy away from critically assessing the roles and responsibilities of the parties involved. In sum, it called spade a spade.

In an unusual demonstration of solidarity, all parties welcomed the Tagliavini report as "balanced" and claimed that it vindicated their respective positions: the Russians were pleased that the report placed the blame on the Georgians for starting the hostilities; and the Georgians were in full agreement with the report's factual findings, in particular its background analysis of the conflict, conclusion that Russia had used disproportionate force, and treatment of Russia's expulsion of the UN and OSCE from Abkhazia and South Ossetia. Domestically, the Georgian opposition seized on the report to attack Saakashvili for unilaterally embarking upon an irresponsible military action. In South Ossetia, its leader, "president" Eduard Kokoity, asserted that the report vindicated his view that Saakashvili was an "international criminal."

Based on these comments and press coverage of the report, it was unavoidable to get the impression that the parties had most likely not read carefully its one thousand pages and took a "pick and choose" approach, disingenuously selecting the passages and findings cited. A careful analysis of the report would have certainly led to slightly different conclusions. While the report pointed out that "the shelling of Tskhinvali by the Georgian armed forces during the night of August 7 to 8, 2008, marked the beginning of the large-scale armed conflict in Georgia, [] it was only the culminating point of a long period of increasing tensions, provocations and incidents." The report also stated that any explanation of the conflict had "to consider, too, the impact of [the] great power's [Russia's] coercive politics and diplomacy against a small and insubordinate neighbour." It further accused Russia of "illegally initiating a conflict in Abkhazia and using false pretexts to invade Georgia." The report also declared illegal and invalid the recognition by Russia of South Ossetia and Abkhazia as sovereign states and the continued presence of Russian forces on their territories as well as the distribution of Russian passports to their inhabitants since 2002. The report further concluded that Russia had been pursuing a policy intended to destabilize the region in order to maintain "privileged spheres of interest, in particular with regard to neighbouring countries, set to deprive smaller states of their freedom of choice and to limit their sovereignty."

In addition, the report warned that "the risk of a new confrontation remains serious." Russia not only continued to occupy parts of Georgia in disregard of the Sarkozy agreement, but also the regional power expanded its military presence in both Abkhazia and South Ossetia. Nor were military forces withdrawn to their positions prior to the outbreak of war as the EU-brokered agreement required; it was simply never done. Rather, Russia concluded military agreements with Abkhazia and South Ossetia, now recognized "states," and took over protection of their borders, air space and, in the case of Abkhazia, its coastline, and established military bases in Gudauta and Tskhinvali. Russia's continued military build-up and presence on Georgian territory itself was a provocation and bound to lead to further incidents involving Georgia.

These actions gave rise to serious political and legal questions: What was the role of the EU in supervising the agreement that it brokered? Did the principle of *pacta sunt servanda* have any meaning, and if so, who was responsible for holding the parties accountable for adherence to its tenets? How did the EU intend to use the Tagliavini report and its unequivocal findings to address the matter? What kind of follow-up was envisioned?

In May 2010, the International Community made the first visible step in this direction. The Council of Europe (CoE) called on Russia to reverse her previous decisions and "invalidate" her recognition of independence of Abkhazia and South Ossetia. It also requested the withdrawal of Russian troops to the prewar line. Russia's foreign minister, Sergey Lavrov, reacted angrily and negatively to those demands.

In Georgia, despite strong anti-Russian sentiments, there was not, at least among the common people, anti-Russian hysteria or hostility. That seemed to be restricted to the president and some in his inner circle, including formerly pro-Soviet members of the communist party. Russian music and songs continued to be played (often) in cafés and restaurants; and Georgians continued to enjoy travel to Russia (at least those with visas), to Moscow in particular, a traditional destination in Soviet days.

"We discussed the matter among the opposition," Keti told me, "and decided to make a clear distinction between the Russian people and Putin's politics, from which we all suffer—to include Russia and its people, even if they do not like to acknowledge it or actively move to change it. Moreover, Russian culture constitutes a part of world heritage. Tchaikovsky, Pushkin, Bulgakov, and Tsvetaeva represent another Russia which belongs to all of us and should be promoted, not rejected.

"Throughout our existence, we have had a troubled history with Russia. We have been occupied, deported, massacred, and abused. But it does not mean that we cannot make a different future, at least we should try. We cannot turn our backs on such an important country and sever all ties with the past—cultural, economic, and political. We have to find a *modus vivendi*, and we have to be serious about it, not adventurous and aggressive like our president."

The lack of open hostility toward Russia among the Georgians did not mean, however, that Russian interference was in any way acceptable.

"Why don't they leave us in peace?" Ruzi said to me despondently shortly after my return to Tbilisi in 2009.

"They always interfere in other people's business. It is a big country, and their own people suffer and live in terrible conditions. Nothing good has ever come from Russia—just abuse, poverty, filth, misery, atheism, and communism. We have our own religion, our own country, and we want to be left in peace. Don't they have enough to do at home?"

Chapter 25

The Rose Revolution: Six Years On

I came back to Georgia in the summer 2009. Rustaveli Avenue was again blocked by demonstrators just as it had been six years ago during the Rose Revolution. But this time, the mood was different. The city was quiet and despondent; the enthusiasm, optimism, and energy had gone. The people were more reserved, less open, and willing to speak freely. They still had yet to recover from the shock of the Russian invasion and the fear and terror it roused the prior summer. Adding to the discontent and somber spirit, the promises of the Rose Revolution had not materialized, but the disappointments had rendered Georgians too tired and pessimistic to act. And what could they do? The proximity of Russian troops complicated matters. Georgians did not like what they had, but they feared Russian interference more; that if they were not careful, Russia would use the opportunity to install a "friendly" government and that the world would remain indifferent. Now, this, they knew for sure.

Walking along Rustaveli Avenue I came across a series of photographs of individuals displayed on the tents of demonstrators. As the captions were in Georgian, I was unable to read them. I asked for translation.

"These are people who died while in police custody," a young woman camping in the street explained. "There have been many more incidents of mysterious deaths among the opposition, but the ones you see here are the cases we know of. In a few instances, we were told later that they had died a natural death or committed suicide."

I looked carefully at the photos. They depicted men of all ages, many young. I felt a chill go down my spine.

"This was not the case in 2003," I said. "So is that what the Rose Revolution was about? It carried the promise of a better life, a more democratic and modern state, and a brighter future for everyone."

"We thought so," she replied sadly. "But our revolution was stolen, and we are ruled by a criminal gang. That's why I am here. I will not leave until Misha goes. Only then can we get back on track and start where we left off in 2004."

Our conversation and a more careful scrutiny of the surroundings made me notice the posters calling for Saakashvili's resignation. Six years ago, they had depicted him as a hero, a savior. It was here, in front of the parliament, where he had had his moment of glory, where he had been cherished, applauded, and supported.

It was apparent that Georgia was going through a period of self-reflection. National solidarity had been strong and support for Saakashvili high during and in the immediate aftermath of the events of August 2008. But now, the time had come to examine precisely what had happened, who had taken critical decisions, and in what basis, to understand the exact nature of Georgian involvement in South Ossetia.

The inquiry was essential to Georgia's political development. As a consequence of the decisions made in those pivotal days, Georgia had lost large portions of her territory. Abkhazia annexed the Kodori Gorge and South Ossetian and Russian forces occupied about 150 villages in the province, rendering it practically sealed off and inaccessible from Georgia. Although Abkhazia and South Ossetia had essentially already been lost, their formal recognition by Russia constituted the last blow to Georgian hopes for reunification. It also opened the door to formal Russian investment and purchase of property in both territories and direct militarization.

The war also disrupted Georgia's generally positive economic development, undermining the confidence of donors and foreign investors. The influx of foreigners and their capital diminished. That combined with the global financial crisis significantly contributed to Georgia's subsequent economic downturn. The thousands of unfinished buildings and abandoned construction sites throughout Tbilisi evidenced this reality vividly.

The prevailing "cold war" with Russia—the lack of diplomatic relations and access of Georgian products to Russia, traditionally their biggest market, in addition to the more stringent visa requirements imposed on Georgians citizens, blocking their ability to access jobs in Russia and the resultant flow of remittances on which many Georgian families heavily relied—further diminished the Georgians' already low living standard.

The foreign policy implications of the war were equally significant. The strained relations with Russia and missteps during the war practically nullified Georgia's prospects of joining NATO and other European institutions. The last thing that Europe wanted was to be forced into a violent conflict with Russia as a result of Georgian adventurism.

Thus, the disastrous events of the last year, combined with the unrelenting cronyism and elite corruption, serious human rights violations, absence of the rule of law and weakening economy, triggered a renewed round of protests and brought the people back into the streets. The discontent, as in 2003, brought visibility to the political opposition and helped motivate its organization. Thus, the original approach of treating any queries related to the 2008 war as unpatriotic or pro-Russian gave way to demands for clarification of not only what had occurred the prior year, but also answers to what had gone wrong with Georgian democracy since the Rose Revolution.

With time, various political parties and groups have emerged to oppose the Saakashvili government. Most formed in the wake of the protests in the autumn of 2007. Among them most visible are the Alliance for Georgia, comprising a few parties, led by Irakli Alasania, the former Georgian Ambassador to the UN, remembered best for his emotional defense of Georgia's position before the UN Security Council during the 2008 war; the Democratic Movement-United Georgia of Nino Burjanadze, the former speaker of the parliament and member of the Rose Revolution triumvirate; the Way of Georgia led by Salome Zurabishvili, the former Georgian Foreign Minister and French Ambassador to Georgia; and the Protect Georgia party of Levan Gachechiladze, a highly successful businessman and member of parliament.

While the opposition groups were united by the singular goal of removing Saakashvili from power, they had neither a consolidated platform nor common plan for future actions. Indeed, it seemed to me that most people, excepting some in the Georgian intelligentsia, did not know what the opposition wanted. Thus, while they were ready to join some actions out of sheer frustration, they did not necessarily see how it might influence their future. Further, given the results of the past six years, there was no mood for another "revolution" or an obvious leader to shepherd it.

I explored these issues further, speaking with both key political players and ordinary people, to see how they understood the issues and envisioned the future of Georgia. What had gone wrong with Georgian democracy, and how it could be corrected?

"It is about direction," Zurabishvili remarked. "Georgia was perceived as a failed state in 2003, but it was more democratic then than it is now. There was freedom of expression and association, and the press was highly critical of the government. After the Rose Revolution, things initially moved in a good direction, toward a Western-style democracy."

The turning point for Saakashvili came in 2006, she said. It became clear at that time that for his government it was more about holding onto power than the future of the country. "There is no contradiction between what the current opposition wants and what it wanted in 2003," Zurabishvili continued. "It is the same. We need truly free elections that will obviously lead to a change in the leadership, to bring the policy line back in order."

"We made a lot of mistakes," Nino Burjanadze admitted during our discussion at her office. "The main mistake was to agree to early presidential elections with a joint candidate of the opposition in 2004. The process was rushed, and there was no reason for it. Shevardnadze's term was up in the late 2004 in any case. We should have used the time to run a multiple-candidate campaign. That would have allowed us to focus on the issues rather than personalities, and test the leadership qualities and programs of the various candidates.

"As it turned out, Saakashvili's 90 percent victory ended up being demoralizing. He quickly used his popularity to dominate the scene. By March 2005, during the parliamentary debate on the constitutional reform, it had already become clear that genuine discussion was impossible, opposing views were dismissed and disrespected. The strong concentration of powers in the president at the expense of the parliament was the first indication that things were going in the wrong direction. Instead of building institutions and ensuring checks and balances were in place, the predominant concern was maintaining the strong position of one individual unabated. That was merely a replication of the situation under Shevardnadze.

"It is hard to understand why strong leaders do not want themselves to be restrained constitutionally. It is healthier for them and better for the society," she concluded.

Vano, a university professor who primarily worked abroad, echoed some of Burjanadze's views.

"We were skeptical even then. We watched it and tried to prevent the departure of Shevardnadze," he reflected. "While we fully supported corrections to the parliamentary elections and the need for a new parliament, there was no need to rush the change in the presidency. Shevardnadze was already powerless. His staying in office for one more year would have enabled well-prepared presidential elections in the autumn of 2004."

In 2009, with the enthusiasm long gone, views on the nature and meaning of the Rose Revolution had also diversified. The majority, like Burjanadze and Zurabishvili, felt that it had been an important achievement, but the process had derailed; some questioned its purpose more generally, yet others ascribed to a myriad of conspiracy theories to explain the events.

"Even before the Rose Revolution, Zhvania had manipulated the media and civil society. It was all orchestrated and paid for by the Americans," one conspiracy theorist opined. "The so-called civil society leaders came directly from the government elite: Saakashvili, Zhvania, and Burjanadze. They left their high-level positions, changed hats, and led the 'revolution.' Afterward, they redistributed the high political posts among themselves. A few years later, they split with some returning to civil society. It is a circus. It is only possible in Georgia."

By 2009, not much remained of the former triumvirate. Saakashvili remained president, though highly unpopular. Burjanadze led one of the main opposition parties. Her composure and professional campaign style made her one of the leading political figures in Georgia. Zhvania was dead, and the circumstances of his death had increasingly become more suspicious with time.

The Georgian prime minister died on February 3, 2005. The official cause of death was accidental carbon monoxide poisoning, but nobody believed it; the circumstances were simply too strange. He died, allegedly, in a room shared overnight with another man—a fact implying homosexuality, which is culturally intolerable in Georgia. The announcement of his death was made the following morning by the Minister of Internal Affairs, Vano Merabishvili. The clarification, which came just a few hours after the alleged accident, was surprisingly quick and definite. Further investigation did not bring about additional information. The push to close the matter quickly, purportedly to avoid embarrassing the family, only heightened the suspicion. Zhvania was a well-known public figure; the story put out by the government was absurd.

Rumored KGB involvement also carried no credibility and was not taken seriously by the public. With time, due to the lack of clarity and transparency, the finger has been increasingly pointed at Saakashvili and members of his inner circle, in particular Merabishvili, as those responsible for Zhvania's death.

Merabishvili, one of Saakashvili's closest allies, had never been considered trustworthy and his ministry had developed a deplorable track record of mysterious deaths among detainees and political persecution. That, however, did not make him responsible for Zhvania's death.

In the absence of reliable facts, some mutual colleagues of Zhvania and Saakashvili offered me the following explanations:

"Years ago, Zhvania convinced Saakashvili to return from New York to join him in removing Shevardnadze, introducing reforms and modernizing Georgia. He knew his own limitations—the lack of appeal and charisma—so he needed Saakashvili to make the breakthrough and lead a popular movement. He believed that he would be able to control Saakashvili but that proved more difficult than anticipated, especially in the long run.

"After the Rose Revolution, Zhvania, a seasoned politician, came to see Saakashvili's increasingly egocentric personality and authoritarian style. He knew that it was neither good for the country nor acceptable to the society. Change was necessary, and he started quietly working toward it. So he became a threat not only to Saakashvili, but also to his cronies as well. That is when the accident happened. But who was responsible will probably remain one of the many unsolved mysteries of Georgia."

The absence of a unifying figure within the opposition, someone who both commanded authority and was familiar with Georgian politics, allowed Saakashvili and his cronies to continue without facing a consolidated challenge. Zhvania would have perfectly filled this gap.

* * *

In 2009, it was difficult to assess objectively what had changed in Georgia since the Rose Revolution, even amid the street protests. The allegations of human rights abuses and anger stemming from the lost war and declining living conditions were clear. However, the general frustration with Saakashvili made some forget that he had inherited a near bankrupted and unmanageable country, came into office with extremely high social expectations (encouraged by Saakashvili himself), and that his government had scored some successes, achievements many in the opposition failed to acknowledge. Saakashvili's successes included:

- Supporting Adjaria's Rose Revolution, which led to the bloodless ouster of Abashidze and reintegration of the province into Georgia early in his presidency.
- Implementing the decision on removal of Russian military basis from the territory of Georgia (reached by so-called OSCE Istanbul Summit in 1999, under Shevardnadze). Salome Zurabishvili, the former Georgian Foreign Minister following the 2003 Rose Revolution, considered it the biggest achievement of Georgian diplomacy under Saakashvili.
- Resolving the electricity shortage problem that plagued the country, bringing an end to the ever-present blackouts.
- Rebuilding the country's deteriorating roads system quickly and efficiently, connecting various parts of the country, and improving transportation conditions for commercial trade.
- Eliminating low-level corruption from administrative, police, and public services. Offices now operate punctually, public servants are polite, and policemen are properly trained. These reforms have brought about a sense of normality to daily life. The police reforms have been particularly exemplary. Compared to 2003—when the image of the typical police officer was that of an unfriendly, half-drunk man clothed in a tattered uniformlike outfit, pressing for bribes—the change was undeniable.
- Transforming Tbilisi from a dirty, neglected, disorganized city with chaotic traffic and high crime into a more presentable and orderly capital with functioning traffic lights and refurbished monuments, fountains and flower beds, among other improvements.
- Solving the problem of internally displaced persons. It was not done in a wholly satisfactory manner, but considering the magnitude of the problem and the fact that it had dragged on since the wars in Abkhazia and South Ossetia in the early 1990s, it was a significant achievement. The inhumane living conditions of IDPs throughout these years and the indifference

and inability of previous authorities to address them made the provision of accommodation, or its monetary equivalent "to many IDPs", a significant step forward.

- Relatedly, providing temporary accommodation for the new wave of IDPs from South Ossetia following the 2008 war. It was done instantly and in accordance with UNHCR standards. Although the houses were of a temporary nature and low quality and living conditions were difficult, the IDPs were far better off in government-financed housing under Saakashvili than the previous generation of IDPs who had lived for almost two decades in the so-called collective centers, facilities often beset with leaking roofs and lacking electricity, water, and proper heating.

Saakashvili inherited a quasi "failed state" in 2003, one which lacked democratic structures and tradition and had a massive corruption problem, to name a few of its many challenges. Despite her strong pro-Western orientation and European-educated elite, Georgia had neither benefited from modern management techniques and a professional civil service nor the rule of law and a strong legal culture. She instead had a tradition of patronage—governance within a system of competing interest groups and clans organized along lines of political and economic interest and kinship.

The Rose Revolution was a populist reaction to the Shevardnadze government's vote rigging and general failures over the prior decade. It was not the product of a democratic, constitutional process. There was no tradition of transparency and public monitoring of government authorities in Georgia, and thus no political accountability. Saakashvili's government followed suit and did not open itself up to public scrutiny.

Certain decisions of Saakashvili's government have not, therefore, exactly comported with traditional notions of constitutional democracy: the amendments to the Georgian Constitution in 2005 were done in a Soviet/Russian manner; the anti-corruption campaign was politically-motivated and not based on the rule of law; the mass media became less critical than under Shevardnadze, either as a result of self-censorship or political pressure; and civil society was weakened. Some groups did not want to criticize the new authorities and rather sought to establish themselves as supporters while others were intimidated or lacked the means to organize an effective opposition.

In this vain, with time, Saakashvili's authoritarian impulses took over as well. Any substantive criticism was perceived by him as a personal attack. He started surrounding himself with people who would not question his views, "yes" men and women: young, inexperienced, unprofessional, and/or corrupt. Saakashvili also quickly established a habit of working behind closed doors with only certain, select staff members, often during the night. There were also frequent changes in his cabinet. Its more experienced and professional members and civil servants began departing, either by resignation or dismissal. Soon, Saakashvili began intervening in personnel matters in all branches of the government.

Although Georgia has been considered a model democracy by the United States and many other countries in the West, she has, in fact, always been far from it. Georgia has been more of an imitation or sham democracy, a country which took on some characteristics of a democratic state in form only. For example, Georgia quickly developed some attributes of a consumerist society, acquiring foreign supermarket chains; an influx of foreign goods, businessmen and capital; modern advertising and electronic communications; and Western-style public relations campaigns. But basic democratic ideas and values respecting the accountability of elected representatives to their electorate; the rights and obligations of citizens, irrespective of their economic, social, or ethnic status; and respect for the rule of law, remained foreign to most of the population and the leadership.

Last, but certainly not least, was the ever-present Russian factor. Saakashvili used the country's strong nationalism as a key unifying force to propel his drive toward full independence and liberation from Russian influence and to seek association with NATO and the European Union. He clearly stated this political objective and was able to pursue it consistently.

While it would not be correct to assume that Russia was behind all Georgia's problems or that of its young president, Russia did not miss any opportunity to discredit him or undermine Georgian attempts to join European institutions. During the 2007 demonstrations, which Saakashvili suppressed with force, the Russian media presented the protests as if they were part of a major revolutionary movement against an authoritarian leader. This differed drastically from Russian coverage of the Rose Revolution, which they portrayed as a few isolated shenanigans instigated by "hooligans" and "Western agents" aimed at undermining stability in the Caucasus.

Georgians' fear of Russia has constituted Saakashvili's strongest source of support. The opposition has often hesitated to challenge him precisely because it might play into Russia's hands. The same motivated, at least in part, the support extended to Saakashvili by the United States and other Western countries. So paradoxically, the two archrivals, the United States and Russia, have helped Saakashvili to remain in power.

But for how long?

Chapter 26

Feeling Abandoned:
The International Community

The persistent poverty and political crisis in Georgia has strongly influenced her people's attitude toward the international community, the United States and key Western countries in particular. Georgians perceived them as uncritical supporters of Saakashvili. When I returned in 2009, people were bitter that their demonstrations, which they had been holding since that April, had produced no results. Nobody was interested in listening seriously to their complaints. The doors of Western embassies were closed to them. They did not want to hear about the Saakashvili government's abuse of power; they did not want to inquire into the matter of political prisoners, eagerly believing Saakashvili government's claim that only common criminals were imprisoned. Saakashvili was, after all, the "beacon of democracy."

The grievances shared with me during my return visit that summer can be summarized as follows:

The Georgian people's voices were ignored.

- Numerous protests and attempted interventions with foreign representatives, diplomats, and intergovernmental organizations fell on deaf ears. No one wanted to read even well-documented reports on human rights abuses, torture, and corruption in Georgia. There was no interest in the facts brought to the attention of the IC by the ombudsman after the government's brutal confrontation with demonstrators in 2007.

Rather, it was an embarrassment that they had been exposed to his briefing at all; they could not deny their knowledge. The IC chose, in any case, to ignore rather than acknowledge what had occurred, lest it require them to take action.

The 2008 presidential election results were falsified.

- That the 2008 presidential election results had been falsified was the common view on the streets of Tbilisi. Yes, he received the majority of votes in the first round, but Saakashvili's vote tally was below the 50 percent mark, so the second round was anticipated. The official result of 52.5 percent reported for him was obviously falsified with the West's blessing.

The IC turned a blind eye to Saakashvili's increasing authoritarianism and political oppression.

- The IC did not want to look behind Georgia's democratic facade and examine the real political mechanisms—Saakashvili's increasing authoritarianism, exclusion of the majority, and suppression of the opposition—and draw policy-related conclusions. Georgia has significantly regressed with respect to the rule of law and transparency under Saakashvili, matters that should be of serious concern to donors. Indeed, some Georgians believed that the foreign aid to the country facilitated the state's militarization and contributed to the security sector's unchecked powers at the expense of democracy, human rights, and legal justice.

Foreign aid was being used to facilitate corruption rather than promote democratic development, a reality often ignored by donors.

- There was deep dissatisfaction with foreign advisers and experts. They have largely been perceived as a collection of uninformed, arrogant individuals focused on pleasing the Georgian government and meeting the expectations of their own capitals and completely detached from the Georgian population and uninformed about its concerns. Not surprisingly, assistance funds have been spent primarily on projects supporting local dignitaries rather than those benefiting the greater populace, to the extent the funds are spent on local projects at all.

- Many believed that most of the foreign aid had "transited" through Georgia and in some form returned to the countries of its origin. "They bring money in with one hand and take it back with the other through putting highly paid advisers, companies, and other people on their payrolls" was an often heard opinion.

- The United States' support of the Georgian government's suppression of political dissent though the provision of modern, high-tech listening devices used to spy on the opposition was another point of contention. I heard often about widespread wiretapping. Salome Zurabishvili, the former Georgian Foreign Minister turned opposition leader, pointed to a hole in the wall of her office. "It is where we found a device. We called the proper authorities who removed it and took it for further examination, which was to be conducted in our presence. It was done a few weeks ago in the presence of the press. Nothing has happened, no action has been taken." I heard similar stories from the ombudsman who had raised the issue officially with Georgian authorities. The opposition club too was bugged. "Our phone conversations, our e-mail, our homes, and our offices are bugged as well," I was told. "That would be illegal in any country. They are ahead of the game using this knowledge to block our demonstrations and arrest and terrorize people on the way home from our meetings."

It was impossible to judge the veracity of some of these views, but that many in the society hold this perception, especially among the political and intellectual elite, is worrisome. The increasingly negative picture of the West and its role in recent Georgian history might, one day, have serious political repercussions. In a society with neither democratic traditions nor transparency, any rumor can easily be generated and believed.

Some conspiracy theorists have already started speaking of an emerging alliance between the "heartless" Western bureaucracy and Saakashvili's regime at the expense of Georgians. Others contemplate the possibility of the West abandoning both Georgia and Ukraine in the event of further trouble. If the two countries continued to be unstable and engage in risky conduct, it may be more practical to simply "return them" to the Russian sphere of influence.

Indeed, dissatisfaction with the West has led some to start considering a Russian option. Irina, an editor, told me that the opposition, to which she belonged, should talk directly to Putin.

"How do you want to do it?" I asked her.

"I do not know, and most people would not like even to hear about it, but here is my reasoning: The West would never sacrifice its good relations with Russia to help Georgia. We still have Russians on our territory after the 2008 war, despite all their promises and agreements with the EU. We have been told repeatedly to be reasonable, to wait, and to understand that antagonizing Russia would not benefit anybody.

"Did you ever think," she said, turning to me, "that we could not join European structures because of a fear of Russia, not because we failed to meet the required standards of democratization under Saakashvili? It seems that in each and every case—NATO, Abkhazia, South Ossetia, you name it—the West had to get Russian approval before it could decide if and how to assist us. So as the key is always in Russian hands, we can deal with them directly without the West as the intermediary.

"We should talk to Putin," she repeated with deep conviction.

I talked to Irina again, two months later. She had not yet spoken with Putin, but her frustration and anti-Western feelings had deepened. She was convinced that with time more people would share her views.

"Can you imagine the Russians not only occupying the area along the South Ossetian 'border,' the conflict line, but also using both territories for military purposes? This is against the agreement with the EU, the so-called Sarkozy agreement. Moreover, the skirmishes and provocations continue, and from time to time, they change the conflict line, pushing deeper into Georgian territory. It does not alter the global picture, but it affects lives of the people who suddenly find themselves under Russian-South Ossetian rule. And nobody is reacting to these provocations. Where is the EU? After all, they should supervise the implementation of their own treaty, correct?

"That's not all," she continued. "Have you followed the visit of Hillary Clinton in Moscow?"

I knew that was coming.

"Unlike Vice President Biden during his visit to Georgia last summer, when she visited Russia, she did not say even one word about the territorial integrity of Georgia as if Abkhazia, South Ossetia, and Russian occupation of our land did not count. She only mentioned that the United States and Russia differed with regard to Georgia. That was all."

Indeed, that was all. I had nothing to add.

Chapter 27

In the Opposition Club

July 2009. Another night at the opposition club, a café bar in the center of Tbilisi, owned by Maja. The place is quiet. It gets busy only in the evening when members of the political opposition start filling it up. They get together to vent their frustrations, share news, and lend support to one another. They know that the club is bugged but, with time, have gotten used to living in the constant presence of the listening devices. For this intrusion, they blame not only Saakashvili's government, but also the United States, the alleged supplier of the devices.

This night, its members were celebrating the public meeting they had successfully organized to welcome the American Vice President, Joe Biden. It was peaceful, and the mood was congenial. The color was white—white blouses, white shirts, white flags—the color of peace. It was well attended although the authorities had changed the venue on short notice from the Freedom Square to an area around the Philharmonic. They wanted to deliver Biden a message: "There is no democracy in Georgia. The US government should stop supporting Saakashvili's autocratic regime. We want our country and the democracy back." Thus, as the atmosphere in the club warmed up, so did Saakashvili's critics.

"The man is crazy," Giga tells me over a glass of whiskey.

"So why did you elect him?"

"We did not know it back in 2003. He was young, dynamic, and strong, all the qualities necessary to throw Shevardnadze and his cronies out. He seemed charismatic, and the others were not. Now we pay for our mistake.

"In any case, we did not elect him the last time. He did not get 52.5 percent of the votes in 2008. It's true that he got the highest number, over 40 percent, but everybody anticipated a second round of elections. That's when the opposition wanted to decide on a common candidate. But there was no second round. Saakashvili's American friends were fast to declare his victory. That is how the election was stolen."

"Didn't you notice that our president is crazy?" Nula, a journalist, asked me.

"No, I did not."

"Then you should look it up on the Internet," she continued. "He has all symptoms of mental illness: he is compulsive, short-tempered, suspicious, and secretive. He is obsessed with conspiracy and loyalty, and he can't control his emotions or resist any temptation. He sees a woman he fancies, he must have her. If he doesn't like something, he must destroy it. He bursts into anger, he eats his own tie."

"What?"

"Check the BBC Web site. You will see." Somebody pulled out a laptop and I was shown a video of Saakashvili chewing on his red tie.

"Is it real or is it doctored?"

"No, it's been shown by the BBC in the past."

"I will tell you what happened to my daughter," Giga continued. "She is a student in the United States. During one of his visits, Saakashvili met with the Georgian students at her university. They were chatting. Suddenly, he turned to my daughter and whispered, 'Give me a call. I want to see you. You can call me day and night' and gave her his business card. Later on, during her vacation in Georgia, she showed me the card with his cell number. I could not believe my eyes. The president! I was turning the card over in my hand in disbelief. He is nuts. This I knew but was still shocked. My daughter learned that two other students at her university were similarly approached."

Goga, the former minister after the Rose Revolution, entered the club. We knew each other from my UN days in Tbilisi and had often discussed possible strategies that could bring the people of Abkhazia and Georgia proper closer together.

"So you are also in the opposition?" I quizzed.

"Where else could I be?"

"How long did it take for you to change fronts?"

"Two years, one month, ten days, and some hours. I do not know how I have survived so long. The guy is mental, completely unpredictable. He says one thing and does another. It is a horror!"

"He is crazy and takes all of us for crazy," Roza, a computer specialist, proclaimed. "Last year, after we had lost the war with Russia and lost territory and were overrun with thousands of displaced people, ruined infrastructures, and Russian troops roaming through our land, he declared victory. Even now he claims victory, just keeps repeating it. Just a few days ago at a meeting in the parliament on the eve of Biden's visit, he again claimed that Georgia was the only country in the world to have stood up to Russia and won the war."

"And our parliamentarians gave him a standing ovation, like during Brezhnev's time," Devi added. "It was totally schizophrenic, their reality versus our reality."

"Does he really believe that it was a victory?" I inquired.

"Yes, because he is insane," a number replied.

"No, but he wants to convince us of it in order to stay in power and avoid political responsibility," said others.

"He is a traitor. He worked it out with the Russians," some claimed. "He is playing into Putin's hands. The whole adventure in August 2008 was pure provocation."

"I thought it was a clever Russian trap into which he fell," I remarked.

"Yes," agreed some of my interlocutors.

"Not necessarily," insisted others. "He is crazy, so nobody really knew what was on his mind."

"But wasn't it a little too convenient?" interjected someone else.

While condemnation of Saakashvili appeared unanimous, at least among the declared opposition, agreement on the way forward seemed more unclear and complicated.

"He has to go," everybody agreed.

"But how? That is the difficulty, correct? He officially won the election. His mandate does not expire until 2013. The parliament is essentially a one-party body, uncritically supporting the president. The real opposition is outside of state institutions, on the streets. So how can it happen?" I pressed.

"The United States should tell him to resign" was one suggestion. "If they really push and accommodate him somewhere else, he will go."

I was a bit surprise by the naïveté of this view. "Why should the United States do that? Isn't that the role of Georgians? Besides, the United States has other problems—Iraq, Iran, Afghanistan."

"The United States helped him win the last round of elections or, rather, helped legitimize their falsified outcome. This guy, Bryza, who had been a friend of Saakashvili's, wining and dining with him in Georgia and liaising with Washington, did it. Once the United States recognized the results, the OSCE did not dare challenge them publicly, so we lost the chance for the second round. The Americans messed it up, so now they should clean it up," a voice from the corner explained.

"Well, not all Americans. It was under Bush. That's why he has an avenue named after him in Tbilisi," another noted.

"I was born on Lenin's avenue," somebody started to sing. "One day it was over, and I started to believe in reason. But not for long. After a while, I woke up on the avenue of George W. Bush."

"They do not care enough about people like us and our lives. They should at least control the money they give to the government. They should react to the human rights abuses, especially now since President Obama has denounced torture," another chimed in.

"They will never do it. Nobody cares about Georgia. Look at the EU. They are not any better. All they are interested in is Russian gas and oil and so-called stability in the region at any price."

"Not all European countries are so bad. Look at Poland and the Baltic states. They know the pain of dependency on Russia. They support us."

"Yes, but they support Saakashvili. Look at this Polish president. He has been to Georgia many times, but he has only interacted with the president as if the society did not exist. They seem comfortable in each other's company—one small, one big, both looking funny."

"I hope he got the message at the end when they got rid of his bodyguards and started shooting on the convoy. That's the kind of fun Saakashvili enjoys."

"So what is the way forward?" I repeated.

"We will go back to the streets, camping out on Rustaveli Avenue in front of the parliament from September on," Gia explained. "By then, people will be back from vacation with no work, no prospects, and no means by which to live. I traveled around the country this summer and the situation is truly awful. You should get out of Tbilisi and see it."

"We do not want any violence or bloodshed," Maja, the café owner, interjected. "But what can we do? We cannot continue to live like this anymore. We just want to have normal lives—normal salaries, schools, health services, functioning courts, security, and dignity. Is that too much to ask for?"

"The opposition is very much aware that the situation can be explosive. People are tired and fed up. A spark can set off a fire. If there is blood, things can get very ugly and out of hand very quickly. We have to be very careful because we are responsible for our actions, and we will be blamed by everybody. But what else can we do other than demonstrate?"

"You are right. We can only count on ourselves. The world has failed us," remarked Giga. "We should try to support the informal initiative to join forces with the people of Azerbaijan and Armenia. Historically, we have been played against each other, and now it is time to change it. Together we might have a sufficient weight to stand on our own feet. But for that we need a leader, not a lunatic."

It was difficult to get something more concrete and specific on how the broader opposition and leaders of the various parties and groups envisioned the process of going forward. There was no agreement even on such essential matters as the forthcoming local elections. Some believed that they should take place as soon as proper arrangements could be made and that they should result in an overwhelming victory for the opposition if properly supervised. Others were more skeptical, doubting the possibility of free and fair elections. All recent elections had been, to a certain degree, falsified; and there was no way to ensure effective supervision and monitoring countrywide. As long as Saakashvili was in power, there was no room for democratic elections, the skeptics argued. New elections should only be held if Saakashvili left office, they believed, and there was no indication that he was inclined to do so.

The major concerns and dissatisfaction with the president expressed at the opposition club were echoed in my conversations on the streets of Tbilisi. Most of my interlocutors were simply tired. They felt that they had no future. They were particularly appalled by the pervasive elite corruption and exorbitant lifestyles of Saakashvili and his cronies. There was neither respect for nor identification with them. They were not perceived as representatives of the people and their interests but, rather, as a greedy, autocratic group preoccupied with defending their power and privilege at any price.

"Look at his palace," a taxi driver told me, pointing to the newly built presidential residence. "It is a shame really. It is bigger than the

White House, and we are a poor nation. I am the only one working in my family. We thought he would make things better, but it has never been as bad as now. He spends foreign assistance money on himself, his clique, and his girlfriends. He travels to foreign countries at our expense. He has his own plane and always takes women along."

"Maybe his wife?"

The driver was amused by my naïveté. "She does not travel with him anymore. These are other women, his lovers."

"How do you know it?"

"Tbilisi is a small place. We know what is going on. Sometimes they even show such things on TV. For example, not so long ago, they showed Saakashvili at a sports stadium in Rome sitting with some Georgian women."

"Was Mr. Berlusconi around?"

"No, it was too much even for Berlusconi. He has his own problems. He does not need to parade around in such company."

"It is nice only on the surface," Ruzi, my former cleaning lady, remarked in reaction to my comments on the changes in Tbilisi over the past six years, its seeming transformation into a normal, orderly city. "We are glad that there are flower beds, functioning traffic lights, and good roads. But we need to eat, live in decent houses, and work, and that is not in the cards. My children have no work, and now I have lost my job because the office closed down. And I do not have anybody to help. My husband and parents are dead. I do not know how I will survive."

Soso, a computer specialist, was able to find a job in Azerbaijan. "I do not want to leave Georgia, but I was lucky to find something," he shared. "I am not employable in Georgia. I belong to the opposition, and I am too old. The new policy is to employ people under forty: the younger, the better. Our president wants to create 'new Georgians,' whatever that means, and only the young ones are deemed sufficiently adaptable and deserving of jobs and humane living conditions. But what should we do? Leave the country to give him enough space for the 'new Georgians'? And from where is he going to import them?"

"Did you know that we won the war, madame?" another taxi driver asked me. "Nobody wants to antagonize Russia—not Europe, not America—only Georgia. It means that we are crazy or, rather, that we have an insane president."

"Why did security block the streets? The whole center was inaccessible. I could not do my business," a street vendor selling fruits complained, speaking of the preparations made ahead of Biden's visit. "America is our friend. Why hide things from the American president? Are they afraid that he will see how poor we are and that the American money is not being used to help the Georgian people?"

Taking me for an American, he continued. "You should tell him what is going on here. He will listen to you. You can go to your embassy and tell him or go see him in America."

I found, however, that general sense of discontent and dissatisfaction did not automatically translate itself into trust in and sympathy for the opposition. I heard varying opinions as to why.

"We do not understand what they want or what they can do for us. They do it for themselves. Most of these people are from the same pack and have personal grievances. They quarrelled with Saakashvili some years ago over dividing the cake. So now they fight him," Vano, a university professor, explained.

"The opposition is divided and cannot get its act together. How long can you talk, agitate, and demonstrate? Time is passing, and we need jobs and stability. Blocking Rustaveli Avenue does not solve our existing problems. What exactly do they propose to change? What is their platform, their program?" Rado, an insurance company manager, queried. "And if I do not know, how can less educated and less informed people know and be willing to join with them?"

"All they want is access to the foreign aid money. That is what they are fighting for," Beko, another driver told me.

While the discontented and fed-up constituted the overwhelming majority of those I encountered, some were pleased with Saakashvili and his policies and appreciative of his achievements.

"Things are wonderful!" Alyena, my real-estate broker friend, exclaimed welcoming me at Prospero, the stylish bookstore and café at the Tbilisi center. "I admire this young man. I never believed that he could achieve so much in such a short time. I can work, I can breathe, I can enjoy the city."

I remember how devastated she was during Shevardnadze's reign and how, reluctantly, she had taken to the streets and joined the protests.

"I am glad for you. But not everybody is pleased."

"Sometimes I do not know what our people want. Why do they make this mess in front of the parliament? It must be personal grievances. And why for heaven's sake do they take to the streets? There are functioning state institutions where their grievances and complaints can be addressed.

"You were here with us in those horrible times," she recalled over an ice coffee, "when nothing worked. You see the difference."

"Of course I see although only on the surface. But the city has changed considerably," I agreed.

"Exactly! I never thought that it would happen in my lifetime. It is safe. I can do my business without pressure and harassment. I simply submit my tax statement once a year and pay accordingly. Nobody ever disturbs me. Before I was audited and questioned every month and pressured to pay bribes. Now I often pay traffic tickets for my daughter. She always parks in the wrong place. The young policemen who cash them are very polite, almost apologetic. You remember what kind of police we had before.

"I enjoy the city now—so clean, so nice, so normal. I love it! I feared before that it would never be possible. We have a lot of quality hotels, restaurants, and cafés. My daughter opened a restaurant in the old city. Now it is possible. It is just a matter of means and initiative. You do not have to go through endless formalities and seek out connections."

"So why are there so many dissatisfied people around?"

"I can't tell you. As you know, I have always stayed out of politics. Sometimes I just think that you cannot satisfy our people. They are not used to taking the initiative, taking responsibility for themselves. They have been demoralized by the Soviet system.

"Some resent our president's style. He is young, energetic, and sometimes arrogant. But then he would not be able to change anything otherwise. We would have stayed mired in the mud, dirt, and corruption as we were during Shevardnadze's time. He wants Georgia to succeed and that requires unpopular decisions. I cannot exclude that some people have been treated harshly in the process. But he is the target of Russia. They will do anything to destroy him. There are a lot of people working toward this end in Moscow, and I am sure that they have some allies in Georgia. His departure would be disastrous for us all," she concluded.

Beso, a private company driver, generally shared this view. "I am fine. I have good work, and I try to do it well. But if necessary, I would be ready to do anything else to earn bread. These have been good years. Our living conditions have improved, the city is nice and normal, and it is safe. I do not worry when my wife and daughter walk around during the night. It is true that since the 2008 war economic conditions have deteriorated, but I am sure it is temporary. The crisis is all over the world.

"I am not interested in politics and all the rumors about the politicians and the president. I just want to have a good life with my family. Since the Rose Revolution, that has been possible."

"Did you vote for Saakashvili?" I asked.

"Yes. For whom else could I vote? And I would vote for him again in the future if given the chance."

Zvano, an owner of a few small hotels, also expressed his satisfaction with Saakashvili. It was under Saakashvili, after the change, that he was able to start building hotels, one by one, step by step. He did not have much money but managed to buy some decaying buildings from the city and renovate them or replace them with new constructions.

"All of my family works. That is why we have something. It is not very Georgian, but in my family, all children have to contribute. And we have a good life as a result. Unfortunately, I do not speak any foreign languages. Only some poor Russian, but my children do speak. You will see. When my daughter comes, you can speak English with her.

"We travel a lot, my wife and I. We try to combine vacation and business. I want to see the world, to know how other people live, and use that knowledge in my business. I want people from all countries to feel at home in my hotels. I am so happy that I can travel. It was not possible in the past, in that surreal land called the Soviet Union. But I have nothing against Russians. They are my best business partners. We understand each other very well.

"If only more people were proactive and enterprising like me," Zvano went on, "we would have a different Georgia. But most people only want things for free. It is because we were part of the surreality that was the Soviet Union. That is why our president has to push these lazy people. Look at the houses falling apart. Nobody bothered to repair them for decades, and people lived in those pig sties."

"But it is quite expensive to repair such neglected buildings," I noted. "I do not think that the elderly or retired could ever have enough money to do it. No maintenance system has been in place, and property rights and responsibilities for utilities are unclear. As a result, buildings are not even fully accessible to perform maintenance. Under these circumstances, it is probably not entirely the fault of the people that they live in such conditions."

"Look at this house. It is not even painted," he continued, undeterred by my arguments. "It would be best just to eliminate it and build something nice and modern in its place instead."

"But it is a beautiful house," I protested. "Quite neglected, that is true, but it is built in the style typical of old Tbilisi. It should be renovated, not destroyed, otherwise Tbilisi will lose its unique character. I do not like most of these modern houses that have appeared over the last few years. They look like houses anywhere else."

"But they are new and nice. I am sure that people who invest their money in them will take good care of them."

*   *   *

The future will bear out which tendency is stronger: the discontent or satisfaction with Saakashvili's policies. Can the opposition get its act together, identify a common leader, and inspire effective action? I doubt it. I do not think that it can overcome the social inertia and apathy and the public's lack of confidence in them. If that is the case, Saakashvili will continue until his current term ends in 2013.

But who knows? It is the Caucasus, and the Caucasus is full of mysteries and surprises with Georgia at its core.

Epilogue

Not much has changed in Georgia during the past few months.

The opposition's anticipation of a massive peaceful protest against Saakashvili which would force him out of power did not materialize.

The feelings of apathy, misery, and resignation continue to prevail in the society.

Economic hardship, unemployment, and insecurity are on the increase.

Daily survival is the main task of the majority; people are tired of politics and politicians and have no confidence in another "revolution."

The suppression of dissent, disregard for human rights, and rule of law by Saakashvili government continue.

The opposition continues to be helpless, unable to change the tide.

Local elections held in May of 2010 again consolidated the position of Saakashvili. The main opposition candidate, Irakli Alasanya, lost the race to the crucial position of the mayor of Tbilisi. It reminded me of the opinion expressed last summer by Nino Burjanadze, former speaker of the Parliament and one of the leaders of the Rose Revolution, and now of the opposition: "We [the opposition] should not take part in elections as long as Saakashvili is in power. We should have learned from the past that there were no prospects for fair elections in [such] circumstances."

On one warm night in June 2010, the monument of Stalin disappeared from the center of Gori causing distress among its inhabitants. It turned out that Saakhashvili had decided to remove Stalin's memorabilia from public places and keep them in museums. It is unclear, what prompted this decision. It may remain one more Caucasian mystery.

Selected Bibliography

Amnesty International, "Georgia: Torture and Ill-Treatment Two Years After the Rose Revolution," 23 November 2005.

Cheterian, Vicken, "The August 2008 War in Georgia: From Ethnic Conflict to Border Wars," *Central Asian Survey*, Vol. 28, No. 2, June 2009, 155-170.

Cheterian, Vicken, "Ethnic Conflict in Georgia," *Le Monde*, December 1998.

Cheterian, Vicken, "Georgia's Rose Revolution: Change or Repetition? Tension Between State-Building and Modernization Projects," *Nationalities Papers*, Vol. 36, Iss. 4, September 2008, 689-712.

Cheterian, Vicken, *War and Peace in the Caucasus: Ethnic Conflict and the New Geopolitics*, Columbia University Press, New York, 2008.

Christophe, Barbara, "Metamorphosen de Leviathan in einer post-sozialistischen Gesellschaft. Georgiens Provinz zwischen Fassaden der Anarchie und regulativer Allmacht," *Global Studies*, Bielefeld, 2005.

Clark, Susan L, "Russia in a Peacekeeping Role," in *The Emergence of Russian Foreign Policy*, Leon Aron and Kenneth M. Jensen (eds.), US Institute of Peace Press, Washington DC, 1994.

Cohen, Jonathan (ed.), "A Question of Sovereignty: The Georgia-Abkhazia Peace Process," *Accord*, No. 7, September 1999.

Coppieters, Bruno (ed.), *Contested Borders in the Caucasus*, VUBPRESS, Brussels, 1996.

de Borchgrave, Arnaud, "Israel of the Caucasus?", *Washington Times*, September 4, 2008.

Ekedahl McGriffert, Carolyn and Melvin A. Goodman, *The Wars of Eduard Shevardnadze*, 2nd edition, Revised and Updated, Brassey's, Washington DC, 2001.

Flikke, Geir and Jakub M. Godzimirski, *Words and Deeds: Russian Foreign Policy and Post-Soviet Secessionist Conflicts*, NUPI, 2006.

Gerber, Jürgen, *Georgien: Nationale Opposition und kommunistische Herrschaft seit 1956*, Nomos Verlagsgesellschaft, Baden-Baden, 1997.

Glenny, Misha, "The Bear in the Caucasus: From Georgian Chaos, Russian Order," *Harper's Magazine*, March 1994, 45-53.

Goltz, Thomas, *Georgia Diary: A Chronicle of War and Political Chaos in the Post-Soviet Caucasus*, M.E. Sharpe, Armonk, NY, 2006.

Jensen, Benjamin, "Demilitarising Demographics: US Policy Options for Strengthening Georgian Internal Security," *Low Intensity Conflict & Law Enforcement*, Vol. 12, Iss. 1, Spring 2004, 51-90.

Jones, Stephen, "Georgia: The Long Battle for Independence", in *Nationalism and the Breakup of an Empire: Russia and Its Periphery*, ed. Miron Rezun, Praeger Press, Westport, 1992, 73-96.

Kapuscinski, Ryszard, *Kirgiz schodzi z konia*, Czytelnik, Warszawa, 1988.

Kharashvili, Julia, "Georgia: Coping by Organizing. Displaced Georgians from Abkhazia," in eds. Marc Vincent and Brigitte Refslund, *Caught Between Borders—Response Strategies of the Internally Displaced*, Pluto Press, London, 2001, 227-249.

King, Charles, *The Ghost of Freedom. A History of the Caucasus*, Oxford University Press, 2008.

Kvarchelia, Liana, "An Abkhaz Perspective," *Accord: An International Review of Peace Initiatives*, Iss. 7, September 1999.

Lynch, Dov (ed.), "The South Caucasus: A Challenge for the EU," Chaillot Paper No. 65, Institute for European Studies, Paris, 2003.

Lynch, Dov, "Why Georgia Matters," Chaillot Paper No. 26, Vol. 86, Institute for European Studies, Paris, February 2006.

MacFarlan, Stephen Neil, "Conflict and Conflict Resolution in Georgia," in Ehrhart, Hans-Georg and Schnabel, Albrecht (eds.), *The Southeast Europe Challenge: Ethnic Conflict and International Response*, Nomosverlag, Baden-Baden, 1999.

MacFarlan, Stephen Neil, "Non-Governmental Organizations as Conflict Prevention Actors in Georgia," in Bonvincini, Gianni, *et al.* (eds.), *Preventing Violent Conflict*, Nomos Verlagsgesellschaft, Baden-Baden, 1998.

MacFarlan, Stephen Neil, "UNOMIG and CISPKF in Georgia: Problems for Task-Sharing and Peace Support Operations," *Stiftung Wiessenschaft und Politik*, Berlin, June 1999.

Mangott, Gerhard, *Der Russische Phönix. Das Erbe aus der Asche*, Kremaair & Scheriau, Vienna, 2009.

Montefiore, Simon Sebag, "Eduard Shevardnadze," *New York Times Magazine*, December 26, 1993, 16-19.

Montefiore, Simon Sebag, *Stalin: The Court of the Red Tsar*, Vintage Books, New York, 2005.

Nodia, Ghia, "Georgian Perspectives," *Accord: An International Review of Peace Initiatives*, Iss. 7, September 1999.

Overland, Indra, "The Co-ordination of Conflict Prevention and Development Aid in Southern Georgia," *Conflict, Security & Development*, Vol. 2, Iss. 1, April 2002, 81-98.

Pelkman, Mathijs, *Defending the Border: Identity, Religion, and Modernity in the Republic of Georgia*, Cornell University Press, Ithaca, NY, 2006.

Politkovskaya, Anna, *In Putins Russland*, Fischer, Frankfurt, 2008.

Politkovskaya, Anna, *The Russian Diary: A Journalist's Final Account of Life, Corruption, and Death in Putin's Russia*, Random House, New York, 2007.

Reitschuster, Boris, *Putins Demokratur: Wie der Kreml den Westen das Fürchten lehrt*, Ullstein Tb, Berlin, 2006.

Rondeli, Alexander, "The Choice of Independent Georgia," in Chufrin, Gennady (ed.), *The Security of the Caspian Sea Region*, SIPRI, Oxford University Press, New York, 2001, 195-211.

Shevardnadze, Eduard, A., *Als der eiserne Vorhang zerriss*, Peter W. Matzler Verlag, 2007.

Shevardnadze, Eduard, A., *The Future Belongs to Freedom*, Free Press, 1991.

Smirnov, Andrei, "North Caucasus Rebels Seek to Expand into Abkhazia, South Ossetia and Azerbaijan," North Caucasus Weekly, Vol. 9, Iss. 36, September 26, 2008.

Socor, Vladimir, "Russia again seeking UNOMIG facade in Abkhazia, Georgia", *Eurasia Daily Monitor*, published by The James Foundation, October 9, 2008, Volume 5, Issue 194.

Suny, Ronald Grigor, *The Making of the Georgian Nation*, Indiana University Press, Bloomington, IN, 1994.

Toft, Monica Duffy, *The Geography of Ethnic Violence: Identity, Interests, and the Indivisibility of Territory*, Princeton University Press, 2003.

Zurabishvili, Salome, *La Tragédie Géorgienne, 2003-2008*, Grasset & Fasquelle, Paris, 2009.

UNOMIG, Tbilisi

The author in Tbilisi

Tbilisi, flee market

The author in Mtskheta the old capital of Georgia

The author on helicopter patrol with OSCE

The author in Batumi

Kitty preparing for a trip to Sukhumi

Travel through Georgia's country roads

High level study trip to Kosovo and Bosnia and Herzegovina lead by Ambassador Heidi Tagliavini, SRSG, UNOMIG (in the middle); the author with members of the team, including delegations of the Georgian and Abkhazian side, in Sarajevo

THIS MONUMENT COMMEMORATES
THE PARTICIPANTS OF A PEACEFUL
RALLY GUNNED DOWN BY THE
SOVIET REGIME ON MARCH 9. 1956

Tbilisi, monument commemorating victims of 1956 massacre

The author at her farewell party at "Petit Trianon", Tbilisi, with
Director Alexander Rondeli and Ambassador Zaal Gogsadze
(in the background), December 2004

Farewell party, the author with friends from the EU Mission

Stalin's State's Museum, Gori

Stalin's museum, gift shop

The "very bad people, who mislead Stalin . . . ."
—Stalin's museum, Gori, 2009

The author in front of Stalin's monument, Gori, summer 2009; the monument was quietly removed in June 2010 on the orders of Georgian government

The veteran of Abkhaz war, Tbilisi, summer 2009

"Cells" of demonstrators camping in front of the Parliament,
Tbilisi summer 2009

Settlements of the "new" IDPs from South Ossetia, victims of the 2008 war, along the road from Tbilisi to Gori

Welcome demonstration to US Vice-President, Joe Biden, organized by the opposition, Tbilisi, July 2009 ("We trust you . . . .")

The author with Nana Kakabadze, a well known human
rights defender

Saakashvili, Zhvania and Gachechiladze—friends and allies
once upon the time

The courtyard of Chavchavadze Avenue 20, Tbilisi, the author's residence in 2003-2004

The author with the former Georgian President, Eduard
Shevardnadze, in his villa in Tbilisi, summer 2009

The panorama of Tbilisi

Abbreviations

CIS-PKF   Commonwealth of Independent States Peacekeeping Force

CoE   Council of Europe

D/SRSG   Deputy Special Representative of the Secretary-General (United Nations)

EU   European Union

IC   International Community

IDPs   Internally Displaced Persons

NATO   North Atlantic Treaty Organization

OSCE   Organization for Security and Co-operation in Europe

SRSG   Special Representative of the Secretary-General (United Nations), Head of the UN Mission

UN   United Nations

UNHCR   United Nations High Commissioner for Refugees

UNDP   United Nations Development Programme

UNGA   United Nations General Assembly

UNMIBH   United Nations Mission in Bosnia and Herzegovina

UNOMIG   United Nations Observer Mission in Georgia

UNSC   United Nations Security Council

About the Author

Dr. Gierycz has had a long and distinguished career in international affairs, peacekeeping, conflict resolution, human rights, and gender equality. For twenty-five years, she worked at the United Nations, serving in senior positions at its headquarters in both Vienna and New York and in numerous missions around the world to include: Head of the Gender Analysis Section at United Nations Headquarters (1998 to 2001); Director of the Human Rights and Protection Section at the United Nations Mission in Liberia, and Representative of the United Nations High Commissioner for Human Rights in Liberia (2004 to 2007); and Deputy Head of Civil Affairs at the United Nations Mission in Bosnia-Herzegovina (2001 to 2003).

From 2003 to 2004, Dr. Gierycz served as a senior political adviser to the Special Representative of the Secretary-General (SRSG) at the United Nations Observer Mission in Georgia (UNOMIG) in Sukhumi and Tbilisi. After leaving the United Nations, she returned to Georgia in 2009 to conduct further research for this book and assess firsthand the outcome of the Rose Revolution and reforms under the Saakashvili government.

Dr. Gierycz holds an MA in public international law and a PhD in political science (international affairs) from Warsaw University in her native Poland. She further studied at the Academy of International Law in The Hague and at Georgetown University in the department of government, the School of International and Public Affairs (SIPA) at Columbia University, and the Watson Institute of International Affairs at Brown University in the United States. Dr. Gierycz has also authored numerous academic articles and regularly teaches and guest lectures at leading universities and institutions around the world.

Recently, Dr. Gierycz has been a senior research fellow at the European Inter-University Centre for Human Rights and Democratisation (EIUC) in Venice, Italy, and the Norwegian Institute of International Affairs

(NUPI) in Oslo, Norway, working on issues of transitional justice and the responsibility to protect. She is also currently associated with the Ludwig Boltzmann Institute of Human Rights, University of Vienna, Webster University, Vienna and European Peace University (EPU), Schlaining, Austria.

Dr. Gierycz presently resides in Vienna and New York.